Sex and International Tribunals

PENNSYLVANIA STUDIES IN HUMAN RIGHTS

Bert B. Lockwood, Jr., Series Editor

A complete list of books in the series is available from the publisher.

Sex and International Tribunals

The Erasure of Gender from the War Narrative

Chiseche Salome Mibenge

PENN

UNIVERSITY OF PENNSYLVANIA PRESS

PHILADELPHIA

Published by
University of Pennsylvania Press
Philadelphia, Pennsylvania 19104-4112
www.upenn.edu/pennpress

Printed in the United States of America
on acid-free paper

10 9 8 7 6 5 4 3 2 1

Library of Congress Cataloging-in-Publication Data

Mibenge, Chiseche Salome.
  Sex and international tribunals : the erasure of gender from the war narrative / Chiseche
Salome Mibenge. — 1st ed.
      p. cm. — (Pennsylvania studies in human rights)
  Includes bibliographical references and index.
  ISBN 978-0-8122-4518-9 (hardcover : alk. paper)
  1. Rape as a weapon of war—Case studies. 2. Criminal investigation (International
law) 3. Rape as a weapon of war—Rwanda. 4. Rape as a weapon of war—Sierra Leone.
5. Women—Violence against—Rwanda. 6. Women—Violence against—Sierra Leone.
7. Rwanda—History—Civil War, 1994—Women. 8. Sierra Leone—History—Civil War,
1991–2002—Women. I. Title. II. Series: Pennsylvania studies in human rights.
  KZ7162.M53 2013
  341.6'9—dc23

                                                            2013012709

To Matilda Mwale, who loved us all

Contents

Gender and Violence in the Market and Beyond

During my first year as a student at the University of Zambia, when I was seventeen, I left campus one Friday for a weekend with my family. It was not yet dark, and the Lusaka Central Market was busy. The lines for the minibus to Kabulonga were extremely long, but I waited patiently for my turn to board. I actually enjoyed the commotion all around.

Then two young men approached me. I recognized one as Chitumba, a friend of my cousin Natasha. They joined me in the line, and we chatted briefly before they invited me to join them in a taxi ride home, at their expense, as they lived beyond my parents' home anyway. I agreed readily, and we walked together, one on either side of me, stepping over vegetables and past vendors until we got into a parked taxi. As we did so, an old woman shouted after my young men, "You've done well. Take her away from here. They were going to strip her naked!"

I remember my shock at realizing that the commotion—whistling and shouting from the young men loitering around the market—had been directed at my legs and thighs. My cotton floral summer dress, a gift from my mother, was apparently attracting mob justice. It is an infrequent occurrence, but an occurrence nonetheless, that an "indecently attired" young woman in Lusaka is pursued by a gang of vigilante youths ostensibly trying to preserve the dignity of Mother Zambia and traditional African values. If she is captured, the woman is normally stripped naked, groped, and roughed up as an appreciative crowd gathers to witness the spectacle. The woman might escape the mob if she is rescued by a shopkeeper and his workers, who will barricade her in their shop until the police arrive to disperse the party.

My two young rescuers were better acclimated than I was to the body and gender politics on the streets of Lusaka and foresaw that I was on the verge of falling victim to a sexual assault. Chitumba admitted that the taxi invitation was a ruse to get me away from danger. I recounted this story to my parents that evening, choking on tears of rage. My father tried to rationalize: "You should understand our culture, mama; those people are grassroots people." I shouted in response: "They're not grassroots! They don't know anything about our culture! They're just thugs!"

In the southern African society of my youth, sexual violence was the bogeyman of morality tales, articulated through commentary or narratives that attached to and sexualized specific body parts and conduct. The shape and tone of these narratives was often censorious of women and girls irrespective of the sex of the narrator. Girls who showed their thighs, girls who stayed out after dark, girls who did not respect themselves—these girls attracted aggressive sexual attention from men, name calling, and ostracism from women's peer groups. If they really pushed the boundaries, they would get the punishment of rape.[1] However, rape was not the ultimate punishment. The ultimate punishment would be that nobody would believe it was rape, or, if they believed it was rape, the conclusion would be that it was well earned by the victim and perhaps even overdue. The social narratives I grew up on often married gender with violence: for example, they easily attached such adjectives as "drunken," "careless," "wild," "provocative," or "stupid" to women victims of sexual violence.[2] These narratives made words such as "no," "consent," "force," and "coercion" ambiguous on my university campus. If I believed in the narratives, I would have had to accept that it was the shapeliness of my bare legs that threatened public morality and order as well as my own dignity and physical integrity in the Lusaka market. However, this acceptance would require submitting to the narratives of gender and violence and their objective of privileging men by policing women's autonomy.

In the almost twenty years since that early evening in the market, my sense of humiliation and rage has passed. What remains with me both intellectually and emotionally is a lasting desire to investigate narratives of gender and their narrators. I am ever watchful to see why and how men and women are influenced and/or bound by the narratives that dictate safe and unsafe expressions of masculinity and femininity. I have found powerful, often coercive expressions of gender wherever my research has taken me over the past decade. In Dutch law faculties, I have been struck by the traditional gender expectations surrounding motherhood versus career progression; to my surprise it is perfectly acceptable to publicly grill expectant Dutch coworkers on personal choices concerning child care and their obligation to "raise their own children." In Bradford in northern England, the gender narratives of "acceptable" dress and behavior for British-born university female students from Pakistani families intrigued me. I was especially amused by a white British librarian who said of a rowdy group of female, British-Pakistani students, "Such a pity, they're just as foul-mouthed as our girls now, sometimes worse. We don't dare to hush them." In Washington, D.C., in the buildup to the 2008 U.S. presidential elections, I overheard many gendered sentiments about the candidates as well as their spouses: "Sarah Palin should focus on her five children and not politics"; "Hillary Clinton lost because of the pantsuits, she should have worn more skirt suits"; "Michelle [Obama] is great because she stands behind her husband, she lets him be the man"; "McCain is an old man, he will make America look weak." I presuppose the existence of narratives about gender in every sociopolitical regime, be it in democratic countries, secular states, war-torn countries, developing nations, or liberal or conservative states.

In this book, my geographical focus is sub-Saharan Africa, in particular, Rwanda and Sierra Leone. My decision to focus on these two African countries, best known in the international community for decades of political violence and armed conflict, was not intended to highlight the most extreme or egregious manifestations of unequal gender hegemonies in wartime. Rather, I chose this focus because postwar reconstruction processes in these two countries provide rich case studies of the many responses to societal gender inequality and discrimination. These responses have taken many shapes, including human rights advocacy, affirmative action, repeal of discriminatory legislation, security-sector reform, demobilization of fighters, civil society activism, education and community sensitization, constitutional amendments, and criminalization.

The Justice Process and Its Dominant Narrative

I concentrate specifically on the justice sector's responses to gross human rights violations and war crimes. This sector interprets human rights norms in order to determine accountability, producing compelling legal narratives that detail and help make sense of the infliction of political violence on men and women. These legal narratives arise from legal as well as factual findings based on evidence that prosecutors, witnesses, and others submit before such mechanisms of accountability as truth commissions and military or international criminal tribunals. The narratives have the power to legitimate victims and condemn perpetrators of human rights abuses. They can produce categories of victims, perpetrators, collaborators, martyrs, traitors, and heroes—all as expressions of "good" and "bad" gender models. For example, a pattern of acquittals or sentences of light community service might affirm the integrity of men who killed their daughters rather than let them be kidnapped and raped by invading armies.

These decision-making processes are not free from bias as the words *law* and *fact* might suggest. Hegemonic power relations contribute to the collation of fact and law, which in turn affect the formulation of the legal narrative. Various stakeholders, including prosecutors, victor states, former colonial masters, nongovernmental organizations (NGOs), and international donors take part in the political negotiation of law, fact, and human rights standards. Political circumstances can constrain the investigative reach of prosecutors and defense counsel, expedite extradition processes, and moderate sentencing practices. Political narratives about the interests of the victor, the needs of victims, and the reckoning with the vanquished are expertly woven by transitional governments; and they color the justice process, which is ultimately the product of a political edict, for example, a peace accord, Security Council vote, or agreement between the state and the secretary general of the United Nations.

Thus, in justice processes, there are a variety of narratives: legal and political, as well as social. By *social narratives* I mean narratives arising from tales, myths, anecdotes, proverbs, and stories that emerge from within a society on any given subject. Scholars, researchers, writers, journalists, human rights defenders, and others codify these usually oral testimonies through a process of interviews, observations, and analysis. These codifiers ultimately produce a social narrative that can become a vehicle for political activism and advocacy. Thus, although I will refer to the narratives of Rwandan and Sierra Leonean men and women on gender and violence, I am really referring to my own appropriation (as scholar, researcher, and writer) of stories I heard during my encounters in Rwanda and Sierra Leone and my arbitrary interpretation and codification of these stories. In sharing these stories with an international and elite audience, the social narrative I tell will have the potential to serve different political purposes.

The narratives of Rwandans and Sierra Leoneans I have selected are by and large not the type that would fall into the category of baleful testimonies about atrocity. Rather, the testimonies I present throughout this book, whether they were collected by me or by other researchers, are contributions not to our collective outrage about war's victims but to a gender analysis of the laws and justice processes that seek to promote human rights. I include them not merely to show that gender is part of the narrative of modern-day postwar reconstruction processes or to add nuance to our understanding of the experiences, both shared and divergent, of men and women in armed conflict. I use narratives to pose a challenge to assumptions and easy conclusions that legal scholars can only draw when relying solely on the case law and transcripts as sources of fact and law. These legal texts have created new crimes against humanity, such as sexual slavery, and in doing so have inscribed femininity and masculinity into our understanding of war's victims and perpetrators. I argue that this inscription has created an essentializing and gendered binary of male abusers and female victims. Further, this binary does not include men and women who do not, cannot, or will not fit neatly into either of these categories. My selection of narratives in this book is motivated by a desire to disrupt the legal text by identifying masculinities and femininities that emphasize other experiences of war yet still warrant inclusion in the process of transitional justice.

I have placed narratives of gender and violence at the center of my research for a number of reasons. Narratives occur within all sectors of society and, because of their authoritative potential, can have an impact on gender roles and relations in periods of violent political transition. And violence ultimately generates and transforms social hierarchies and perceptions within and between groups.[3] An example of a violent transformation of social hierarchies is the image of an armed child soldier arresting or facilitating the passage through a checkpoint of frightened adult civilians in their vehicles. And in the aftermath of violence, communities shape collective narratives that can represent a cultural remembrance of the violence and its significance for the group identity, including gendered identities. However, narratives can be contested and may be a source of conflict between members of a society. I can illustrate this by recounting conversations with two Sierra Leoneans I encountered on a field visit in February 2007.

I was the guest of Paramount Chief Sesay.[4] He told me that he had survived the war because, as rebels advanced, he was able to escape to a rebel-free zone where he stayed during the years that the rebels occupied his chiefdom. On his return to his chiefdom, he held several meetings with his people. Apparently, the men of the village asked the chief to thank the rebels for their benevolent rule during the occupation. According to the village representatives, apart from a few killings at the start of the occupation, life under the rebels had been peaceful and secure.

The chief later introduced me to Bintu, a mother, wife, and grandmother who had recently been elected the first woman local representative in the area's political history. She had been supported in her campaign with leadership training and funding by several local women's NGOs. In a private conversation with her, I mentioned that "some men" had told me that apart from killings in the early days, rebel occupation had been secure. As I anticipated, Bintu exploded in anger: "Who told you that? It's a lie! We women were slaves! Wake up in the morning to farm for them, collect their water, we had to feed them! Those rebels! They raped us in front of our husbands, and our husbands did nothing."

In the same way that I extracted conflicting social narratives of gender and violence from the incident in the Lusaka market and a father and daughter's struggle to draw meaning from it, I extracted from conversations with Bintu and Chief Sesay social narratives of gender and violence. Bintu's outburst and the chief's claim present views that are different yet similar. Both assert that gender shaped the way they experienced insecurity within armed conflict, and indeed gender continues to shape the way they experience the peace process and nascent democracy. Bintu speaks of herself and other women as slaves. The chief, however, describes men and women going about their everyday business. Bintu describes not only rape but also rape as theater, as husbands were forced to watch the rape of their wives. The chief refers to "some killings" and his probable assassination had he remained in a rebel stronghold. The absence of sexual violence in the chief's account is in itself a valuable narrative of masculinity and patriarchy that demands a gender analysis (though far from the only point to raise the gender flag).[5]

The juxtaposition of Bintu and Chief Sesay's responses raises a number of questions about gender and violence. Some of the questions are too simple and too obvious to build a thesis upon. For example, one might conclude that Bintu leads us to a narrative on suffering that is asking rhetorically, "Who suffers the most in war, men or women?" This contest can be observed between victims, victim organizations, humanitarian organizations, the media, and human rights advocates, depending on their specific political agendas. Some argue that men suffer the worst human rights abuses; after all, they are killed, unlike women, who are only raped.[6] The image of Srebrenica, for example, where thousands of men and boys were led to an execution ground while their women were only put on buses and exiled from their village, bolsters this view.[7] Others torment the public with images of abandoned or orphaned children, conveying the message that children suffer the most, that they are the most vulnerable to exploitation.[8] Still others tell us that actually women suffer the most atrocious violence, often in the form of rape. They are raped because it is a fate worse than death; perpetrators of rape tell women they will die from sadness, and there is no need to waste bullets on them. Women, especially widows, are left to head households and rebuild shattered families and lives.[9]

This is not the contest Bintu's outburst drew me toward. Bintu's and the chief's separate yet related accounts raise the key questions that concern me throughout this book: How did men and women experience violence and human rights violations? Which men and women have their narratives privileged by the prosecutor's investigation? Who is representing or giving voice to victims' experiences, and how do they edit out "inconsequential" details from the formal processes of justice?

In responding to these questions, I will reveal a dominant narrative of gender and violence emerging from the legal and justice process, a dominant narrative that is wont to represent African women not only as victims of armed conflict but as rape victims of a militarized African masculinity. This narrative essentializes women as a monolithic victim group and gender as a unitary ground of discrimination. In essentializing women's gender role thus, this dominant narrative fails to acknowledge variance within the group and ultimately variance in the experience and impact of gender-based violence on women and men.

While it is important for me to focus on the men and women excluded from the justice process, I also examine what I call the price of inclusion in an essentializing justice process for women victims of gender-based violence. The dominant narrative requires a "perfect" or "legitimate" victim who is allowed to gain access to justice but required to adjust their testimony of atrocity in war to fit the script provided by the dominant narrative. The legal narrative of the "perfect victim" is a well-known phenomenon in the domestic sphere; it varies from society to society and is dynamic. In the context of U.S. legal and justice narratives of the 1970s, Alice Sebold described herself as the perfect victim because of an important set of facts:

"I was a virgin. He was a stranger. It happened outside. It was night. I wore loose clothes, and could not be proven to have acted provocatively. There were no drugs or alcohol in my system. I had no former involvement with the police of any kind, not even a traffic ticket. He was black and I was white. There was an obvious physical struggle. I had been injured internally. . . . I was a young student at a private university. . . . He had a record and had done time."[10]

I am concerned with the impact of the "perfect victim" narrative on the experiences of women who are included as well as excluded: the wartime experience of both groups is never fully authenticated by a legal narrative. Even as I identify and distinguish between "perfect victims" and "imperfect victims," I recognize the vacuity of the terms beyond their malleability as research tools. The women I met in Rwanda and Sierra Leone are survivors. These survivors live firmly in the present and look back at the upside-down world of war only when prodded by researchers such as myself to (against their better judgment) look backward and not forward. As I acknowledge this awkward transaction between scholar and survivor, I recall a vow made by Albie Sachs, a South African Constitutional Court justice and an iconic victim of apartheid. Sachs vowed that he would not make himself an exhibit, even when asked to speak subjectively of his victimization by the apartheid state (Sachs 1997: 20). And even as I place my body and the bodies of other African women and men into this book, I vow not to make myself or others exhibits. The exhibit in this book is law and its enforcement of human rights.

The ad hoc criminal tribunals for the former Yugoslavia and Rwanda brought gender, violence, and armed conflict into the lexicon of international jurists. The initial response by legal scholars was to focus on the interpretation of the statute and rules of evidence and procedure. Literature flourished on landmark interpretations and definitions of sexual violence, and on admissible defenses for rape and the inclusion of evidence of rape trauma syndrome by medical experts.[11] The scholarship then began to focus on the needs of victims and witnesses of gender-based violence, and scholars have discussed the support services provided by the victim and witness unit and the tone of examinations by prosecutors and defense counsel. They have raised the issue of reparations for victims and witnesses, invoking this as a form of social justice, for example, suggesting the provision of housing and medical treatment.[12]

There is a curious research gap between legal scholars at the domestic and international levels. In the case of gender-based violence at the domestic level, criminologists, in particular, have exposed how race, ethnicity, and class can limit or improve the prosecutor's odds of securing a conviction on behalf of the victim. Facts such as the victim being Hispanic, the community being white, the accused being a surgeon, the jurors being working class, the police precinct being located in a black neighborhood, and the judge being a conservative can influence prosecutorial strategy and judicial processes and outcomes. At the level of international armed conflict, social scientists have led the way with studies of how the state, media, and propaganda include and exclude victims of gender-based violence from narratives of victimhood in the former Yugoslavia, South Africa, and other transitional societies (Zarkov 2007; Ross 2002 and 2005). However, legal scholars have lagged in producing a comparable body of work within their discipline that reveals those factors that disadvantage victims of gender-based violence from accessing effective justice. My research in this book responds to the apparent need for legal researchers, such as myself, to pose the gender questions surrounding victim participation in processes of international criminal law.

Factors such as stigma or ignorance of the workings of the legal system are regularly put forward as obstructing women from seeking justice at the international level. However, this view focuses on projecting fear or reluctance onto women as victims and witnesses, and placing the responsibility for accessing justice exclusively on them. Little energy is directed toward investigating the international tribunal and its unwillingness or inability to give an audience to women on discriminatory grounds. Few scholars have empirically investigated whether an international criminal tribunal is sexist, racist, or ageist, for example. As a legal scholar, I draw the jurist or legal scholar toward a serious self-examination that could reveal the reasons why women might shun the legal system. I have encountered the assumption that international processes of justice, in contrast to the domestic level, are immune from projecting gender, race, and other forms of bias on victims and witnesses. While there is an understanding that elderly, poor, and illiterate women may lack the means to access justice, there is no examination of whether prosecutors might arbitrarily deem poor, illiterate, and elderly women to be unreliable witnesses or simply implausible victims of rape. Bias emanating from the international justice process has yet to be thoroughly interrogated by legal scholars, and my objective with this book is to contribute to this interrogation.

Defining the Terms and the Structure of the Book

Mass violence and its avoidance have held central places in nations' framing and ratification of international laws that supersede their own domestic laws and sovereignty. By the twentieth century, the international community unanimously agreed that crimes such as piracy and slavery violated international custom and the standards of civilized nations. Law students may take for granted that UN General Assembly declarations, UN Security Council resolutions, reports by truth commissions, and decisions of international criminal tribunals clearly state that sexual violence against women committed in armed conflict is a form of gender-based discrimination. However, the legal and political processes that brought gender into the framework of international law depended on the birth and maturity of a new body of international law, namely, international human rights law after World War II. This new law brought the rhetoric of universalism, nondiscrimination, and equality to all members of the human family. Over a span of more than sixty years, certain family members have called attention to unique challenges posed to their enjoyment of human rights as a result of their membership in subgroups. Disabled people, migrant workers and their families, refugees, children, domestic workers, women, and many other groups have advocated for the establishment of thematic human rights norms beyond an international bill of rights stating government's responsibility to prevent actions that discriminate against them specifically.

The inclusion of gender into the international human rights law framework is a recent and ongoing process that I am contributing to with this work. By *gender* I refer broadly to the socially constructed roles ascribed to women and men, as opposed to biological and physical characteristics under the banner of *sex*. The social worth of men and women is closely tied to their ability to internalize, perform, and fulfill idealized gender roles. Gender expectations shape the ways in which men and women interact in every sphere of social activity, such as those that determine access to resources, security, power, and participation in political, cultural, and religious activities (Pankhurst 2003: 166). Although the details vary from society to society and change over time, gender relations always include a strong element of inequality between women and men and are influenced strongly by ideology (ibid.).

Gender groups are traditionally divided into two monolithic units: men and women. This division is erroneous as it tends to make invisible subgroups and cultures within a dominant gender group and also conceals the hierarchies and hegemonic power within a single gender group. Thus, within the supposedly monolithic group of men, there is an idealized man who fulfills the gender expectations dictated by society. Those men who aspire to conform to this model of masculinity would enjoy greater civil, political, economic, and social freedom than men who deviate too far from the idealized model. However, men may feel ambivalent and even oppressed by their conformity, even when it reaps rewards such as increased social standing and economic gain.

There is no universal model of the idealized male. In one society he could be Muslim, heterosexual, a father, self-employed, married, and faithful to his wife; in another, he may be Protestant, educated to college level, heterosexual, a father, married, and casually but discreetly involved with multiple sexual partners. And those women who complement and enable men's performance of an idealized masculinity are promised greater security and bargaining power in a patriarchal universe and privileged access to contested or scarce resources. Equality requires that the gender roles of both women and men who do not fulfill and/or complement the idealized male gender role model are awarded comparable status as those of the idealized male and entitled to equal access to rights and resources.

Many inequalities in the enjoyment of human rights arise from gender-based discrimination, which is an umbrella term for any harm that is the result of power imbalances that exploit distinctions between men and women and among men and women. Gender-based discrimination or the threat of gender-based discrimination can press "deviant" men and women to conform to acceptable gender roles. Thus, a woman may conceal that she is gay in order not to jeopardize her appointment as a partner in a law firm, or an unmarried woman may wear a wedding band in order to gain the respect of colleagues in an office. Gender-based discrimination often occurs as a combination of both sex and gender bias. For example, a company may refuse to employ young women because of an expectation that they will get pregnant and prove a liability. This form of discrimination is based on women's sexual reproductive potential, that is, their biological sex. It is also based on the common belief that professional women (rather than professional men) should take primary responsibility for child rearing, household chores, and other domestic roles perceived to be natural and gender appropriate but incompatible with the pursuit of a career outside of the home.[13]

Discrimination can manifest itself as violence against men and women.

Gender-based violence takes many forms, including sex-selective abortions, gay bashing, honor killings, and sexual harassment. There is often a continuum of harm and magnification of scale with regard to violent forms of discrimination. Thus, discriminatory hiring practices against "girls," "gays," "pregnant ladies," and others can foster a hostile work environment where sexual harassment is not only prevalent but condoned by management.

The international community has recently accepted unanimously that sexual violence in armed conflict is a weapon or strategy of war[14] and, further, that the egregious nature of gender-based violence, particularly sexual violence, is aggravated by the prima facie coercive nature of armed conflict.[15] The judicial processes of accountability in postconflict societies that I describe in this book are responding in part to widespread acts of sexual violence and other forms of gender-based violence. According to the case law, gender-based violence characterizes abuses such as the conscription of child soldiers, disappearances, detention, torture, genocide, and enslavement.

My study of gender and violence in Rwanda and Sierra Leone takes place in peacetime, but I bear in mind the popular truism that war is not over with the last bullet. This truism has come to signify the ongoing gender impact of conflict on women's insecurity and vulnerability to violence and exploitation.[16] In Rwanda and Sierra Leone, and indeed in many countries that have experienced widespread and systematic violations of human rights, women's security remained—long after demilitarization—precarious and marginalized from the core peace processes and reconstruction projects.

Human rights instruments have played an important role in blurring the dichotomous peace-war framework. This traditional framework allocated abuses committed in peacetime to the jurisdiction of the human rights law framework and wartime abuses to the jurisdiction of international humanitarian law. This delineation between war and peace allowed states to summarily "suspend" fundamental rights of civilians in times of emergency or conflict and to put civilians under the less humane protection of the laws of war. Until the early 1990s, at the international level, little recognition was made of the scale of the insecurity women experienced in the various gray zones that mark the continuum of violent economic, social, and political upheavals caused by armed conflict.

The term *wartime rape* is very revealing of the gray zones. It suggests that there is something called "normal rape" that happens only occasionally in peaceful societies. "Normal rape" suggests an apolitical offense that does not traumatize or offend the sensibilities of civilized peoples and its victims in the same way that wartime rape does. And indeed, the distinction between peace and wartime rape is often emphasized by observers, such as scholars and the media, by the attachment of adjectives such as "heinous," "egregious," "atrocious," and "brutal" to rapes occurring in armed conflict. Differentiating between rape in war and peace carries the danger of prioritizing sexual assaults so that rape that is used as a tactic of ethnic cleansing evokes moral outrage but forced sex in the privacy of family life is accepted (Nordstrom 1991, quoted by Sideris 2001b: 146). Tina Sideris points out that ultimately this view allows lawmakers, the police, and communities to explain ordinary rape in terms of dysfunctional and pathological relations and attitudes between men and women. The idea of "ordinary rapes" in peacetime separates violent sexual relations and the construction of masculinities and femininities from an analysis of power relations. Deprived of such an analysis, the task of transforming social relations becomes more difficult (2001a: 61).

The idea of something called ordinary rape is propagated at the highest levels of international influence. In what was then a leading report on sexual violence in armed conflict, the Council of Europe described wartime rape as "worse than 'ordinary' rape because it is accompanied by other war-related trauma: loss or death of husbands, children, parents or friends, loss of property, etc." The report emphasizes that "wartime rape differs from sexual assault in peacetime in that it is committed in a political context which often engenders organized violence," and, further, peacetime rape is isolated and frequently punished.[17] These claims do not take into account the organized nature of trafficking in women and girls in peacetime, domestic courts' systemic discrimination against victims of domestic violence, wardens' sexual exploitation of female detainees, or police ambivalence about following correct forensic and investigative procedures when women report sexual violence. I do not need to name a specific country or region where such phenomena occur simply because they are pervasive in developed and developing countries. Rape and other forms of gender-based violence in peacetime are also committed in a political context of hegemonic power, which has serious repercussions for gender equality and nondiscrimination in women's enjoyment of fundamental human rights.

Undertakings to establish accountability for war crimes and crimes against humanity have become a feature of negotiated peace. Mechanisms of accountability, such as truth commissions in South Africa and Liberia and ad hoc criminal tribunals for Rwanda and the former Yugoslavia, operate at the official close of armed conflict but often during a state of insecurity for civilians, particularly displaced persons. Bearing this in mind, I choose to collapse the temporal zones of peace, the immediate aftermath of armed conflict, the postconflict, into a zone broadly referred to as conflict. Conflict may precede armed conflict or it may follow the signing of a peace treaty. It is often the site of continuing violence by covert means; however, it is violence tempered by a wide range of developments having an impact on security, such as a partial demilitarization and demobilization process or the wholesale exporting of armed conflict to a third territory or a border region.

Throughout the escalation or transition of conflict to armed conflict; rumors or threats of violence; pockets of violence; arbitrary curfews; shortages of such basic amenities as electricity and water; disruption to daily rituals such as attending school, community meetings, or prayer groups; and battle-rousing propaganda and images destabilize the daily life of the civilian population. Propaganda easily coopts gender into its narrative. Even as masculinity and the male body are aggressively militarized, femininity and women's bodies are transposed onto the identity of the nation: the vulnerable mother nation must be protected from violation, and the enemy nation must be violated (raped even) and conquered.[18]

Throughout the deescalation and demilitarization of armed conflict into conflict, the situation of the civilian population can be as dramatic and precarious as during the period of armed conflict, and in some cases worse. The risk of renewed hostilities is high so that the application of the term *peacetime* is no more than a fleeting fiction. The crime rate goes up, infrastructure (water, health, education, justice, security) has been destroyed, homes lie in ruins, problems of a humanitarian nature are rife, the economy is paralyzed, and the international aid is often woefully inadequate.[19]

Women's living conditions in conflict zones are very revealing of the gendered outcomes of violence and their impact on survivors of armed conflict. Violence in the conflict zone is often concealed in private women's spaces and such acts as child bearing. Thus, women in a war zone experience the collapse of primary health-care services most cuttingly through high levels of maternal and infant mortality and morbidity (Jacobson 1999: 180, quoted by Cockburn 1999: 11). Domestic and community violence against women increases after armed conflict.[20] Women, particularly those widowed by the conflict, are exposed to violent altercations over land with strangers as well as relatives, in-laws, children, and aggressive suitors. The adoption of often unfamiliar head-of-household roles for many women who have no sustainable livelihood opportunities and the burden of providing for war-affected dependents may increase vulnerability to exploitative relationships.

Humanitarian workers have gradually expanded their profile of internally displaced persons and refugees to include women with individual as well as gender-specific needs. This inclusion is a marked shift from an androcentric lens that viewed refugees primarily as men plus their dependents (children and wives). A sustained gender assessment of refugee policy has led to a deeper understanding of the ways in which displacement increases women's vulnerability to exploitation and abuse.[21] Women displaced by armed conflict are especially vulnerable to sexual abuse and exploitation in camps and when they attempt to return and reclaim their homes.[22]

Advances in media technologies that facilitate live reporting of conflicts mean that we see just how the lives of civilians are marked by gross violations of human rights. The testimony from victims and witnesses before tribunals such as the International Criminal Tribunal for Rwanda (ICTR), the International Criminal Tribunal for the Former Yugoslavia (ICTY), and the Sierra Leone Special Court (Special Court) reveal that armed conflict takes place in the homes, classrooms, front gardens, fields, and churches of civilians as combatants occupy towns and villages and effectively hold their occupants hostage. These texts or transcripts complement the change in the research focus from battlefield casualties to civilian casualties on the home front. To call armed conflict "armed" conflict is actually misleading because the civilian hostages targeted for enslavement, amputation, mutilation, rape, torture, abduction, summary execution, forced labor, and other gross violations of human rights are for the most part unarmed.

Feminist scholars have led the way in displacing two powerful gendered narratives that undermined the development of relevant international law protection for women in armed conflict. The first narrative restricted women's victimhood to the loss of husbands and sons on distant battlefields. Scholars do not deny that the loss of male heads of household is a devastating loss for women; however, they have provided the cultural, economic, and legal implications of such loss for individual women. The loss of social status is closely linked to the loss of civil status where, for example, women's property rights or citizenship rights depend on a male guardian.

The second narrative dispelled is that rape is the only gender-based violation that distinguishes women's experience of armed conflict from men's. While research may reveal that rape predominantly targets women, there is a tendency to ignore that a gendered analysis of armed conflict requires an understanding of how cross-cutting issues, such as housing rights, food insecurity, health care, and the loss of one's livelihood, shape gender-based violence but also exist independently as human rights concerns of women separate from rape or the threat of rape (Pankhurst 2007; Enloe 2007). Further, rape is one of many forms of sexual violence that women as a gender group experience. Feminist legal scholarship increasingly calls on the legal recognition of acts such as forced nudity and separation from infants to be recognized as egregious forms of sexual violence and, more broadly, gender-based violence (Ní Aoláin 2000b). Like most studies on gender and armed conflict, mine focuses on women. Even as I caution against losing men's stories, I acknowledge that the recent and drastic changes in the understanding of the impact of war on civilians but particularly on women civilians intensified my interest in civilians and particularly women survivors, such as Bintu, and their stories about war. And it is women's relationship to law and justice that takes center stage in my overview of the international human rights law framework and the processes of transitional justice addressing, among other abuses, violence against women.

In Chapter 1, I introduce violence against women as an extreme form of inequality and discrimination against women because of their gender. I outline the evolutionary process that put gender into the discourse of human rights law and subsequently within the jurisdiction of legal and judicial responses to war crimes and crimes against humanity. The laws of war are activated by armed conflict, and my case studies of Rwanda and Sierra Leone are decidedly conflict or postconflict societies. For this reason, I also present a brief overview of the feminist critique of international humanitarian law prohibitions against rape and other forms of sexual violence against women in wartime.[23] My focus will, however, remain on human rights law instruments and not the laws of war because even as international humanitarian law seeks to minimize the civilian population's vulnerability to the vagaries of war, it is in fact military expediency that lies at the heart of its objectives. This prioritization of military interests over civilians' explains in part its limited relevance to my discussion in Chapter 1. Further, I demonstrate in Chapter 1 the unabashed and important trespass of human rights discourse into the jurisdiction of international humanitarian law. I argue that unlike the laws of war, human rights have responded substantively in the postwar period to the reality of belligerents that willfully target civilians as proxies for enemy combatants. This response has helped keep civilian women's experiences of atrocity in war in the imagination of international humanitarians advocating for the rights of women in peace and war.

In Chapters 2, 3, and 4, I describe the ways in which gender and violence have been included or excluded from the processes of the ad hoc criminal tribunals in Sierra Leone and Rwanda and the Truth and Reconciliation Commission in Sierra Leone (TRC). My selection of mechanisms of accountability privileges judicial or quasi-judicial processes. Although many other nonjudicial mechanisms have operated or are operating in Rwanda and Sierra Leone, I chose judicial processes because I am aware of their power to create a historical account of atrocity and justice. Even into the new millennium, apologists and revisionists attempt to rewrite or deny historical facts of the Holocaust and World War II.[24] Most people would agree, however, that the prosecution and conviction of those most responsible for crimes against peace, war crimes, and crimes against humanity as part of the Nuremberg Trials helped confirm the fact of German aggression.[25] The Nuremberg process of justice establishing individual criminal accountability laid the foundation for the creation of the ad hoc criminal tribunals as well as the permanent International Criminal Court. The convictions have also provided a historical record of war crimes, war criminals, and their victims.[26] Like the Nuremberg trials, justice processes in Rwanda and Sierra Leone are setting historical legal precedents and are contributing to a historical account of conflict and peace in their respective regions. I argue that women's narratives belong in this historical account, and in these chapters I look at narratives and examine the extent to which they represent gender and violence.

My exercise is spurred on by the fact that Nuremberg's judicial-historical narrative of gender-based violence is far from satisfactory. While historians and other social scientists have amply documented the widespread and systematic nature of gender-based violence in World War II and its aftermath, a binding legal narrative does not affirm it. While French and Soviet prosecutors wrote evidence of mass rape into the trial record, the Nuremberg Trials did not explicitly criminalize rape and other forms of sexual violence as either war crimes or crimes against humanity.

The absence of specific prosecutions for sexual violence from the Nuremberg Trials was a great omission and a poor precedent for the ad hoc criminal tribunals. The prosecutor and trial chambers of the Yugoslav and Rwandan tribunals were unable to rely on judicial precedent from international criminal process when trying to define and interpret rape and sexual violence as international crimes. The decisions of the ad hoc criminal tribunals have remedied this omission, and broadly defined elements of rape and other forms of sexual violence are now part of the emerging body of international criminal law.

Tribunals and national courts have begun to refer to the ICTR and ICTY statutes and decisions, and in particular their definitions of sexual violence and rape are being coopted into national and international justice processes. The case law of the Sierra Leone Special Court, the final report of the Sierra Leone Truth Commission, reports of the special rapporteurs, general comments of the treaty bodies, and Security Council resolutions all specifically refer to the case law of the ad hoc tribunals. The doctrinal achievements of these tribunals are contributing to a growing awareness of a gendered experience of war and other forms of political violence. I am joining the growing number of legal scholars in assessing our profession's competence and consistency in doing justice to framing the intersection of gender and violence in Rwanda, Sierra Leone, and other countries and regions that have granted jurisdiction to prosecute war crimes and crimes against humanity to ad hoc international tribunals.

In Chapter 2, I focus on gender and violence in the context of an ethnic conflict. I use gender as a lens through which the dominant narrative of the authentic man and the authentic woman (his wife) are dethroned as the universal models of mankind to which human rights laws first tailored their protection mechanisms. I argue that one's categorization as the authentic man and/or his wife is a dubious privilege. In the context of armed conflict, the authentic man and his powerful and inviolable body make acts such as castration and other sexualized forms of torture such a potent attack. Conversely, it is this inviolable body that conceals castration from the investigation and prosecution process. I argue further in this chapter that the narrative presents the wife of the authentic man as valuable yet infinitely vulnerable—the better to complement the authentic man's power. This infinite vulnerability makes sexual violence such an incontestable and dominant narrative in peace and war. In peace, she must avoid public spaces such as the workplace and be indoors before dark in order to avoid the advances of predatory men. And in war, the enemy must rape her. In this narrative, the anticipation of sexual violence is a pervasive fear shared by the woman and her community. The legal framework's privileging of her vulnerability over other less valuable women's security guarantees that only her victimhood is acknowledged but not necessarily with an effective legal remedy. I will demonstrate that in fact such acknowledgment may result in more severe forms of self-cloistering and restricted movement. Using such categories as "small woman," "big man," and "big woman," I will introduce those victims that the International Criminal Tribunal for Rwanda could not accommodate in its narrative of genocide, which privileged ethnicity as a category of bias to the exclusion of gender and class.

In Chapter 3, I move from Rwanda's tribunal to Sierra Leone's TRC. Truth commissions do not produce judgments or case law. Rather, their legal and factual findings are presented in voluminous reports, and my discussion is based on the final report of the TRC. There is a great body of critical writing on the gendered processes and outcomes of truth commissions, largely produced by anthropologists, ethnographers, political scientists, and other social scientists.[27] My focus on the report is an important contribution to legal scholarship because substantive research on the findings of commission reports is minimal compared to research on the case law of tribunals. This oversight by legal scholars is surprising considering that recommendations made by truth commissions are far-reaching and, some would say, inventive: they can include demands for apologies and reparations to victims, petitions for commemorative monuments, and curriculum changes that would bring subjects such as conflict and peace building into elementary and high-school classrooms. However, these recommendations often remain unenforced because they are vested with moral and not legal authority, and governments and identified perpetrators are not compelled to take any positive action to redress the rights of victims. The disproportionate attention paid by legal scholars to case law is influenced by a tribunal's authority and stature in the hierarchy of mechanisms of accountability. For example, ad hoc criminal tribunals use their legal authority to convict and sentence public officials or other perpetrators for human rights abuses.

I argue in Chapter 3 that the TRC final report produces a human rights narrative of gender and violence that essentializes Sierra Leone's culture as harmful and inherently violent toward women. Building on this argument, I pay attention to the government's and the international community's representation of the TRC as a restorative and indigenous model of justice and the impact this has had on the commission's specific framing of gender and violence in Sierra Leone. In particular, I show how the report's rights based emphasis on forced marriage and early marriage as forms of gender-based discrimination produces a problematic narrative of marriage as an oppressive institution for women. As in Chapter 2, I introduce narratives in contradistinction to the dominant narrative. I create such categories as "adulterous wives," "cuckolds," and "merry widows" to illustrate that women do exercise agency, even from within oppressive social structures. In this chapter, I borrow heavily from narratives produced by ethnographic researchers embedded in

Sierra Leonean society whose work inadvertently but importantly disrupts the dominant legal narratives that I question.

In Chapter 4, I remain in Sierra Leone but move my focus to the Sierra Leone Special Court. A review of this court is important because its statute creates an extraordinary and broad gender mandate. The statute specifically calls for the Office of the Prosecutor to adopt measures that ensure the justice process realizes women's and girls' specific needs. In light of this mandate, I critique the decision-making process of the prosecutor, which I argue discriminated against female victims and witnesses and negatively affected their ability to participate in the justice process. I also critique the Special Court's narratives around forced marriage and sexual slavery as crimes distinct from the customary international law crime of slavery. This distinction made by the court relies on reducing crimes, such as forced marriage and sex enslavement, to multiple incidents of the rape of women. In so doing, the law avoids a broader gender analysis that would reveal the complexity of the crime of enslavement and the ways in which an enslaved person, irrespective of gender, experiences the loss of sexual reproductive health and autonomy, sexual autonomy, physical integrity, and dignity. Using a historical perspective, I borrow from the gender analyses of scholars who have studied transatlantic slavery and colonial wars to support my critique of legal categorizations such as "sexual slavery."

In Chapter 5, I provide a final roundup and review of my narratives and arguments. It is important for me to add at this stage that during my field work, I came to consider all Rwandans and Sierra Leoneans, who had lived in their respective countries or even the region during any period between the outset and the close of the armed conflict, as survivors of the conflict. I use the term *survivor* to convey that the civilian population was disproportionately targeted for and affected by human rights violations and war crimes committed by the conflict. Despite the targeting, they survived.[28] This approach in the field allowed me to avoid categorizing individuals dichotomously as either victims (women) or perpetrators (men).

Finally, I am guided in my selection of narratives and alternative narratives by Poyi Soyinka-Airewele's reminder that "in the narrative of African societies the invocation of the past is most intense when it is embodied within the discourses and memories of violent struggles, of communities emerging from and through collective traumas, of oppression, violent resistance and the continuity of pain on the minds of those who have suffered" (Soyinka-Airewele 2004: 7).

The Women Were Not Raped: Gender and Violence in Butare-Ville

In May 2004, a decade after the genocide, I sat with Aimable, a state prosecutor at the Office of the Prosecutor of Butare-Ville in Rwanda. I asked him for his thoughts on why prosecutors failed to pursue allegations of sexual violence. He answered with a story, describing a curious incident:

A detainee confessed to having raped a number of women. Aimable immediately recognized that this was an incredible confession considering that the death penalty was still in place in Rwanda for those who confessed to sexual violence and other crimes listed as category one offenses. Confessions for lower level crimes were frequent in 2004, but Aimable had not yet encountered a confession to a category one crime. The detainee made a full disclosure, and he listed the names of his accomplices and of the women, living and murdered, he had raped. Aimable duly commenced an investigation into these claims, starting with statements taken from the survivors. However, Aimable was faced with the unexpected predicament that the alleged victims denied that they had been raped by the accused or his accomplices. The women completely refused to cooperate with the Office of the Prosecutor. Consequently, Aimable was forced to withhold the rape charges from the dossier, although he did not doubt their veracity. I asked Aimable why the women reacted as they did, and he responded with a nod in my direction: "*You* should know why."

I assumed at the time that "I should know why" because I am a woman, and as my introductory chapter reveals, I received an early education in "rape fear." Therefore, I could easily place my rape fear into the context of a postconflict, yet still insecure society, where reprisal killings of women alleging rape were widely reported. However, I also assumed that "I should know why" because as a guest of the Office of the Prosecutor I resembled Aimable more than I resembled the raped women: I shared Aimable's academic and professional training as a lawyer and his experience of the criminal justice process. I understood as well as he did the opportunities and the challenges women genocide survivors would encounter when accessing that process. Some challenges stemmed from convoluted procedural issues and others from the substantive complexity of sexual violence as a crime against humanity and an element of genocide.

I have used Aimable's anecdote as well as the story of the denial of the women victims in lecture halls in Europe and the United States, and have thus produced a narrative about justice, gender, and violence. While I can quote or at least paraphrase Aimable's words, I produce a silence when it comes to the women. A gender analysis of the silence of the women victims is, however, also essential because their resistance to speaking within the criminal justice machinery produces a gap that acts as a challenge or counterweight to the promise (made by the likes of Aimable and me) of human rights law and transitional justice interventions to prevent or punish violence and other forms of discrimination against women.

The gap I describe also reveals the underlying political context that engenders violence against women in conflict as well as peaceful societies: Annemiek Richters's study of rape survivors in the United States showed that their experience made them aware of the "little rapes" that plague women on a daily basis. "Little rapes" were defined as encounters with such phenomena as sexist jokes and pornography, which were only perceived as negative after the experience of rape. Survivors realized that their real life world and their language are full of symbols of objectification and degradation of women, out of which the potential for rape arises. They became acutely aware that they were victims not only of an individual perpetrator but of male hegemony within society at large and of the social and political constructions that enable and even sanction gender-based violence (Richters 1998: 114).

Similarly, Susan Brison, a philosopher and survivor of sexual violence and attempted murder, describes her subsequent awareness of a pervasive culture of violence against women broadcast innocuously by the media in the United States. She explains that events such as the trials of the defendants in the Central Park jogger case, the controversy over the book *American Psycho* (and subsequently its film version), the Kennedy rape case, and the Tyson trial triggered "debilitating flashbacks" and a "visceral" reaction (Brison 1998: 21).[1] And Brenda V. Smith, a professor of law, describes how she has been able to place an abusive relationship between her parents within the context of a number of other equally violent experiences in her life, such as racial segregation, poverty, and a fear for her safety with people outside of her home (2003).

Richters, Brison, and Smith politicize what might otherwise be regarded as "ordinary violence." They push the reader to grasp the gravity and pervasiveness of violence, or the threat of violence in "peacetime," and its objective of maintaining gender inequality. The "little rapes" perpetuate violence against women such that the insecurity that women experience in peacetime is commensurate with that in a conflict. I believe that Aimable's victims, a decade after the genocide, were aware of the "little rapes" in their society, seen in the essentialization of genocide survivors by local and international media as "brutally gang raped and dying of AIDS";[2] the escalation of sexual abuse of the girl child in the home; and the examination and cross-examination of women before the International Criminal Tribunal for Rwanda and domestic courts often perceived by survivor groups as humiliating.

In 1994, Rwanda's legal system lay devastated by a long civil war, a swift genocide, and a judiciary that had lacked independence for decades. This situation resulted in impunity for state sponsored violence. In spite of this legacy, the transitional government known as the Broad-Based Government of National Unity (1994–2003) dedicated itself to renewing public faith in the judiciary, putting justice at the center of the country's democratization and peace process. A strong human rights discourse buttressed this call for far-reaching judicial and legislative reform. This governmental commitment mandated that prosecutors investigate sexual violence as an element of the genocidal massacres.

Human rights defenders in all conflict zones refer to the "culture of silence" surrounding sexual violence. Victims and their communities are said to refuse to disclose sexual violence to authorities, such as prosecutors, international investigators, the media, and human rights defenders. In contrast to these common assertions, I was taken aback during my research at the National University of Rwanda's Center for Conflict Management by the forthright manner in which Rwandans, male and female, discussed sexual violence as it was perpetrated during the 1994 genocide and as it had proliferated in postconflict society. In private as well as public spaces, such as the police station, Office of the Prosecutor, and the university's department of law that I visited, there was no culture of silence. I attribute this openness to the fact that rape in Rwanda was a public act, committed by light of day in classrooms, open fields, and even outside government offices where female internally displaced persons converged to seek refuge from militias and other *genocidaires*. At the same time, however, the high public visibility of rapes largely not only precluded discussions of specific cases of the rape of individual women but also made little impact on the prosecution of perpetrators of these rapes. A decade after the genocide, the gap between documented cases of sexual violence and criminal prosecutions of this crime was unacceptably wide.[3]

Since the 1994 genocide, some notable gains have been made in strengthening the human rights law framework at the domestic, regional, and international levels. However, these gains apparently were not enough for "Aimable's victims." They, and many other women, continued to choose to remain outside the parameters of formal legal redress offered by the state. Can silence create a narrative? In my experience, yes. The silent narrative of these women undergirds my review in this chapter of the international human rights law and international humanitarian law frameworks for the protection of women against violence, particularly gender-based violence. It suggests a gap between the imperatives of legal process and those of its intended beneficiaries.

In order to address this gap, I explore two important legal approaches to eradicating gender discrimination: the application of "formal equality" and the "single category axis."[4] Formal equality implies that women have equal rights and are treated as equal to men. Throughout the twentieth century, the formal equality approach to redressing the denial of women's human rights played an important role in combating inequality and discrimination against women. A popular example of its application could be seen in the post–World War II era when many European women were granted the legal right to vote.

A limitation of formal equality is that granting everybody the same rights does not ensure that these rights have an equalizing effect since everybody is not similarly situated. Thus, despite the legal award of formal equality, it may well be that some women still require the implicit or explicit permission of a guardian (such as a father or mother-in-law) before registering to vote. Or women citizens (unlike men) who marry foreign nationals may immediately lose their citizenship and the attendant right to vote. It may also be that as a result of a discriminatory education system, women's literacy levels are dramatically lower than those of men's, making them less informed about candidates' policies and reducing their inclination or ability to independently register as voters. Thus, realizing equality beyond formal equality requires complex and long-term gender-specific measures before the electoral process is a truly participatory one for both men and women.

The application of a single category axis analysis entails that lawmakers center their response to inequality and discrimination on one feature, and in the case of armed conflict, we see the recurring imagery of an essentialized female measured against an essentialized male.

Both formal equality and the single category axis approach result in legal responses that can only effect cosmetic or limited challenges to gender inequality, for example, by creating formal *de jure* equality between men and women. Further, the positive outcomes of the legal responses privileges a limited and usually elite group of women and not a wider demographic. Women's identities are multidimensional, which means that a combination of factors intersect with gender to shape and distinguish inequality and discrimination for individual as well as collective groups of women. Multiple identities in the gender group could refer to religion, civil status, age, race, ethnicity, nationality, disability, caste, and sexual orientation. Intersecting identities can aggravate as well as mitigate gender-based discrimination against women depending on the social and political context in which a woman is located. Overturning essentialism and understanding the role of intersecting identities is crucial for the human rights law framework to meet effectively the concerns of women at all levels (universal, collective, and individual).

To clearly illustrate the human rights law framework for the purposes of a gender analysis, I have created a three tiered structure of rights. In the first part of this chapter, I divide international and regional laws into three "tiers" representing a progression of the inclusion and exclusion of women as a gender group and gender-based violence into and from the human rights discourse. My examination of the trilevel framework also reveals the gradual trespass of human rights law into situations of armed conflict and the jurisdiction of international humanitarian law, also known as the laws of war. I begin with the caveat that my selection of the various human rights instruments should not be read as a chronological or linear evolution of human rights legislation. For example, a 1948 declaration should not immediately be viewed as less gender inclusive than a 1978 declaration. Rather, what guides my chronology from the first to the third tier is the inclusion of gender into the ambit of the instrument in question. Further, the instruments I refer to in this study should not be regarded as exhaustive. I have selected representative laws that provide clear illustrations of a shift toward gender awareness in the interpretation and application of norms that ostensibly protect women against discrimination.

In the second part of this chapter, I discuss two key features of the feminist legal critique of international humanitarian law. The first relates to the reductionist presentation of women as vulnerable mothers, and the second to the interpretation of violence against women in wartime as an honor crime against the community. I support the feminist critique in its call for individualizing the multiple harms women experience in war, but I also argue that the critique should not totally ignore women's identities in the collective, and women's own valorization of motherhood and their reproductive capacities. An elaborate intersection between individual and collective harm shaped ethnic violence in Rwanda, and in order to describe it, I refer extensively to the feminist critique of legal scholarship on the Holocaust for its failure to unpackage the harm Jewish women suffered as mothers and caregivers of children. I also use the repatriation of Korean women after World War II and Indian women after partition as comparative examples that demonstrate that women's roles are multidimensional and that a strong individual identity does not have to exclude a woman's membership in a group or her desire to fulfill the gender roles within her community.

First Tier

The first tier of international human rights law was enacted shortly after and was greatly influenced by World War II. The Universal Declaration of Human Rights (1948) (UDHR) has influenced the development of subsequent human rights treaties, codes, declarations, and proclamations since its adoption. In particular, the International Covenant on Civil and Political Rights (1966) (ICCPR) and the International Covenant on Economic, Social, and Cultural Rights (1966) (ICESCR) greatly elaborated on the principles and protections laid down by the UDHR. Together the three documents are referred to as the International Bill of Rights.

The UDHR states that all human beings are born free and equal in dignity and rights and that everyone is entitled to all the rights and freedoms without distinction of any kind, such as race, color, sex, language, religion, political or other opinion, national or social origin, property, birth, or other status (UDHR, art. 1 and 2; ICCPR, art. 2[1] and 3).[5] While the ICCPR and ICESCR provide greater elaboration of women's rights than does the UDHR, the focus remained on women's biological differences from men, particularly their sexual reproductive potential. This focus is apparent in the ICCPR, which prohibits the execution of pregnant women (art. 6[5]). Apart from this reference to the pregnant woman felon (and the desire to protect her fetus), the larger question of gender discrimination and how it might affect women's enjoyment of the right to a legal remedy or equality before the law is ignored by the International Bill of Rights. For example, women do not have legal standing in many societies despite formal equality in constitutions and national laws, and, without such standing, a woman would require a male custodian to pursue an action on her behalf.

The role that gender plays in criminal actions where a woman is the accused is also inadequately provided for by the gender neutral human rights law provisions. Are jurors more hostile to women felons than men? Are women defendants more likely to be indigent than men? Is a female prostitute more likely to be arrested and prosecuted than her male client? Responding to such questions with an analysis of social constructions of masculinities and femininities brings the principle of formal equality and nondiscrimination before the courts into doubt. Further, it demands that human rights instruments respond to women as belonging to a gender group and whose performance of gender roles has serious consequences on their relationship to justice processes.

The ICESCR provision that women enjoy just and favorable conditions of work and remuneration equal to that of men for equal work is another case in point (art. 7). The protection fails to address pertinent gender issues, such as working hours that do not take into account women employees' prescribed gender role as the primary caregivers to children, partners, elderly parents, and sick or otherwise dependent family members. Such an omission treats women's choice to work part time or to leave the workforce altogether as personal decisions that reflect women's natural lack of ambition or failure to meet the rigors of professional life. Companies are exempt from charges of direct or indirect indiscrimination or from investing in support systems that might ease women's disproportionate domestic burden.

Apart from the justice system and the workforce, another institution left unchallenged by the International Bill of Rights is the family, referred to as the "natural and fundamental" group unit of society (UDHR, art. 16; ICESCR, art. 10). The rights of women in relation to family life when elaborated upon by these first tier instruments refer typically to marriage and child care, signifying those areas defining women's sexual and reproductive functions (ICCPR, art. 23). The focus on protecting women's reproductive and sexual potential assumes that the heterosexual, married couple biologically certifies the family as natural and, if not pro-woman, then at least benign. This normative assumption that women belong in relationships with men—within the marriage union—fails to examine how heteropatriarchy creates a context of risk for women. Such risks to women are seen as aberrations rather than forms of violence in a continuum of various forms of violence that affect women's lives (Wilkerson 1998: 131).

This idea of promoting formal equality between women and men while subjecting women to the control and even tyranny of the family and other community based institutions is a typical feature of first tier human rights instruments. Within these legal frameworks, women belonged or were relegated to the (private) home "for their own protection" owing to their biological and/or sexual vulnerability and in order to nurture their childbearing and maternal instincts. The first tier human rights instruments with their formal equality approach fell short of effectively identifying the gendered nature of human rights violation and could not produce effective remedies. This shortcoming led to the depoliticization of private acts of violence and other forms of discrimination and left the structural inequalities intact.

The single-axis approach was also evident in the first tier. The failure of the International Bill of Rights to recognize inequalities among women within the universal category of "woman" poses a challenge to subsequent first tier human rights instruments, such as the Convention on the Elimination of All Forms of Racial Discrimination (1965) (CERD) and the African Charter for Human and People's Rights (1981) (Banjul Charter).

The Banjul Charter is Africa's first regional human rights instrument. Enacted forty years after the UDHR, the Banjul Charter's political backdrop is not the Holocaust but rather the colonization of African peoples by European nations, especially France, Britain, Belgium, and Portugal. With the rapid liberation of many African countries throughout the 1960s and 1970s, it is unsurprising that national sovereignty, control of mineral wealth, development, and reclaiming values and cultures that had been besieged by the colonial experience were central objectives of the Banjul Charter. The charter represents a claim by Africans that their experience of human rights denial, characterized chiefly by their historical subjugation and exploitation on racial grounds by Europeans, was so unique and specific to the African continent as to require not only a universal human rights framework in the shape of the International Bill of Rights but also a regional one.

Banjul's provisions on equality and nondiscrimination mirror those of the International Bill of Rights (Banjul Charter, art. 2). The trademark feature that makes the Banjul Charter a first tier instrument is the assumption of a universal experience of rights enjoyment and denial for the Pan-African family. While Africans are distinguished from the universal family envisaged by the International Bill of Rights, Banjul does not evince that human rights violations overlap and affect African groups in specific ways according to their gender, race, religion, color, and so on. In Banjul's narrative, Africans are presented as a monolithic family united against the colonizing West. However, Banjul never envisages the reality of human rights abuse by legitimate African governments. The general prohibition of discrimination against "ethnic groups," for example, does not lead to any elaboration on how these groups can be more vulnerable to human rights denial and abuse when political allegiance forms along tribal lines. Banjul has no provision against state authorized land grabbing from indigenous groups, for example, or forced relocation arising from development projects agreed on by the state and international donors that deny these groups the exercise of their cultural livelihood.

The Banjul Charter does, however, make an effort to emphasize the rights of women beyond the generic salute to nondiscrimination and equality. States are called on to ensure the elimination of every form of discrimination against women and to ensure the protection of the rights of the woman and the child according to international declarations and conventions. However, this call is made while invoking the family as the natural unit of society and custodian of community morals and traditional values (art. 18[1]). It is a disingenuous protection that places women within a private space governed apparently not by law or state but by the community's customs and traditions. The family and the community are given free rein over the delineation of women's freedoms according to their discretion and guided by malleable traditional morals and values. This provision within Banjul gives a nod to traditional practices that violate women's rights but places such violation beyond the public space that demands state intervention. Whether at the international or regional level, there was a first tier tendency to "protect" women as a reproductive source by placing them within a private space overseen by parents, guardians, and husbands. This tendency affirms Thomas McClendon's point that while African men and the state had their long-standing conflicts, they agreed that the subordination of African women through control of their mobility from rural to urban areas and reproductive rights maintained patriarchy and other forms of male privilege (2002: 164–79).[6]

The presumed universality of the Pan-African family makes belonging to the African group the single axis on which rights protections are elaborated. Thus, racism apparently has no linkage to sexism and other bias. Within this human rights law narrative there is no room for human rights protections that respond to gender discrimination experienced by men and women in their homes, in prisons, in the military, in the workforce, in accessing health care, in accessing maternal health care, and so on. Banjul creates a human rights law narrative in which African men, women, and children suffer (colonial) persecution as a universal or monolithic experience.

CERD is one of several thematic human rights instruments expanding on a specific area of discrimination referred to broadly by the International Bill of Rights. It is rooted in the fundamental equality principle of the International Bill of Rights, although it focuses exclusively on the prohibition of discrimination on the grounds of race, color, descent, and national or ethnic origin (CERD, art. 1). Like the Banjul Charter, CERD is located in social and political structures, such as apartheid and segregation, that led to wide-scale racial discrimination. However, as race is taken as the single category axis, no effort is taken to investigate the ways in which racial discrimination combines with such intersecting features as caste, class, gender, and religion. In this way, CERD could fail to effectively protect, for example, Dalit Christians in India, Malaysians with Chinese ancestry, or African American women from discrimination in the workforce or school system. There is a uniformity assumed in groups targeted for racial discrimination but no attempt to disaggregate these groups in order to see how multiple identities might exacerbate or mitigate discrimination.

The Banjul Charter and CERD made substantial advances from their precedent in the first tier of human rights, the International Bill of Rights. They provide clearer definitions of discrimination, and while they do not refute the universality of human rights, they deny any uniformity in the ways in which freedoms are enjoyed and denied. In the case of Banjul, rights are placed in the context of African culture, history, and politics. CERD focuses on specific groups who suffer discrimination on the grounds of race and the political regimes that make widespread racism possible. Banjul and CERD begin the task of disaggregating victims of discrimination; however, like the International Bill of Rights, they fail to expose gender-based discrimination as a pervasive human rights violation.

Second Tier

The advent of the Convention on the Elimination of All Forms of Discrimination Against Women (1978) (CEDAW) represents the evolution from first to second tier instruments marked by the prominent location of women's rights in human rights law. CEDAW, the central second tier instrument, made several bold moves away from the approach of the International Bill of Rights to eradicating gender inequality and discrimination. It provides an important substantive definition of discrimination against women as follows: "Any distinction, exclusion or restriction made on the basis of sex which has the effect or purpose of impairing or nullifying the recognition, enjoyment or exercise by women, irrespective of their marital status, on a basis of equality of men and women, of human rights and fundamental freedoms in the political, economic, social, cultural, civil or any other field" (art. 1).

The indivisibility of economic, social, and cultural rights from civil and political rights is affirmed by this definition, and although the term *sex* rather than *gender* is used, CEDAW does not underestimate the socially constructed gender roles and expectations that constrain women in their enjoyment of human rights. CEDAW urges states to end prejudices and harmful stereotypes of women based on the idea of their inferiority in all spheres of life, specifically in the field of education (art. 5 and 10[c]). In a revolutionary step revealing its recognition of the unevenness of the playing field between men and women in the enjoyment of their rights, CEDAW provides for temporary special measures such as affirmative action to facilitate women's attainment of gender equality with men (art. 4).[7]

Despite its status as the International Women's Bill of Rights, CEDAW has not escaped criticism for maintaining elements of the formal equality approach to attaining gender equality, particularly with respect to the right to employment and participation in political life and omissions relating to forms of gender-based violence, such as domestic violence. CEDAW calls for women's equal participation in the workforce and the political realm, areas traditionally dominated by male employers and employees, without addressing hostile hegemonic responses such as sexual harassment. Sexual harassment was not acknowledged as a human rights abuse in CEDAW's narrative on women and their enjoyment of human rights, despite it being a long-standing barrier for many women to enter, excel, and be retained in the workforce or in political life. And indeed, women who experience harassment from subordinates, peers, and superiors may have no option but to opt out of a hostile work environment. This "free choice" is not far removed from the "voluntary" decision taken by Prosecutor Aimable's victims to opt out of the justice process in Rwanda. Human rights instruments may grant equal rights to men and women but then leave women ill-equipped to navigate the hostile repercussions from colleagues, family members, governmental authorities, and others that constrain them from fully realizing their rights.

CEDAW provides extensive protection for women as a unitary and universal group. However, it is limited in its efforts to acknowledge that within the universal woman group there are differences that can increase vulnerability to human rights abuse. It restricts this recognition to married women, rural women, prostitutes, and trafficked women (art. 6, 14, and 16). The selection is in its own way a caricature of the different roles that women may play in a society and may even be understood to suggest that a married woman, for example, cannot also be both a prostitute and a rural woman. The complexities of women's multiple identities are far from encompassed by first and second tier instruments. These groups identified by CEDAW inarguably require special attention; however, their inclusion cannot be justified when migrant women, domestic workers, displaced women, LGBT (lesbian, gay, bisexual, and transgender) women, disabled women, women living with HIV/AIDS, refugee women, and other groups of women are not considered.

With regard to CEDAW's reference to prostitutes and trafficked women, in particular, the failure to address the intersection of gender discrimination with other bases of discrimination, in particular race discrimination, weakens any protection measures. The international traffic in women is in many cases embedded with beliefs in the racial inferiority of women, whether they are trafficked Slavic women being received in the Netherlands, Filipino women in the United States, Korean women in Japan, Senegalese women in Spain, or Albanian women in Italy. In order for states to respond effectively (and not only with the arrest and/or deportation of prostitutes and trafficked women), international norms that recognize the intersecting and complex issues that lead to violations of the rights of women must guide them.

A founding principle of the women-of-color movement states that the struggle against patriarchy is linked to the struggle against all forms of subordination, and therefore all forms and patterns of oppression and subordination are interlocking and mutually reinforcing.[8] Similarly, the theories of Third World feminists have insisted on the complex interrelationships between feminist, antiracist, and nationalist struggles (Ferguson 2003, quoted in Anghie 2008: 46). CEDAW's narrative of discrimination against women and inequality suggests that the subordination of women on the grounds of sex and gender occurs along a single category axis. Kimberlé Crenshaw argues that this axis "erases black women" in the conceptualization, identification, and remediation of race and sex discrimination by limiting inquiry to the experiences of otherwise privileged members of the group (1989: 139–40). Crenshaw points out that this approach, when applied to feminist theory and antiracist politics analysis, creates a paradigm of sex discrimination that tends to be based on the experiences of white middle-class women while the model of race discrimination tends to be based on the experience of black middle-class men (ibid.: 151).

The Human Rights Committee (HRC) and the CERD Committee are committees for the ICCPR and the CERD, respectively. The HRC was established to monitor the implementation of the ICCPR, and the CERD Committee monitors implementation of the CERD. The General Comments passed by the HRC and the CERD Committee are widely accepted as interpretative sources of human rights substantive law, and within my trilevel framework, their comments represent the most (gender) developed spectrum of the second tier of human rights instruments.

However, the foremost comments made by the HRC and the CERD Committee neglected to put gender into the interpretation of their respective conventions. Like the first tier instruments before them, the treaty bodies were criticized for failing to recognize that gender adds a significant dimension when defining the substantive content of individual rights or that it should affect the choice of methods that must be adopted by states to ensure that all individuals within their jurisdiction enjoy those rights equally (Byrnes 1988: 216).[9] Andrew Byrnes aims this criticism specifically at HRC General Comment 16 (1988) on the right to privacy, which ignores the importance that this right has assumed in the struggle of women for control over their reproductive lives, for example, with respect to abortion or the spacing of children (HRC General Comment 16, art. 17).[10] Instead, traditional (androcentric) concepts, such as the inviolability of the home from state interference and restrictions on the use of sensitive personal information by governments and others, were the major preoccupation of the HRC (Byrnes 1988: 217). The narrative arising from the HRC General Comment on the issue of privacy privileges the concerns of men.

However, with the passage of time committee members have come to place gender at the core of their comments. Through these General Comments, first and second tier human rights instruments have been elaborated upon in order that women's multiple identities are identified and considered. General Comments have become an important means of normative development in a regime that is frustratingly limited in this respect (Otto 2002: 10). The HRC, earlier criticized for failing to take gender into account, produced the far reaching General Comment 28 (2000) addressing article 3 of the ICCPR on equality between men and women. Gender is squarely addressed as grounds for discrimination, and its impact on vulnerability to discrimination as well as the shape of discrimination is discussed within this comment. States are instructed by General Comment 28 that combating inequality in both public and private spaces is the responsibility of the state and cannot be limited to formal equality but requires multiple responses, including the removal of obstacles to the equal enjoyment of such rights, the education of the population and of state officials in human rights, the adjustment of domestic legislation, and affirmative action for the advancement of women (art. 3 and 4).

General Comment 28 goes on to prohibit states from justifying unequal treatment and opportunity for women on the grounds of tradition, history, and culture or religious attitude. Dowry killings, clandestine abortions, prenatal sex selection, and the abortion of female fetuses are condemned as a manifestation of discriminatory attitudes that subordinate women (art. 5 and 10). General Comment 28 describes how poverty and deprivation, armed conflict, and states of emergency can compromise women's rights and increase their vulnerability to discrimination, often in the shape of violence, such as sexual violence and abduction (art. 10).

As I stated earlier, CERD had ignored gender related aspects of racial discrimination. The CERD Committee replicated this omission in all nineteen of its General Comments passed before 1996. At one stage, the CERD Committee chairperson made the astounding declaration that he rejected directives to integrate gender issues into the CERD's work as "fundamentally misconceived" and considered that it was the CEDAW Committee's job to deal with women (Gallagher 1997: 304, quoted in Otto 2002: 27).[11] This statement was even more astounding considering that in 1995 the chairpersons of the treaty committees had endorsed a shared commitment to "fully integrate gender perspectives into their working methods, including identification of issues and preparation of questions for country reviews, general comments, general recommendations, and concluding observations."[12]

It is notable, therefore, that in the past decade the CERD Committee has surpassed the HRC in its efforts to incorporate gender into its treaty. Indeed, the CERD Committee has introduced a gender analysis of human rights into various comments and not only a thematic comment on gender. In General Comment 25 (2000), the CERD Committee notes that there are circumstances in which racial discrimination only or primarily affects women, or affects women in a different way or to a different degree than it affects men. Such racial discrimination will often escape detection if there is no explicit recognition or acknowledgment of the different life experiences of women and men, in areas of both public and private life (art. 1). Further, certain forms of racial discrimination may be directed toward women specifically because of their gender, such as the coerced sterilization of indigenous women and the abuse of women workers in the informal sector or domestic workers employed abroad by their employers (art. 2).

The CERD Committee's General Comment 25 (2000) elaborates that racial discrimination may have consequences that affect primarily or only women, such as pregnancy resulting from racial bias–motivated rape; in some societies, the women victims of such rape may also be ostracized (art. 2). Women may also be further hindered by a lack of access to remedies and complaint mechanisms for racial discrimination because of gender related impediments, such as gender bias in the legal system and discrimination against women in private spheres of life (art. 2). General Comment 25 clearly states that gender discrimination is highly likely to intersect with racial discrimination and urges states to investigate this intersection in a consistent, systematic manner (art. 3). This is a landmark interpretation, and analysis of racial and gender discrimination as indigenous women, minority women, displaced women, imprisoned women, women before a prejudiced justice process, women political prisoners, women in armed conflict, and other unspecified groups are envisaged by the committee as falling within the mandate of CERD.

The CERD Committee succeeds with this General Comment in enhancing its efforts to integrate gender perspectives, incorporate gender analysis, and encourage the use of gender inclusive language in its sessional working methods, including its review of reports submitted by states' parties, concluding observations, early warning mechanisms and urgent action procedures, and general comments (also known as general recommendations) (art. 4). This is a remarkable commitment, and since it was made, the CERD Committee has passed two other General Comments that show a sophisticated analysis and mainstreaming of gender issues. General Comment 27 (2002) on discrimination against the Roma provides states with measures for the protection of Roma communities. It also refers in several instances to Roma women who are often victims of "double discrimination" (art. 6). In the area of education, for example, states are urged to take responsibility for the high drop-out rates of Roma children and to take into account gender issues that might force girls out of school far earlier than boys (art. 17). The comment calls on government programs, projects, and campaigns in the field of education to take into account the "feminization of poverty" (art. 22). The committee also urges that health programs implemented by states to service Roma communities factor into their policy and administration cultural attitudes that subordinate women and girls and contribute to their lower levels of education (art. 34).

CERD General Comment 29 (2002) focuses on the unique oppression caused by descent based discrimination, discrimination on the grounds of caste and analogous systems of inherited status.[13] Discriminatory practices against affected communities might include the restricted ability to alter inherited status; socially enforced restrictions on marriage outside the community; private and public segregation, including in education and access to public spaces, places of worship, and public sources of food and water; subjection to debt bondage; and subjection to dehumanizing discourses referring to pollution or untouchability (art. 1). Moving further and further away from the monolithic construction of women seen in first tier instruments, General Comment 29 also identifies the particular vulnerability of women to multiple forms of discrimination in the areas of personal security, employment, and education (art. 12).

The comment goes on to identify discrimination in education based on perceived gender roles for girls as well as caste or descent (art. 44). General Comment 29 specifically refers to sexual exploitation and forced prostitution as gendered experiences for women discriminated against on account of descent. The comment encourages states to account for such abuse and respond to it in projects designed to support these groups (art. 11). Both General Comments 27 and 29 with their careful attention to multiple and intersecting forms of discrimination have been successful in acknowledging claims of Third World feminists and the women-of-color movement that fighting discrimination requires an evaluation of interlocking forms of oppression. The CERD Committee also provides a gender analysis in General Comment 31 on the prevention of racial discrimination in the administration and functioning of the criminal justice system (2005).[14] It is certain that in future comments gender will remain central to any analysis of racially discriminatory practices.

The CERD General Comments focus chiefly on discrimination that can be traced to state policy, for example, discriminatory entrance requirements for schoolchildren or discriminatory selection criteria for public housing. However, less attention is paid to investigating and naming inequality and discrimination as it manifests itself in formal and informal community institutions, including the home and places of worship. Thus, issues such as high incidence of domestic violence or early marriage within marginalized minority groups or cultures are overlooked because the focus of the General Comments is fixed on the position of vulnerable groups vis-à-vis oppressive state policy. Gender discrimination emanating from within the group is studiously avoided in the human rights narrative of second tier rights in an effort to avoid further stigmatizing such groups as the Mormons in North America, the Roma in Europe, and aboriginal peoples in the Pacific region. This omission inadvertently mirrors the omission of first tier rights to subject the family and other private institutions from any serious scrutiny of institutionalized violations against women and girls, particularly those arising from custom and religion.

The second tier instruments also continue to evade issues of sexual autonomy, thus leaving the enjoyment of this freedom in the custody of matriarchs and patriarchs in the family and the community. LGBT communities are well aware that their status as subaltern sexual minorities combined with race, color, descent, nationality, or ethnic features can greatly magnify hostility and even violent reprisals from their own ethnic but heterosexual community as well as from the dominant heterosexual community. This omission places the reality of discrimination on the grounds of race and sexual orientation out of sight and reach of human rights protections.

Third Tier

The distinguishing feature of third tier human rights instruments is that they are focused foremost on gender. Gender is not an afterthought but the core element shaping discriminatory practices against women. Third tier instruments view women's rights away from the mirror reflection that is a man (formal equality) or the uniform representation of a woman as Everywoman (single category axis). I focus in particular on the Protocol to the African Charter on Human and People's Rights on the Rights of Women in Africa (2003) (Maputo Protocol);[15] CEDAW General Recommendation 12 (1989)

on violence against women, Recommendation 14 (1990) on female circumcision, and Recommendation 19 (1992) on violence against women; the
CERD General Comment 25 (2000) on gender related dimensions of racial
discrimination; and the reports of the UN Special Rapporteurs, particularly,
the Special Rapporteur on violence against women and its causes and consequences.[16] Rather than providing a descriptive account of each provision
within these instruments, I analyze the most profound distinction between
third tier instruments and earlier instruments, namely, the expansion of third
tier rights into the private sphere. This move has brought once invisible forms
of gender-based discrimination, particularly familial and intimate partner
exploitation, abuse and violence against girls and women to the forefront of
human rights discourse. Most important, I look at the way in which third
tier instruments have brought violence against women into the narrative of
human rights law.

The CEDAW Committee's General Recommendations and the provisions of the Maputo Protocol supply some of the most innovative normative and interpretative protections against inequality and discrimination on
the grounds of gender. In 1989, the CEDAW Committee's General Recommendation 12 specifically called on states to protect women against violence,
including sexual violence, abuses in the family, and sexual harassment in the
workplace. It also recommended that CEDAW signatories include in their
periodic reports to the committee information about the legislative and other
measures in force to protect women against violence; the existence of support services for women who are the victims of aggression or abuses; and
statistical data on the incidence of violence of all kinds against women and on
women who are the victims of violence (art. 1–4).

And in 1992, the CEDAW Committee's General Recommendation 19
extended CEDAW's general prohibition on sex discrimination to include
gender-based violence, "that is, violence that is directed against a woman
because she is a woman or that affects women disproportionately." General
Recommendation 19 states that CEDAW's definition of discrimination prima
facie includes gender-based violence, including acts that inflict physical,
mental, or sexual harm or suffering; threats of such acts; coercion; and other
deprivations of liberty (art. 6). General Comment 19 provides an illustrative list of those fundamental rights and freedoms that can be impaired by
gender-based violence: the right to life; the right not to be subject to torture
or to cruel, inhuman, or degrading treatment or punishment; the right to
equal protection according to humanitarian norms in times of international

or internal armed conflict; the right to liberty and security of the person; the right to equal protection under the law; the right to equality in the family; the right to the highest standard attainable of physical and mental health; and the right to just and favorable conditions of work (art. 7).

It is a defining feature of third tier human rights instruments such as CEDAW General Recommendations that "private" violence is not only identified as a human rights violation but that state parties have an obligation to protect victims, punish abusers, and eliminate the practice in communities (art. 9).

The preamble to the Maputo Protocol points out that "despite the ratification of the African Charter on Human and Peoples' Rights and other international legal instruments by the majority of States parties, and their solemn commitment to eliminate all forms of discrimination and harmful practices, women in Africa continue to be victims of discrimination and harmful practices." This statement reminds us that the subject of human rights law and gender equality in Africa cannot be discussed without acknowledging the civil, political, economic, social, and cultural realities that women in sub-Saharan Africa continue to confront despite the existence of a human rights law framework at the international, regional, and domestic levels.

The Maputo Protocol defines violence against women as all acts perpetrated against women that cause or could cause them physical, sexual, psychological, and economic harm, including the threat to take such acts, or to undertake the imposition of arbitrary restrictions on or deprivation of fundamental freedoms in private or public life in peacetime and during situations of armed conflicts or of war (art. 1[j]).The preamble to the protocol defines violence against women specifically as a form of gender-based discrimination.. A rather bold entry into the private sphere and, particularly, into the family quarters allowed the protocol to emerge as the first international convention to explicitly articulate a woman's right to a medical abortion when pregnancy endangers the life or health of the pregnant woman or when it results from sexual assault, rape, or incest (art. 14[c]). It provides a far reaching construction of violence against women, including verbal attacks, sexual violence, and harmful traditional practices, conducted in public as well as in private spaces (art. 3, 4[2][a], 5, 11, and 12). Thus, it not only prohibits female circumcision as a harmful traditional practice; it also defines it as an act of violence against women. The Maputo Protocol is important in its emphasis that sexual violence is discriminatory against women. Elderly women are specifically provided for as vulnerable to violence, including sexual abuse (art. 22[b]).[17] This emphasis allows for the inclusion of women beyond reproductive age as targets for specific forms of sexual violence. Violence is not compartmentalized into states of peace and war or into private and public spaces.

The Maputo Protocol's condemnation of harmful traditional practices was preceded by CEDAW's General Recommendation 14 on the subject. General Recommendation 14 notes its reliance on the work of experts such as the Special Rapporteur on Traditional Practices Affecting the Health of Women and Children. These precedents as well as Maputo's location as a regional human rights body allowed it to place the prohibition on harmful traditional practices into early drafts and to negotiate agreements from member states at the signing and ratification stages. Inclusion in the main body of the Maputo Protocol has given the issue greater prominence; however, it is CEDAW's General Recommendation 14 that provides an extensive, layered interpretation of the cultural, traditional, and economic pressures that allow female circumcision and other harmful traditional practices to flourish. The recommendation identifies partners with whom states can cooperate in the eradication of harmful traditional practices, including traditional birth attendants, universities and other research centers, artists, religious leaders, and local and national women's networks. This particular focus emphasizes that the home, the community, and other previously "private" spaces are not exempt from the standards of equality and justice and are critical stakeholders in righting inequality.[18]

Like the CERD Committee through its General Comments, the Maputo Protocol is cognizant of the multiple forms of discrimination that women experience as a gender group and as individuals. It moves away from formal equality and attempts to engage with the multilayered genres of women in order to better serve women's interests and concerns with regard to the enjoyment of their human rights. The protocol calls on African states to take special measures to protect women in distress, including elderly poor women, women heads of families, women from marginalized population groups, and women with disabilities (art. 22 and 23). States are called upon to provide these women with an environment suitable for their condition and their special physical, economic, and social needs. It takes into account that formal equality will not suffice for women who are historically and systematically subordinate to men and to other women and who require special assistance to overcome physical, economic, and social disadvantages before they can begin to compete on a level playing field (art. 24).[19]

Feminist Critique of International Humanitarian Law

Before the consolidation of an international humanitarian law framework (and long before the consolidation of an international human rights law framework), international law did not directly address the status of women in armed conflict, although implicitly it reduced women's vulnerability to rape and other forms of violence. The Japanese Army's enslavement of Korean and other women in the 1930s and then throughout World War II is a good example of the outcomes of this exclusion of women from the public realm. Because women and girls were perceived as private objects rather than public subjects in law (Mitchell 2005: 236–37), the fact that they suffered extreme physical and mental anguish as a result of their enslavement was irrelevant. Military commanders saw this system of military enslavement as vital to maintaining troop discipline, public health, and public order in occupied areas. And even though the sexual violence was illegal, it was seen as inevitable during armed conflict.

Sadly, the Allied response to war crimes committed by the Axis Powers affirmed this position. The military trials in Tokyo and Nuremberg represent the first international effort to establish individual criminal accountability for war crimes and crimes against humanity. The prosecution of German and Japanese leaders showed that the enforcement of human rights could be possible with political will and international cooperation. An international treaty prohibited slavery in 1926, and yet the narrative of the international criminal justice process ignored well documented evidence of the systematic enslavement of Asian girls and women in World War II.[20] The first comprehensive legal narrative condemning the Japanese Army's enslavement of up to two hundred thousand women during World War II was promulgated in 1994, nearly fifty years after the fact. The International Commission of Jurists (ICoJ) commissioned a study that led to a mission to the Philippines, the People's Republic of Korea, and Japan (Dolgopol and Paranjape 1994).

All laws are products of their place and time. The atrocities committed by the Axis Powers, particularly the Holocaust, influenced the four Geneva Conventions (1947).[21] While little reference is made of it in the Nuremberg judgment, women's experience of anti-Semitism and of the Holocaust was a gendered experience. Fionnula Ní Aoláin provides one of the few gendered legal analyses of the Holocaust. She describes in particular how traditional attitudes toward women, their gender, and unique maternal responsibilities heightened the vulnerability of women living in ghettos (2000b: 53–55). Many of the atrocities committed against women in the Holocaust centered on their maternal position and included the deprivation of the reproductive rights of women through enforced sterilization, abortions, and separation from their children (ibid., 54, 57, 58). Women with young children were usually selected for extermination upon their arrival at camps. Their maternal status and their continued attachment to their children made them uniquely assailable and defenseless (ibid., 53, 56). Ní Aoláin's insightful gender analysis of the Holocaust explains in part the preoccupation of the Geneva Conventions with the protection of women as mothers. Few of the several specific references to women in the Geneva Conventions and the Additional Protocols (1977) transcend the woman-as-mother model of vulnerability and victimization in armed conflict.

This maternal narrative of women and their experience of war predates World War II and the Holocaust. Article 46 of both the Hague Conventions of 1899 and 1907 also provided an "honor based" construction of sexual violence. They asserted that "*Family honor and rights* [my emphasis], the lives and persons, and private property, as well as religious convictions and practice must be respected." This opaque language conceptualized sexual violence as a crime offending the virtue of women as opposed to a crime of aggression violating the human dignity and physical integrity of women. Family honor connotes the chastity of women and the potency of men to penetrate as well as protect "their" women from impure relations with rival men, and it is rooted in such patriarchal considerations as fear of miscegenation.[22] At its most basic construction, this is based on the idea that women raped by the enemy army/nation/race will bear children that will be alienated from the targeted group. Conversely, the symbolic poisoning of women by the enemy rapist makes them physically, psychologically, or socially infertile.[23] When enemy belligerents kidnap, rape, marry, or impregnate women, the fear that men will be deprived of a reproductive asset solidifies the construction of rape as an honor crime that primarily befalls menfolk as well as their communities. The patriarchal anxieties ignore the violent and traumatizing impact of rape on individual women. Ultimately, concepts of virtue and family honor objectify "pure" women and stigmatize "impure" women according to the gender standards of the day (Turshen 2001: 65). Both objectification and stigmatization are tools for the policing of women's sexual autonomy, economic productivity, and sexual reproductive potential in conflict.

Similarly, the exclusive portrayal by the laws of war of all women as "mothers," "nursing mothers," or "pregnant women" strips women of individuality and focuses legal protection on women's sexual reproductive potential.[24] This presumes and perpetuates the patriarchal claim of guardianship over the sexual and reproductive function and potential of women, an androcentric view of women's central role in society.[25]

The legal implications of reducing sexual violence to an honor crime are evident in the categorization of crimes. While the Geneva Convention (IV) prohibits rape, the category of crimes known as grave breaches does not include rape. The legal significance of this omission is that in the case of violations categorized as "grave breaches" of international humanitarian law—the *erga omnes* principle obliges states to prosecute violators or extradite them for prosecution in another jurisdiction. The placement of rape outside the category of grave breaches signified that sexual violence was subject to domestic jurisdiction only at the discretion of national prosecutors and not as a positive obligation.

The International Committee of the Red Cross (ICRC) attempted to remedy this miscategorization in 1958. The ICRC Commentary on the Geneva Convention (volume IV) recognized that the grave breach of "inhuman treatment" should be interpreted in the context of Article 27 (which prohibits rape) (Uhler and Coursier 1958). However, this contribution was ignored by the Diplomatic Conference on the Reaffirmation and Development of International Humanitarian Law Applicable in Armed Conflicts (1977) on the enactment of the Optional Protocols (I and II of 1977) to the Geneva Conventions. These protocols were introduced in order to increase the scope of international humanitarian law from international conflicts between states to non-international conflicts, such as civil wars and armed resistance against colonial domination and alien occupation.

The only provision applicable to non-international armed conflicts before the adoption of Protocol II was Article 3, common to all four Geneva Conventions of 1949.[26] This article proved inadequate since the majority of the victims of armed conflicts since 1945 have been victims of non-international conflicts and non-international conflicts are more likely to target civilians than are international conflicts.[27] The aim of Protocol II relating to the protection of victims of non-international armed conflict was to extend the protections of international humanitarian law to internal wars fought between "government's armed forces and dissident armed forces or other organized armed groups which, under responsible command, exercise such control over a part of its territory as to enable them to carry out sustained and concerted military operations and to implement this Protocol" (art. 1).

Despite the unprecedented attention the Diplomatic Conference raised around the experience of civilians in contemporary armed conflicts, the humanitarian law narrative remained fixated on women as mothers and generally marginalized any wider interpretation and analysis of gender and its interface with armed conflict.

Since the mid-1990s, there have been impressive gains whereby the trial chambers of ad hoc criminal tribunals have clearly adjudicated rape and other forms of sexual violence as acts of aggression against individual women. And the human rights discourse also increasingly eschews the narrative of vulnerable mothers in favor of civilian women navigating and challenging the insecurity of armed conflict. The gendered human rights critique at present requires scholars to privilege individual harm over collective harm, and at times it denies the collective harm altogether. This approach is said to provide women with the full recognition their war experience merits.

These positions, however, have left little room for an inquiry into the intersection between what Tina Sideris (Sideris 2001a: 57) refers to as the individual psychic injury and collective social traumatization caused by political violence. Entirely erasing the intersection between communal and individual harm makes it difficult for scholars to analyze the root causes, the motive behind and the impact of war crimes and crimes against humanity. The widespread repercussions of sexual violence, such as when women are raped in order to force an entire community to flee a region, cannot be entirely categorized as attacks against the individual. Particularly in the case of crimes against humanity, where a threshold of "widespread or systematic" attacks must be attained, the collective social trauma must necessarily be incorporated into the legal narrative. Introducing the collective impact of gender-based violence need not negate women's individual suffering, and it can enhance an understanding of the extent of harm and aggravating ramifications for women survivors.

The gender critique has focused its gaze on international humanitarian law and the way it constructs women chiefly as mothers and wives in relation to men. What is missing from this critique is women's own perception of their gender roles regarding, for example, the care and protection of children and the self-sacrifice of personal interests over those of their families and communities. I introduce the following three examples of women's experience of conflict in Asia and Europe to illustrate timely disruptions by scholars of the dichotomous construction of violence against women as either individual or communal in nature. The studies of the repatriation of abducted Indian women from Pakistan, the repatriation of Korean women from enslavement by the Japanese military, and the detention of Jewish women in ghettos and in the Holocaust provide vastly different contexts of armed conflict but raise related questions about constructions of gender and violence and the most effective responses to the harms suffered by women.

Ritu Menon and Kamla Bhasin have analyzed how women themselves do not necessarily separate their individual and communal identities from their experience of gender-based violence. Menon and Bhasin describe the political capital gained by the Indian government in its response to abducted women through the Central Recovery Operation carried out between 1948 and 1956.[28] The rescue was bitter and painful for many women: the women were abducted as Hindus, converted and married as Muslims, then repatriated where they reverted back to Hinduism; but they were required to relinquish their children because they were born to Muslim fathers and subsequently disowned as impure and ineligible for membership within their erstwhile family and community. Their identities were in a continual state of demolition and reconstruction by others (1996: 3 and 16).

The individual harm that some "rescued" women experienced cannot be grasped without an understanding of gender constructions governing the trajectory of women's lives within both Hindu and Muslim communities. Individual and communal ideas about gender roles, particularly relating to motherhood and marriage, shaped women's resistance to rescue. Thus, Menon and Bhasin's research shows that many Hindu women expressed a desire to remain with their husband-captors in order to preserve relationships with their Muslim children and/or to preserve the status and protection provided by Muslim husbands within the sacred institution of marriage. An intimate knowledge and even acceptance, in part or in whole, of communitywide ideas of motherhood, marriage, chastity, and honor shaped these individual choices to resist repatriation. The failure of the state's remedy (a recovery operation) to take this confluence of individual and community harm into account resulted in the pain and bitterness that Menon and Bhasin so poignantly recount.

Testimonies taken by the ICoJ from Korean victims of Japanese wartime military enslavement reveal the interconnectedness of individual harm and community harm in women's narratives of gender-based violence. ICoJ reports, in contrast to the scholarship of Menon and Bhasin, focus on a legal narrative and the need to insert both an individual and collective standard of harm when understanding women's war experiences. Because the ICoJ testimonies were collected decades after the period of enslavement, they prominently featured the hardship that women experienced after their liberation and repatriation. Society's rejection and the women's internalization of this rejection were responsible for much of this hardship. Sexual violence summarily and irrevocably deprived them of the honor and inviolability that attaches in patriarchal societies only to unmarried virgins, wives, and mothers.

I selected this first narrative because it so clearly emphasizes the interruption of motherhood and its fruits through stigmatization, ostracism, and a perpetual sexual objectification of the survivor of enslavement.

> When I reached my house, my husband received me very warmly while in the presence of the American soldiers. However, when the soldiers had left he immediately distanced himself from me. He told me to sleep in a separate room and made it very clear that he would not share a bedroom with me anymore. I swallowed this insult because of the fact that I could at least be near my children. However, he would not allow me to share my children's bedroom. I was thus isolated in my own house. Thereafter, I noticed that my husband also treated me just like a comfort woman. He would come to me whenever he felt the need for sex. He said he did not want to restore our original relationship because he termed me as a leftover of the Japanese soldiers. He could not reconcile himself to the fact that it was not my doing and that I was not at fault. My husband never fully understood or even tried to understand my plight. (Dogopol and Paranjape 1994: 74)

Another woman's testimony describes the interruption of motherhood through the loss of reproductive potential: "Because of her experiences she had to have a hysterectomy and continues to rue the fact that she has never been able to have children. At the age of 28 she married a man twenty-three years her senior and lived with him and his five children for three years, but as she had not been able to have any children, his family refused to give her any property after his death. She lived for many years in a Buddhist temple, helping the monks by cooking and cleaning and doing general chores" (ibid., 81). The ICoJ report places the sexual abuse of women into a patriarchal framework where male hegemony is absolute. The report duly decries this structural inequality yet also shows that the victims of sexual violence recount their experience of rejection long after the armed conflict in the patriarchal language of "shame," "virtue," "honor," and "impurity." The loss of access to family life and marriage, sexual intimacy, childbearing, and child rearing is lamented throughout the testimonies. This gendered presentation of victim testimonies does not obscure the fact that many women do in fact embrace the gender roles of mothering and childbearing as sites of social affirmation and personal fulfillment. Without acknowledging this, the resultant legal narrative of justice and remedies would have missed the fact that "the acts of brutality committed against these women go beyond the immediate suffering of having to endure a continuous rape . . . the pain these women endured has continued throughout their lifetime" (ibid., 57).

Ní Aoláin's study of a gender and sex based view of the Holocaust, which I have referred to above, also responds to the postwar enterprise of justice, which fell short of naming many harms that women experienced. To illustrate the failure of the laws of war to engage with the totality of harm experienced by women, Ní Aoláin focuses particularly on the harm arising from the separation of mothers from their children upon arrival at concentration or labor camps (2000b: 63). She makes clear that mothering is a gendered undertaking and both the Nazi captors and their victims understood it as such (ibid., 58).

Ní Aoláin recognizes the problematic nature of privileging motherhood over individual personhood; however, her analysis individualizes the harm of forcible separation by arguing for its categorization as another quantifiable harm occurring in the realm of the sexual self and not exclusively in the realm of the familial self (ibid.). Ní Aoláin points out that many women also articulate such separation from children as a physical act of aggression against their own person, concentrated on their own experienced sense of being female, aimed at undermining their sexual identity by taking away the expression of that reproductive self or product of sexuality, namely, the child (ibid., 61–62). I fully concur with Ní Aoláin when she judges the laws of war a failure in the wake of the Holocaust because they did not recognize forced separation as sex based harm targeting the woman's body, both in its symbolic and actual manifestations (ibid.).[29]

Sexual violence, whether inside or outside of armed conflict, carries a unique stigma because of its general perception as a specifically sexual violation, a view that tends to subsume its violent nature and gravity as a gender-specific offense (Mitchell 2005: 247). There are few modern societies that do not valorize purity and fertility in women. Acknowledging this valorization is a necessary step toward investigating the power of rape to destroy the fabric of society through the gendered targeting of women and, more important, toward finding social, political, and legal responses that can diminish this power. The call for the individualization of gender-based violence within international humanitarian law and a focus thereon as an act of aggression rather than an honor crime or a crime against a community is a valid one. However, a focus on the individual need not exclude her relationship with her community and its dominant constructions of gender, be they contested or accepted in whole or in part.

My brief accounts of the repatriation of Indian-Hindu-Muslim women and of Korean women highlight the fact that women's experience of gender-based violence is not extinguished with the end of armed hostilities. Hostile legal, social, and political responses often pursue women survivors of violence such that a state of conflict persists, at least in their private lives. It is therefore a striking omission that while international humanitarian law protections have moved from international conflicts to encompass internal conflicts involving nonstate actors, they have failed to expand their temporal jurisdiction, which is restricted to active hostilities. Thus, the scope of protection provided by international humanitarian law ends abruptly with the official ending of hostilities. The resultant narrative suggests that gender-based violence is temporal and unique to armed conflict. This short-sightedness results in a lost opportunity for policy makers (such as members of the Council of Europe responsible for the drafting of reports on sexual violence in armed conflict), who are charged to dismantle and reconstruct political and social structures that contribute to the conditions for the perpetration of widespread sexual violence against women in war and its aftermath. Leaving these structures intact generates new forms of sexual exploitation exacerbated by postconflict conditions.

Sexual exploitation proliferates in the immediate aftermath of armed conflict. Peacekeepers, humanitarian workers, invaders, occupying forces, demobilized fighters, and retreating forces are regularly implicated in the sexual exploitation of women and girls made vulnerable by months or even years of armed conflict. In the aftermath of World War II, Susanne Zwingel (2004: 8) describes how in the French, British, and American occupation zones, the situation of material deprivation generated considerable dimensions of "occasional prostitution" in exchange for basic goods.[30] Richard W. McCormick (2001: 106) reviews Helke Ander's film *BeFreier und Befreite* (1992) (U.S. title: *Liberators Take Liberties*) and presents as evidence of mass rapes an interview with a doctor who treated German women raped by the French on a massive scale in Freudenstadt, a town in the Black Forest, as a reprisal for atrocities committed against French civilians.

Yuki Tanaka has written about the widespread incidence of sexual violence by Allies in occupied Japan. He describes American soldiers breaking into the homes of civilians and raping women and girls, fondling girls and women clerking in public offices, and abducting girls and women for sexual violence (Tanaka 2002: 121–22). Most disturbing, however, is Tanaka's revelation that the defeated Japanese government created a "comfort woman" system for the occupation forces. Duplicitous police officers recruited Japanese geishas and prostitutes and coerced women and girls impoverished by the war into volunteering for a "special task" (ibid., 136–39). GIs typically gang raped "volunteers" repeatedly before they were sent to comfort stations also referred to as "recreation" and "amusement" centers (ibid., 140). Tanaka's account of the normalization of widespread and systematic sexual violence by Allied occupiers emphasizes that women's security remains precarious even as transitional governments appear to commit to democracy, rule of law, and good governance projects.

These postwar situations of gender-based violence are equal in scale to violence committed against civilian populations in armed conflict. And yet civilian women and their families were not able to seek justice from occupying powers responsible for the violence. Reporting sexual violence to the military police was futile, and the liberators and victors abused women and girls with impunity.

Human Rights Law Responses to Gender and Violence in Armed Conflict

As a state fluctuates unpredictably between war and peace, human rights advocacy has played an important role in bringing such forms of abuse to light. Human rights laws play an important role in the response to the harms women suffer. In the decades since the ratification of the Universal Declaration of Human Rights and the Geneva Conventions, the human rights law framework has developed at a faster rate in response to global trends in warfare than the more conservative international humanitarian law. It is fair to say that third tier instruments, in particular, have encroached on the territory of international humanitarian law standards and in many respects have overtaken international humanitarian law in protecting women against violations in "war," particularly with respect to the periods preceding and following war.

The committees for CERD and CEDAW have provided important

interpretations of the relationship between human rights and conflict, and world conferences have acted as a platform for states, civil society, and NGOs to affirm their shared commitment to human rights and to broaden their understanding of rights and duties. The impact of war on women's human rights has become a central point of advocacy and activism at these conferences.

The End of Decade Conference held in Nairobi in 1985 and the Forward Looking Strategies for the Advancement of Women referred to the especially vulnerable situation of women affected by armed conflict, including threats of physical abuse.[31] However, violence against women was not specifically linked to widespread and systematic violence in armed conflict nor was there a strong affirmation that violence against women was prima facie a human rights issue (UN Division for the Advancement of Women, 1988: 13). The reference to vulnerability implied that the concerns of international humanitarian law over women's honor remained the dominant area of concern.

To counteract the invisibility of abuses against women in the mainstream human rights discourse, the Center for Women's Global Leadership with a consortium of hundreds of women's organizations worldwide launched a global campaign for women's human rights to influence the Second World Conference on Human Rights in Vienna (1993) (Dauer 2001: 68). Their campaign goal was to give visibility to forms of violence against women that UN experts in human rights and governments had failed to include as part of human rights, especially those occurring in the community, family, and private sphere, and to demand government accountability for eradicating them (ibid.). To do this, the global campaign organized a series of (nonbinding) tribunals around the world, culminating in the Vienna Tribunal for Women's Human Rights, in which thirty-three women testified to firsthand experience of violence, including war crimes against women, political persecution, and discrimination (ibid., 66).[32]

An audience of NGOs and country delegates heard the testimonies while a panel of judges presided. The judges concluded that the failure to recognize violence against women and to protect their human rights was pervasive and required urgent attention. They identified three reasons for this general failure: a lack of understanding of the systematic nature of the subordination of women and of the social, political, and economic structures that perpetuate such subordination; a failure to recognize the subordination of women, particularly in the private sphere, as a violation of their human rights; and state neglect in both condemning and providing redress for discrimination and other violations against women (Dauer 2001: 68, citing Bunch and Reilly,

1994: 3). The judges made several recommendations, including the appointment of a Special Rapporteur on Violence Against Women at the UN Human Rights Commission; General Assembly approval of a UN Declaration on the Elimination of Violence Against Women; and the recognition of war crimes against women in an international criminal court (Dauer 2001: 69).

The General Assembly did go on to approve the UN Declaration on the Elimination of Violence Against Women (1993), and it provided that acts of violence included physical, sexual, and psychological violence occurring in the family, including battering; sexual abuse of female children in the household; dowry-related violence; marital rape; female genital mutilation and other traditional practices harmful to women; nonspousal violence; violence related to exploitation; sexual harassment and intimidation at work, in educational institutions, and elsewhere; trafficking in women; and forced prostitution (art. 2).

And although the declaration had no binding force, its influence can be detected in subsequent human rights conventions and the work of treaty bodies. The declaration's preamble referred to an increased vulnerability to violence that women belonging to minority groups, indigenous women, refugee women, migrant women, women living in rural or remote communities, destitute women, women in institutions or in detention, female children, women with disabilities, elderly women, and women in situations of armed conflict experience. However, it did not make the link between sexual violence and war crimes.

Further, the UN Human Rights Commission approved the appointment of an expert referred to as the Special Rapporteur on Violence against Women, who has produced various studies focusing on sexual violence in armed conflict. The International Criminal Court, established in 2000, includes in its jurisdiction rape and other forms of sexual violence, such as enforced prostitution, forced pregnancy, and sexual slavery, as crimes against humanity and as war crimes when committed in the context of international or internal armed conflict (Dauer 2001: 69).

The UN World Conference on Human Rights adopted the 1993 Vienna Declaration and Program of Action, and it also confirmed that violations of the human rights of women in situations of armed conflict are violations of the fundamental principles of human rights and humanitarian law and that they require a particularly effective response (Vienna Declaration, art. 30). The Vienna Declaration describes massive violations of human rights, such as genocide, ethnic cleansing, and the systematic rape of women in war situations as "abhorrent" and calls for the punishment of perpetrators (art. 28). It lists discrimination against women among some of the most egregious forms of gross and systematic violations of human rights alongside such crimes as disappearances and arbitrary detentions, crimes that are associated with armed conflict, particularly internal armed conflicts (art. 28 and 30).

At the Fourth World Conference on Women (Beijing Conference, 1995), the topic of sexual violence against women during armed conflict occupied a prominent position.[33] The Beijing Declaration and Platform for Action (Beijing Declaration) identified women and armed conflict as one of the twelve critical areas of concern that member states, the international community, and civil society should address (Beijing Declaration, para. 131–49). The Beijing Declaration defines violence against women as any act of gender-based violence that results in, or is likely to result in, physical, sexual, or psychological harm or suffering to women, including threats of such acts, coercion, or arbitrary deprivation of liberty, whether occurring in public or private life (para. 114). Violence against women in armed conflict is expressly referred to: "Other acts of violence against women include violation of the human rights of women in situations of armed conflict, in particular murder, systematic rape, sexual slavery and forced pregnancy" (para. 115).

The Beijing Declaration places violence against women in armed conflict within a structural hegemonic framework that subordinates the gender role of women in society (para. 136). It describes rape as a tactic of war and terrorism. The impact of war on women is described in terms of displacement, loss of the home and property, the loss or involuntary disappearances of close relatives, poverty, and family separation and disintegration (ibid.). Women are described not only as rape victims but also as victims of acts of murder, terrorism, torture, involuntary disappearance, slavery, sexual abuse, and forced pregnancy in situations of armed conflict.

The Beijing Declaration describes violence against women in armed conflict, foreign occupation, and other forms of alien domination not as a limited temporal event but as one having enduring social, economic, and psychologically traumatic consequences (para. 136). This recognition is integral to understanding testimony from women speaking years after the cessation of hostilities, as in the testimony I referenced above. The Beijing Declaration pays particular attention to the enhanced vulnerability to abuse and exploitation that refugee and internally displaced women experience (para. 137).[34] It shines some light on sexual violence against uprooted women and girls employed as a method of persecution in systematic campaigns of terror and intimidation that forces members of a particular ethnic, cultural, or religious group to flee their homes (ibid.). The declaration describes gender as a ground for persecution and transcends the temporal jurisdiction of international humanitarian law by pointing out that women persecuted on grounds of gender, for example, through acts of sexual violence, continue to be vulnerable to violence and exploitation while fleeing, in countries of asylum and resettlement, and during and after repatriation. It further states that women often experience difficulty in some countries of asylum in being recognized as refugees when the claim is based on such persecution (ibid.). An unequivocal recognition such as this is pertinent when recalling the invisibility of enforced prostitution, rape, and exploitative sexual bartering that so dominated the landscape of occupied and liberated Europe after World War II.

The Beijing Declaration is one of the first rights instruments to refer to the positive roles women play in mediating conflict and mitigating its harmful impact on themselves, their wards, and community. It states that during times of armed conflict and the collapse of communities, the role of women is crucial. They often work to preserve social order in the midst of armed and other conflicts and they make an important but often unrecognized contribution as peace educators both in their families and in their societies (para. 141 and 138). The Beijing Declaration also salutes refugee, displaced, and migrant women for their endurance, resourcefulness, and positive contribution to countries of resettlement or the country of origin on their return. The declaration calls on states to involve these women in shaping policy that affects them (para. 138).[35] More broadly, the declaration calls on states to mainstream a gender perspective into all programs responding to armed conflict and to increase the participation of women in conflict resolution at decision-making levels (para. 143).

Taking into account the violent power struggles that many African countries have undergone since the inception of the Universal Declaration, at the regional level, the Maputo Protocol pays specific attention to the protection of women affected by war, including those seeking asylum, refugees, returnees, and internally displaced persons, against all forms of violence, including rape and other forms of sexual exploitation. The Maputo Protocol uses the term *women* to include both women and girls; however, at times girls are given special mention by virtue of their status as minors, particularly with respect to their special vulnerability in armed conflict to sexual violence and recruitment for child soldiering (art. 11[3] and 11[4]). The Maputo Protocol, in the manner of third tier instruments, asserts that the perpetrators of such violence (gender-based violence as a war crime, genocide, and/or crimes against humanity) will be brought to justice (art. 11[3]).

References to violence against women in armed conflict in international human rights documents became more specific in the 1990s, with the media devoting attention to gender-based violence as a form of genocide and ethnic cleansing in Rwanda and the former Yugoslavia, respectively. In 2000 the Human Rights Committee noted the particular vulnerability of women in times of internal or international armed conflicts and called on state parties to inform the committee of all measures taken to protect women from rape, abduction, and other forms of gender-based violence (General Comment 28, art. 3[8]). Interestingly, the CEDAW Committee does not focus on making a "war" and "peace" distinction but leans toward describing hegemonic relationships, for example, those arising in occupied territories, where women may be especially vulnerable to sexual abuse and exploitation. In highly specific gendered language, the CEDAW Committee states that wars, armed conflicts, and the occupation of territories often lead to increased prostitution, trafficking in women, and sexual assaults against women, which require specific protective and punitive measures (General Recommendation 19, art. 16).

CERD General Comment 25 provides that certain forms of racial discrimination may be directed toward women specifically because of their gender, such as sexual violence committed against women members of particular racial or ethnic groups in detention or during armed conflict (art. 2). General Comment 25 also calls for accountability for abusers and makes an unprecedented demand by a treaty body for the establishment of an international tribunal to prosecute genocide and crimes against humanity, including murder, extermination, enslavement, deportation, imprisonment, torture, rape, and other inhumane acts directed against any civilian population on political, racial, and religious grounds. Not surprisingly, CERD's comment was made following the Security Council Resolution establishing the International Criminal Tribunal for the former Yugoslavia.[36]

The UN Office of the High Commissioner for Human Rights defines "special procedures" as those mechanisms the Commission on Human Rights established to address either specific country situations or thematic issues.[37] Although they may be constituted in any manner, special procedures are commonly either an individual, called a special rapporteur or representative or an independent expert, or a group of individuals, called a working group.[38]

These experts, whether individually or as a group, examine, monitor, advise, and publicly report on human rights situations in specific countries or territories, known as country mandates, or on major phenomena of human rights violations worldwide, known as thematic mandates. Experts can conduct studies, provide advice on technical cooperation, respond to individual complaints, and engage in general promotional activities. Thematic subjects taken up by experts have included investigations into trafficking in persons, child prostitution and child pornography, the human rights of internally displaced persons, and violence against women. These experts' reports include much needed interpretations of human rights instruments, and many include gender analyses that take into account the different ways girls, boys, men, and women experience human rights abuses on a day-to-day basis, including in armed conflict.

The work of the special rapporteurs and other human rights experts has added texture and depth to the international community's understanding of gender-based violence and its victims. Their elaboration on the shape and impact of gender-based violence is possible through country visits that allow a contextual analysis of harms, and often a critique of the failure to prevent and punish abuses through the implementation of the existing legal framework. The Special Rapporteur on violence against women provides far reaching analyses of violence against women in armed conflict. This body of work provides an unprecedented portrait of sexual violence as a weapon of war. Evidence collected from country visits she conducted under her mandate, particularly to Rwanda and Sierra Leone lays the groundwork to my discussion on justice, gender, and violence in these countries in Chapters 2, 3, and 4.

Following a country visit to Rwanda after the 1994 genocide, the rapporteur substantiated existing definitions of sexual violence with the testimonies of Rwandan women describing their personal experiences of genocide. Forced nudity appeared as a recurring theme in many of these testimonies. In one case, women were forced to strip naked as they dug graves and buried the corpses of their husbands (Special Rapporteur 1998: para. 78). In another case, a woman was forced to strip naked and walk for thirty kilometers; she told the rapporteur of the humiliation she continued to feel when she encountered people who had witnessed her nudity during the genocide (ibid., para. 34). The rapporteur referred to these experiences as not simply humiliation but as *sexual* humiliation that has resulted in mental health disturbances. The country visit allowed the rapporteur to write the continuum of harm into the narrative of gender-based violence, emphasizing the individual harm women experience as well as the aggravating nature of women's perceived sense of rejection and censorious judgment by their communities. Further, because of her physical presence in Rwanda, she was able to discern the violent and sexual nature of forced nudity and its cultural context from the victim's perspective. The rapporteur's report also provides insight into existing structural inequalities in Rwanda before the genocide, such as women's lack of access to land rights and poorly developed reproductive health care.

The special rapporteur's mission to Sierra Leone in 2001 also produced a gendered analysis of violence against women in armed conflict. As with the Rwanda report, the rapporteur sought to describe violence against women in armed conflict as well as to underline the fact that the aftermath of the armed conflict posed gendered obstacles to justice for human rights violations, social and psychological rehabilitation, and political and economic empowerment for women. Rape and other forms of gender-based violence are described as constituent elements of crimes against humanity and war crimes. The special rapporteur identifies specific groups that she determined were especially vulnerable to violence, including women and girls abducted by the armed forces, women and girls forced into sexual relationships with combatants, and women in internally displaced persons' camps. The rapporteur's interviews with women survivors of war revealed accounts of sexual violence and other heinous abuses, such as when an abducted teenager was made to carry her father's decapitated head in her arms on a forced march (Special Rapporteur 2002: para. 8).

As with the Rwanda mission and report, the rapporteur identified preexisting inequalities and discrimination against Sierra Leonean women that made postwar redress difficult: "Even before the conflict, women in Sierra Leone had been marginalized in all spheres of life. Some of the reasons for this were low or no literacy, poverty, lack of capacity to participate in decision-making and cultural constraints, all of which contributed to the low status of women in society. The conflict has exacerbated the problem by creating many female-headed households which face, among other things inappropriate shelter conditions, family separations and legal inequality, for example discrimination under the law in regard to property ownership and inheritance rights" (para. 34). The Security Council's Resolution 1820 (2008) can be seen as the culmination of decades of efforts to place gender-based violence within the narrative of gross human rights violations. The resolution's preamble specifies the significance of early instruments such as the obligations under CEDAW and the commitments under the Beijing Declaration to condemn, protect against, and punish sexual violence in armed conflict. Resolution 1820 displays the international community's comprehension that sexual violence is a weapon of war: "Women and girls are particularly targeted by the use of sexual violence, including as a tactic of war to humiliate, dominate, instill fear in, disperse and/or forcibly relocate civilian members of a community or ethnic group . . . rape and other forms of sexual violence can constitute a war crime, a crime against humanity, or a constitutive act with respect to genocide" (preamble and art. 4).

The gravity of sexual violence as a war crime is emphatically expressed through the resolution's exclusion of crimes involving sexual violence from amnesty provisions in the context of conflict resolution processes (art. 4). The resolution notes the continuum of (sexual) violence into the aftermath of conflict, and as a result indicts not only belligerents but "peace building" actors, such as local police officers and UN personnel as perpetrators of sexual abuse and the exploitation of women, particularly displaced women. Security Council Resolution 1820 has been the launch pad for increased Security Council intervention in conflict areas where sexual violence is widespread and systematic and where impunity for these crimes is the norm. Security Council Resolution 1888 and 1889 go so far as to acknowledge nontraditional gender roles of women, for example, as combatants who need full access to disarmament, demobilization, and reintegration programs, as refugees with specific humanitarian needs, and as partners in the peace and mediation process (Security Council 1889: art. 12–14).

Conclusion

Some substantive transformations have occurred in the laws of war as the impact of war, particularly, civil war on civilians has been acknowledged by the international community. Humanitarian law, however, has yet to make the transition from the category of tier one instruments with respect to gender. It still sequesters women in the private sphere but fails to acknowledge the trespass of war into that gendered space. It denies the central role that women's bodies have always occupied in warfare and thereby depoliticizes their experience of violence in contemporary conflicts.

I could categorize Security Council Resolutions 1820, 1888, and 1889, with their focus on international peace and security, as a new tier of the laws of war squarely addressing women's experience of armed conflict. However, these resolutions are clearly products of the human rights discourse and sustained advocacy that committee members of the human rights treaty bodies, special rapporteurs, feminists, and women's rights activists have generated. By strategically infiltrating and influencing political fora (such as world conferences, the General Assembly, and the Security Council) traditionally reserved for statesmen and jurists, these stakeholders in the movement to prevent gender-based violence in conflict are not elaborating on international humanitarian law but rather extending human rights law into zones of conflict. The Geneva Conventions, like the International Bill of Rights and other first tier human rights instruments, were unsuccessful in articulating violence against women as a gendered phenomenon in a structural continuum of oppression. To their credit, human rights instruments have dramatically outpaced the laws of war in bringing gender into the mainstream human rights discourse.

Conversely, the narrative of gender and violence that has emerged from first to third tier instruments tells us that violence against women is strategic in peace and war. The objective of perpetrators of violence is to maintain their own hegemony, which includes discrimination and the perpetuation of women's inequality in a widespread and systematic fashion.

In Chapters 2, 3, and 4, I move on to processes of retributive and restorative justice. In as much as justice is a process governments administer, the social outcry against transgressive behavior also drives it. Although I have shown in this chapter that third tier instruments have overwritten the traditional temporal jurisdiction of humanitarian law and exposed the structural systems behind gender-based violence, I have also argued that domestic and international tribunals prosecuting war crimes, crimes against humanity, and genocide have only recently begun to internalize these developments, and they have done so inconsistently. The women who denied rape and resisted Aimable's investigation are aware of the political and legal discourse that categorized sexual violence as an element of genocide that warranted the death penalty for perpetrators. And at the same time, they are hostile to the promise of justice. They expressed their agency as survivors not through participation but by withholding their testimony from the legal narrative. Their choice of privacy over publicity, of being silent victims over iconic victims, runs counter to the policy driven third tier instruments' call for the involvement of women in postconflict processes. However, I view it as a challenge to the legal practitioner and scholar alike to scrutinize the tribunals that are promising not only justice but also gender justice: their rules and procedures, participatory processes, and most important, their categorization and interpretation of gender and its intersection with violence.

Chapter 2

All the Women Were Raped: Gender and Violence in Rwanda

Lynette, a Rwandan girlfriend of mine, survived the genocide because at its onset she was attending a boarding school in Kenya. Neighbors, some of whom were relatives, massacred her parents. She returned to Rwanda after the genocide and reunited with those relatives who survived persecution. She studied law and on graduation was appointed as a state prosecutor. She recounted for me a conversation she had had with her Aunt Hermien nearly a decade after the genocide. Like Lynette, Aunt Hermien was a genocide survivor, the difference being that Hermien had been in Rwanda during the genocide. Lynette expressed her concern about Anna, Hermien's teenaged daughter. Anna's behavior had become increasingly erratic, to the point where Lynette suspected that her young cousin was mentally unhinged. Aunt Hermien listened to Lynette's concerns but eventually interrupted with a question: "Well, how do you expect Anna to behave after the rapes?" Lynette replied, in shock: "My cousin was raped!" Calmly, her aunt challenged her: "Lynette, show me a woman who wasn't raped."

In the last chapter, I described a prosecutor faced with a world where apparently none of the women were raped. Here I contrast the denial of these women with Aunt Hermien, who cries rape on behalf of all the women. She poses a daunting challenge to legal scholars and practitioners who believe that it is essential that all victims enjoy equal access to mechanisms of justice. In Aunt Hermien's response, I see a metaphor for the typical binary posi-

tions from which narratives on gender and violence lie within the sociopolitical discourse of a postconflict society. One position at the local level readily
accepts the narrative provided by Aunt Hermien: a casual acknowledgment
that Aunt Hermien and her daughter(s) were raped; all of us were raped; all
Rwandan women were raped; every Hutu woman and every Tutsi woman was
raped. In this wildly inclusive narrative of gender and violence, the woman
who was not raped is the exception.

As discussed in the previous chapter, the CERD Committee recognized
the intersection of gender with race discrimination and the ways in which
this impeded women's enjoyment of human rights (General Comment 25).
The committee also made the link between gender and its significance in the
commission of crimes such as ethnic cleansing in conflict and armed conflict.
In this chapter, I heed the CERD Committee's call for an acknowledgment of
the different life experiences of women and men, but I also move beyond the
double discrimination framework (i.e., ethnicity and gender) in order to reveal multiple forms of discrimination unexamined in the case law of the UN
International Criminal Tribunal for Rwanda (ICTR). I argue, in the same vein
as Aunt Hermien, that gender and other systemic forms of social discrimination made all women in Rwanda vulnerable to sexual and other forms of violence during the genocide, irrespective of their ethnicity. Even as I make this
argument, I must add that vulnerability to violence is never uniformly dis-
tributed among and between women because identity marks (none of which
were static), such as ethnicity, religion, nationality, class, race, and age, in the
context of the Rwanda genocide greatly enhanced or mitigated vulnerability.

The difficulty in my alignment with Aunt Hermien in this chapter is that
her powerful challenge from the local level to "show me a woman who wasn't
raped" is diametrically opposed to a second position at the international level
and, more specifically, at the substantive and procedural level of international
criminal law. International criminal law reframes the challenge in this way:
"Show me a woman who was raped." This challenge asks Aunt Hermien and
other survivors of wartime rape to try and place their experience within the
parameters of the mandate of the ICTR. Thus, allegations of rape must satisfy
the requirements of articles 2 (on genocide), 3 (on crimes against humanity),
and 4 (on violations of Article 3 common to the Geneva Conventions and of
Additional Protocol II) of the ICTR statute. The statute provides definitional
boundaries and thresholds that victim testimony must meet in order for their
allegations of violence to fall within the jurisdiction of the tribunal. Prosecutors and trial chambers' narrow interpretation of these boundaries has con-

tributed to low conviction rates for sexual violence, such that the resulting transitional justice narrative proclaims that "the woman who was raped" is the exception.

In this chapter, I argue that the ICTR's dominant narrative of gender and violence is monolithic and overtly exclusive. Through the analysis of case law from the ICTR, I show how the narrative of ethnic genocide, by privileging ethnicity as the requisite condition of sexual victimization, denies gender-based discrimination. The narrative suggests that sexual violence against Tutsi women is a type of ethnic violence rather than gender-based violence. Further, the privileging of ethnicity has led to an undue focus on women and their biological capacity to reproduce and, in so doing, has reduced the ICTR's gender narrative to a focus on women's sexual reproductive function. This form of reductionism closely resembles the traditional international humanitarian law preoccupation with protecting "mothers" and "nursing women" that I described in some detail in the preceding chapter. Moving away from the laws of war and human rights laws in this chapter, I extract the narrative on gender and violence from the work of the tribunal and, specifically, the Office of the Prosecutor and the decision-making process of the trial chambers.[1] The tribunal's narrative on gender and violence is important because it is a crucial determinant of which aspects of women's experience of armed conflict are actually investigated, charged, and prosecuted. Ultimately, the narrative determines which victims of sexual violence have access to international criminal justice and what aspects of their testimony are deemed valuable.

The role of my gender critique in this book is to affirm existing gender inclusions in the case law as well as to point out the exclusionary practices and interpretations that render the narrative on gender and violence incomplete. I use the critique to produce alternative texts and theories of gender and violence, which scholars and practitioners should read not as ancillary but as equally essential legal and pedagogical sources for application in subsequent tribunals' prosecutions of gross human rights violations.

In this chapter, I disrupt the dominant narrative by revealing the narrow interpretation of gender and violence in the following cases: Akayesu,[2] Muhimana,[3] Gacumbitsi,[4] Niyitegeka,[5] Ntuyahaga,[6] Bagasora,[7] and Ndindiliyimana and others.[8] I use these cases to create alternative narratives that illustrate the negative consequences of a restrictive construction of gender-based violence for women as well as men victims. I then subject my alternative narratives to a broad gender analysis of violence against women that I argue should be included in the dominant narrative already produced by the trial chamber.

I am creating and drawing my alternative narratives from a jurisdiction that is not domestic but international: substantively, the statute of the ICTR is rooted in international law norms that include customary international law. Thus, even as the statute consists of a "fusion and synthesis" of the common law and civil law traditions, it qualifies as a source of international law in conformity with Article 38 of the Statute of the International Court of Justice.[9] The case law or judicial decisions of the ICTR also qualify as a source of international law, either as international customary law or as a general principle of law (De Brouwer 2005: 27, 29).

The Security Council took the extraordinary step of establishing the ICTR under Chapter VII of the United Nations Charter.[10] The Security Council justified this executive action because the genocide in Rwanda posed a threat to international peace. The Chapter VII resolution created a binding obligation on all states to cooperate in the enforcement of justice in Rwanda, an obligation that was not dependent on states voluntarily ratifying a treaty as is the case with the International Criminal Court (ICC). This binding obligation gave the impression that the international community unanimously accepted the legitimacy of international criminal justice. More significantly, Security Council Resolution 955 (1994) specified that the government of Rwanda had requested the establishment of an international tribunal for the prosecution of war criminals. However, the Rwandan government's submission to the Security Council Resolution was short-lived. Its objections to various provisions of the statute of the ICTR regarding temporal jurisdiction, the severity of penalties, and the location of the seat of the tribunal outside of Rwanda (in Arusha, a town in northern Tanzania) were ignored by other Security Council members. The drafting of the resolution and the ICTR statute grew to be so contentious that Rwanda, which had a seat on the Security Council at the time, cast the sole vote opposing the adoption of the resolution.[11]

This ominous start emphasized the tensions among the local, national, and international stakeholders in the crafting of a narrative on ethnic violence through the international criminal justice process. Having said that, a narrative about local events that emanates from an international organization is not necessarily disconnected from the stories of local people. However, the location of the tribunal in Arusha created an insurmountable physical and psychological disconnection between the international community's pursuit and process of justice and the expectations of the Rwandan government and the local populace in Rwanda.[12] While Security Council Resolution 955 claimed that the establishment of the ICTR would contribute to peace and reconciliation and end impunity for violations of human rights in Rwanda, its extraterritorial status alienated it from the local and daily realities of Rwandans attempting to rebuild a society destroyed by a near successful genocide and a civil war that for all intents and purposes continued even with the launch of the ICTR's first indictments.

Although I opened this chapter with Aunt Hermien's story, a local narrative, I do not mean to hold up her narrative as representative of widely accepted accounts in her community. Clearly, among genocide survivors, there are diverging accounts of gender and violence. Otherwise, her aunt's story would not have so shocked Lynette. It is of course quite possible that Lynette's understanding of the widespread nature of sexual violence shifted drastically when she realized that her own female relatives had been raped.

In addition to my conversations with Rwandans in the field, I have drawn on the works of anthropologists such as Christopher C. Taylor (1999a and 1999b), Lisa Malkki (1995), and Johan Pottier (2005). These social scientists do not focus exclusively on women, gender, or gender-based violence, but their wider perspective of the creation and performance of national identity has deepened my critical observation of the ICTR narrative. Their scholarship provides insight into the complexity of local identity formation (beyond sex and ethnicity) in Rwanda—a perspective largely absent from legal literature on the Rwandan genocide.

Until 1960, a Tutsi king under the tutelage of the Belgian colonial administration ruled Rwanda.[13] The Tutsi group was pastoralist and a minority in Rwanda, constituting 15 percent to 20 percent of the population. The Hutu group was agricultural and constituted about 80 percent to 85 percent of the population. There was also a third group called the Twa, who were potters and foragers, constituting about 1 percent of the total population. The Tutsi held the overwhelming majority of posts in the indirect rule state apparatus under the Belgians.[14] In the 1950s, educated Hutus sought a greater role in the Rwandan government and became increasingly politically active. Their movement, aided by the Rwandan Catholic Church and later supported by the Belgian colonial administration, culminated in the replacement of Tutsi administrators with Hutus. Thereafter, the system of Tutsi dominance was overthrown, and the Tutsi king abdicated.

The violence of this transition, which began in 1959 and continued until 1964, claimed the lives of tens of thousands of Tutsis. Thousands fled to neighboring countries, creating a sizable diaspora. During the 1980s, some of these refugees sought to return to Rwanda. When their overtures to the

Habyarimana government met with political and legal obstruction, they decided to return to Rwanda by force. Their movement, the Rwanda Patriotic Front (RPF), drew support from some Hutus disaffected from the Rwandan regime and more significantly from an alliance with Uganda's national army. The RPF invaded Rwanda from Uganda in October 1990. Peace accords ending this war were signed in Arusha, Tanzania, in August 1993 and gave the RPF most of what it had fought for: the right to Rwandan citizenship, the right to take up permanent residence in Rwanda, and a role in a broad-based government. Implementing the peace accords, however, proved another matter as Habyarimana and his supporters proclaimed that the Arusha Accords were toothless documents. Hostilities between the two sides resumed on 7 April 1994 after President Habyarimana was killed when his aircraft was shot down by extremist elements within his own circle (Taylor 1999a).

The first victims of the massacres by the interim government that was formed following Habyarimana's assassination were Hutus known within political circles as opponents of the Habyarimana government and not necessarily as Tutsi sympathizers. Within twenty-four hours, Prime Minister Agathe Uwilingiyimana, President of the Supreme Court Joseph Kavaruganda, and several other prominent members of government, together with ten Belgian members of the United Nations Assistance Mission for Rwanda (UNAMIR), were shot or bludgeoned to death by civilian militias known as the *interahamwe*.[15] The massacres spread through the country as the Rwandan army's (Forces Armées Rwandaise) war strategy against the RPF degenerated into the massacre of every Tutsi man, woman, and child in Rwanda. The highest levels of the interim government incited the general Hutu populace to join in the carnage with absolute impunity. Many did so armed with rudimentary weapons, such as machetes and other farming tools.[16] The genocide ended when the RPF invaded and occupied the countryside and Kigali, and the Rwandan army fled into the neighboring Democratic Republic of Congo along with up to one million civilians. Approximately one million Tutsis and Hutus had been killed in a three-month period (April to June 1994).[17]

On 1 July 1994, the UN Security Council adopted Resolution 935 in which it requested that the secretary-general establish a commission of experts to determine whether serious breaches of humanitarian law had been committed in Rwanda. The commission reported that genocide as well as systematic and widespread violations of international humanitarian law had been committed in Rwanda, resulting in a massive loss of life.[18]

The ICTR and the Gender Critique

Almost twenty years after the establishment of the ICTR, there is an impressive and still growing body of scholarly work reviewing the interpretation of gender and sexual violence in the statute, rules, decisions, and case law of the ICTR. The ICTR's early landmark convictions for sexual violence as a constituent element of genocide and a crime against humanity were applauded but also subjected to critical review (Cole 2008; Goldstone 2002; Askin 1999 and 2003; De Brouwer 2005). There have been many comparative and complementary studies of the ICTR's judicial interpretations and case law with other ad hoc tribunals and the ICC. However, as the ICTR nears its completion date, there is a resounding verdict from legal commentators that the early convictions were no more than an anomaly in the record of the ICTR prosecution of sexual violence (Nowrojee 2007: 110). The larger body of case law does not reflect the high levels of gender-based violence committed in Rwanda during the genocide.

Binaifer Nowrojee (2005 and 2007) has criticized the tribunal for a systematic lack of gender-based violence charges in its indictments and for the high numbers of acquittals for sexual violence charges in genocide cases. Nowrojee noted as of March 2004 that an overwhelming 90 percent of judgments handed down by the ICTR contained no rape convictions.[19] Further, she noted at the time that there were twice as many acquittals for rape as there were rape convictions. Four years later, Doris Buss pointed out the contrast between the hypervisibility of sexual violence as a backdrop to genocide with the striking invisibility of sexual violence in indictments, sentences and verdicts.

> The numbers tell the story. As of December 2008, the Tribunal has overseen the completed trials and guilty pleas of 48 men, only 15 of whom went to trial on charges including rape or sexual violence. Only five men in total have been found guilty of rape related charges. Further, eight men have pleaded guilty before the Tribunal, five of whom were charged with sexual violence crimes. All five were able to have their sexual violence charges dropped in exchange for guilty pleas on other counts. No one has pleaded guilty to any sexual violence offences. (2009: 151)

The Office of the Prosecutor has been accused by scholars such as Nowrojee of lacking gender competency in fulfilling its mandate, particularly with respect to investigating gender-based violence. Nowrojee (2007) charges that investigators and prosecutors have lacked the skill and political will to identify, cultivate trust among, and interview victims of sexual violence. In its defense, the Office of the Prosecutor has blamed Rwandan women for their cultural sensitivities, which prevented them from disclosing sexual violence.[20] Numerous researchers and human rights investigators have disproved this claim. They based their conclusions on thousands of testimonies collected from survivors of sexual violence in Rwanda and throughout the Great Lakes Region from 1994 until the present day. I argue that the prosecutor regarded sexual violence charges as the least relevant of the grave crimes being investigated and in many cases sacrificed them in the interest of expediency.[21] In the final analysis, it can be said that gender-based violence has never emerged as central to the ICTR's prosecutorial strategy. The prosecutor has not consistently pursued a comprehensive prosecution strategy or a precise working plan to properly document and bring the evidence of sex crimes into the courtroom for the considerable number of years that the ICTR has been at work.[22]

Legal commentators have also criticized the manner in which judges have presided over cases involving gender-based violence. Rwanda's survivor groups have rebuked them for permitting the retraumatization and humiliation of victims of sexual violence during "inept" and "insensitive" cross-examination by defense counsel.[23] The post-trial interviews of women survivors of sexual violence who testified as victims and witnesses before the ICTR also reveal a disenchantment with the international criminal justice process. A recurring complaint is that despite protection and confidentiality measures before the tribunal, witnesses were exposed to political and social repercussions on returning to their communities.[24]

Common wisdom suggests that punishing individual perpetrators of gross violations of human rights has a deterrent effect such that governments and others engaged in warfare will observe more closely the rules of war and duties toward civilians. However, any such impact of the convictions for sexual violence before the ICTR in Rwanda and in the Great Lakes Region is negligible. The civil war that began in 1990 has continued intermittently between Rwanda's government and *interahamwe* to this day. With the RPF takeover of government, the *interahamwe-genocidaires* established a military and political base in the Democratic Republic of Congo (DRC) that soon formed deadly alliances with various Congolese insurgent groups.[25] This war has continued to threaten regional security as other African countries, overtly and covertly, ally themselves militarily with the governments of the DRC or Rwanda or insurgents. A widespread, unprecedented, and well documented campaign of terror, often in the shape of sexual violence, against Congolese and Rwandan women caught in the crossfire has been a constant reality of the conflict in the Great Lakes region.[26] Observers report that the DRC government forces, insurgents, Rwandan forces, and *interahamwe* are all responsible for the widespread rape of women and girls in the DRC. This backdrop to the ICTR decisions undermines daily any significance of the prohibition and punishment of sexual violence as a crime against humanity, a war crime, and a form of genocide in the Great Lakes region and elsewhere.

Genocide and Its Intersection with Sex, Gender, and Ethnicity

The Genocide Convention (1948) describes five acts that amount to genocide if committed with intent to destroy, in whole or in part, a national, ethnic, racial, or religious group: killing members of the group; causing serious bodily or mental harm to members of the group; deliberately inflicting on the group conditions of life calculated to bring about its physical destruction in whole or in part; imposing measures intended to prevent births within the group; and forcibly transferring children of the group to another group (art. 2).

With a long history of the persecution of European Jews as its reference point, the international community experienced, analyzed, and constructed the violence in Rwanda as a fundamentally ethnic or racial conflict. Thus, the international community's framework for its understanding of the range of crimes against humanity and genocide, was that the perpetrators of civilian massacres were overwhelmingly ethnic Hutus and the civilian casualties of the massacres were overwhelmingly ethnic Tutsis. The language of Security Council Resolution 955 encoded this construction of the conflict.[27] Its reference to the ICTR's jurisdiction over "genocide and other serious violations of international humanitarian law" privileges the investigation and prosecution of ethnic persecution in the shape of genocide as the chief crime committed in Rwanda and the Great Lakes region.[28]

Throughout the case law of the ICTR, the language of ethnic persecution compellingly frames the factual events and the prosecutor's legal findings. The Gacumbitsi case is an excellent case in point. The Gacumbitsi indictment describes the RPF as "predominantly Tutsi," the target of violence as "Rwanda's civilian Tutsi population," and "the ordinary citizens of Rwanda, primarily

Hutu peasantry," as the killers (Gacumbitsi Indictment 1 June 2001, para. 3). The prosecutor substantiates the ethnic violence thesis through the selection and examination of victims and witnesses of genocide. Eyewitness accounts of the attack on the parish of Nyarubuye, where up to thirty thousand Tutsi and Hutu displaced persons sought refuge from violence, described how the Hutu were ordered or invited to separate themselves from the Tutsi before the massacre could begin in earnest (Gacumbitsi Judgment 17 June 2004, para. 108, referring to the Gacumbitsi Indictment 1 June 2001, para. 15). A particularly poignant testimony from witness TAQ describes how a young woman and child came out of the church when Hutus were ordered to separate themselves from the Tutsis. The attackers pushed the child back toward the refugees because they judged him to be a Tutsi. He was killed by grenades they lobbed into the crowd of refugees (Judgment, para. 113).

Through such testimony we see the "gender neutral" narrative of genocide where machetes, grenades, and gunfire fell Tutsi children, men, and women indiscriminately. There is a formal equality to the collectivization of Tutsi victimhood within the legal narrative. As I mentioned in Chapter 1, the limitation of formal equality is its obscuring of difference in identifying and redressing human rights abuse. The assumption by the prosecutor of a universal Tutsi experience of genocide compromised the legal categorization of gender-based violence, obscured important differences in victim typology, and had serious repercussions for men and women in the ICTR narrative of violence.

The intersection of race and gender marked women's experience of the Rwandan genocide in analogous ways to women's experience of violence during World War II in European ghettos and the Holocaust. Fiounnuala Ní Aoláin's (2000b) study of women and the Holocaust describes how women in ghettos and concentration camps experienced separation from infant children, forced abortions, forced nudity, and other abuses as specifically attacking their gendered and sexual identities constructed both at societal and individual levels. Ní Aoláin (2000b: 58) demonstrates that the legal formulation of the protection of women did not address the specific harms women suffered because they retained the narrow prewar construction of women in their "familial" role. The emphasis of these descriptors rested on women as sexually reproductive vessels regenerating the racial, national, ethnic, and religious group.

Ní Aoláin criticizes the laws of war, in particular, the 1977 Geneva Conventions, the supplementary Additional Protocols, and the jurisprudence of the Nuremberg Trials. Guided by Ní Aoláin's critique and conclusions, I focus my criticism here on the material jurisdiction of the Genocide Convention, which the Statute of the International Criminal Tribunal and the case law of the ICTR, in particular, the Akayesu case, replicate. The Akayesu case is the landmark ICTR case because it defined sexual violence as an element of genocide and produced a broad definition of rape and sexual violence at the level of international law.

I argue that the focus on women in the Genocide Convention, the Statute of the ICTR, and the case law on sexual violence as genocide (represented by the Akayesu case) privileges the biological function of sexual reproduction and to a lesser degree the attendant gender role of women as primary caregivers of children over other harms women experience and which the perpetrator intends.[29] According to the logic of the law and case law, the persecuted woman is foremost a mother. Without her, the Tutsi group would no longer be able to regenerate itself and would become extinct. The harm then is to the ethnic group. This legal construction is an important but far from individualized construction of the scope of gender-based discrimination within the act of genocide.[30] Ní Aoláin (2000b: 56 and 61) points out that both the perpetrator and the Holocaust victim understood how acts of violence attacked complex, intersecting strands of a victim's gender identity and sexual autonomy. Likewise, testimonies from survivors of Rwanda's genocide clearly show that both victim and perpetrator are conscious of multiple, complex meanings behind the nature of gender-based violence and the intent of the perpetrator to harm the victim, her immediate family, and her community. Testimonies collected by the Special Rapporteur on Violence Against Women during her mission to Rwanda illustrate the gendered and sexed spaces from which women's multiple harms arose. A victim known as JJ, who also testified as a witness before the ICTR, provided this testimony: "A young man rushed at me. He led me to the corner of the room. He undressed and put his clothes on the ground. I asked him what he was doing; he said I had no right to ask him anything. In fact, he did humiliating things to me even though I was a mother."[31]

Placing the legal analysis of witness JJ's testimony within a social and cultural context demands that we acknowledge or even privilege "motherhood" as a category of persecution. Doing so is problematic, as Ní Aoláin writes: "Defining harms that categorically or even partially place the women in a maternal context is not without theoretical or practical complications. Feminist theory continues to struggle with and to rally against the essentializing of the female person to her unique biological capacities" (2000b: 58). However, Tutsi women were raped on a widespread, systematic scale in part because as women and mothers they would bear future generations of Tutsis. When considered in isolation, this fact leads to the single-axis and androcentric legal analysis of any testimony of sexual violence in the context of ethnic cleansing, genocide, or holocaust. Ní Aoláin's analysis presses the legal scholar of gender and violence to understand the attack against "women mothers" not only as a nationalistic construct of the extremist ideologues but also from the micro-level of the individual victim and the individual perpetrator.

Reading the testimony of witness JJ, it is not clear to me whether she was fourteen or fifty years of age. What is clear is her belief that the perpetrator is aware that she, his rape victim, is a mother and he is a youth. In the major cultures of the world, her societal status as a "mother" far exceeds that of women who are unwed or childless. And certainly, her status exceeds that of a young man. The status of motherhood would in a civilized society protect her from sexual advances from men outside of her matrimonial home. This shared awareness of society's positive and empowering construction of women as wives and mothers should be a strong influence on our interrogation of the nature of witness JJ's harm and the perpetrator's motivation. Witness JJ suffers an individual harm, and the perpetrator aggresses an individual woman in the corner of a room filled with male (presumably) Hutu aggressors and female (presumably) Tutsi victims. However, witness JJ in her testimony appraises the attack and the humiliation it brings as an attack on the sexual inviolability her status as a mother bestows on her.[32] In as much as some feminist theorists might frown at any focus on women as mothers, there is a need for us to explore and deeply analyze the ways in which victims and perpetrators understand motherhood as a gender, sex, and sexual construct. Doing so is a necessary step in identifying the limitations of the law's categorization of gender-based violence and how these limitations affect women's experiences in armed conflict and its aftermath.

Under article 2(2)(b), the statute mandates that the ICTR prosecute acts causing serious bodily or mental harm to members of the group as genocide. The trial chamber found that serious bodily or mental harm included rape and other forms of sexual violence (Akayesu Judgment 2 September 1998, para. 688 and 731). Further, sexual violence as a form of serious bodily or mental harm was described as the physical and psychological destruction of Tutsi women, their families, and their communities (para. 731). The trial chamber's elaboration of gender-based violence in the commission of genocide was sensitive to physical, spiritual, and psychological harms. Its reference to mental trauma was an important feature of the chamber's analysis of individual harm.[33] However, it stops short of describing the source of trauma separate from the physical act of rape.

The nationalization of the Rwandan state was produced by political elites in social spaces, including in the private sphere and in the location of the female body, most highly prized for the ability to reproduce children. Motherhood is a critical social identity and an esteemed status for women (Baines 2003: 482). It is this exalted state that is cordoned off by genocidal rape and its reproductive harms, such as infertility and sexually transmitted infections, including HIV. It is of course not the case that every woman who was raped became infertile or developed a sexually transmitted infection. However, among local, national, and international commentators, this belief is widely held. Legal analysis has failed to address the issue of symbolic and social death resulting from an irreversible interruption to the gendered trajectories of life. Social and physical death can at times be closely interwoven. Béatrice Pouligny points out that the field of transitional justice has developed in almost total disconnection from other fields of expertise—more particularly anthropology and mental health studies. Pouligny (2007: 7) calls for a closer scrutiny of the relation between legal or paralegal (such as truth commissions) processes and social and psychological processes.

In describing rape as a form of ethnic persecution, the trial chamber demonstrated its awareness that it was negotiating a delicate balance, struggling not to erase the individual even as it described communal violence. In its legal analysis, the trial chamber states that for any of the acts charged under article 2(2) of the statute to be a constitutive element of genocide, the act must have been committed 1) against one or several individuals; 2) because such individual or individuals were members of a specific group; and 3) specifically because they belonged to this group. Thus, the victim is chosen not because of her individual identity but on account of her membership in a national, ethnic, racial, or religious group. The victim of the act is therefore a member of a group, chosen as such, and so it follows that the victim of the crime of genocide is the group itself and not the individual (Akayesu Judgment 2 September 1998, para. 521). In a footnote, the trial chamber reveals that it is guided by the fact that victims as individuals "are important not *per se* but as members of the group to which they belong" (para. 521 [at note 100]).

This unabashed emphasis on women's ethnicity as the essential component in prosecuting genocide against the Tutsi group was also evident in the prosecution of sexual violence as a crime against humanity. The trial chamber in the Akayesu case determined that the various acts of sexual violence, such as forcing Tutsi civilian women and girls to strip naked and parade before crowds, were crimes against humanity under article 3(i) of the statute (other inhumane acts). And the trial chamber deemed the *interahamwe* rape of Tutsi civilian women and girls at the bureau commune in a nearby field and forest to amount to rape as a crime against humanity under section 3(g) (rape) of the statute.[34]

In describing sexual violence, the chamber highlighted individual indignity, such as being forced to sit in the mud before being raped or being raped in a position that forced the victim to witness the concurrent rape of a female relative. The chamber stressed the idea of rape as an individual harm and an act of aggression against women (as opposed to an honor crime against her tribe or race). But, ultimately, as with genocide, it constructed rape as a crime against humanity as an *ethnic* attack. It determined that for sexual violence to be a crime against humanity, it must have been committed as part of the widespread or systematic attack against the civilian ethnic population of Tutsis in Rwanda, between 7 April and the end of June 1994 (Akayesu Judgment, 2 September 1998, para. 598 and 695).

Alternatives to the Narrative of Ethnic Persecution

Historical and anthropological accounts taken from the postcolonial era suggest that in Rwanda, male dominance was maintained by patriarchal customs legitimized by discriminatory parliamentary enactments or omissions. Sexual violence was arguably also in part emblematic of an older conflict surrounding social inequalities in Rwanda. Women's subordination was a legal reality and women in most cases lacked legal capacity. They could not, for example, own property except through male guardians, such as a father, an adult son, or a husband. This construction of gender had implications in increasing women's vulnerability to sexual exploitation and abuse by men seeking to acquire property (Rose 2005: 911–36).[35] Traditionally, Rwandan women were seen as primary caregivers and homemakers. Thus, women holding public office could be regarded as violating social norms and even challenging male dominance in the public sphere. This hostile view of women in public or traditionally male spaces made woman more vulnerable to sexual violence in armed conflict by men seeking to maintain their dominance in the formal sector and public life while confining women to the unthreatening conjugal role of reproduction, production (farming), and domestic service.

I argue here that these narratives of structural inequality are present in the case law of the ICTR. However, the exclusive focus on ethnicity or the sexual reproductive potential of women, or both, obscures the narratives' significance as indicators of gender, class, and other grounds of discrimination fomenting violence. The scale of sexual violence committed against women during the genocide should not be understood purely as acts of genocide against women as reproductive resource. The construction of sexual violence in Rwanda as a weapon of war is rooted in two highly gendered and interwoven hypotheses. First, extremists used sexual violence to reclaim the lost ground of patriarchy and reassert a male dominance over Rwandan women. Second, sexual violence was supposed to perpetuate Hutu dominance and destroy all threats to racial purity and unity.

Despite institutionalized and social challenges to the advancement of women in the public and private sphere, women, and especially those living in urban areas, made steady gains to such an extent that it created resistance: "To many Rwandans, gender relations in the 1980s and 1990s were falling into a state of decadence as more women attained positions of prominence in economic and public life, and as more of them exercised their personal preferences in their private lives" (Taylor 1992: 130). Christopher Taylor recounts an incident that occurred throughout Rwanda's cities in the 1980s and that highlights the perceived threat that women's sociopolitical and sexual freedom posed to Rwanda's gender regime. He writes: "Scores of young Rwandan women, virtually all residents of Kigali, Butare and other cities in Rwanda, had been arrested and placed on 're-education farms' outside of Kigali. All were accused of 'vagabondage' or prostitution and some were indeed prostitutes. Others, however, were guilty of nothing more than having European boyfriends or consorting with Europeans socially." Taylor concludes: "An underlying fear that motivated the campaign was that a national reproductive resource was gradually being lured away by the blandishments of foreigners' money. In addition, [men] lamented the dissolution of patriarchal authority and the diminishing control that older women exercised over younger women" (ibid.).

Taylor's account of the arrests of women helps us begin to understand the complex construction of women's gender and sexuality in the ideology of male hegemony. These events occurred in the 1980s when the prospect of rape as a tool of genocide was still inconceivable in Rwanda. It is perhaps for this reason that there is no allusion in Taylor's account as to the ethnic composition of the "vagabonds" and "prostitutes" rounded up. It is therefore striking that in a subsequent work published soon after the genocide, Taylor revisits this incident and adds the surprising conclusion that "the most enduring consequence of the repression was to plant the idea in the minds of many Rwandans that single Tutsi women were likely to be prostitutes (Taylor 1999b: 162). Taylor's implication in the subsequent (postgenocide) account of the same incident is that Tutsi women were the chief targets of this police harassment and arbitrary arrests. Taylor's gender analysis shifted to one of the sexuality of Tutsi women in the ideology of Hutu supremacy.

Taylor's shift from a gender-based analysis of the incident to an exclusively ethnic-based analysis is analogous with the international community's reduction, for the purposes of the international criminal justice process, of gender-based violence and all other forms of violence in Rwanda to ethnic persecution. This genocide/ethnic framework for prosecution has the effect of granting immunity to perpetrators who raped for reasons that were not ostensibly ethnic persecution. Peyi Soyinka-Airewele (2004: 27) explains that girls and women were obliged to "offer themselves" to the RPF soldiers in order to avoid being regarded as sympathizers of the deposed Hutu government. Such claims are well beyond the legal categorization of sexual violence as a form of ethnic persecution and are invisible from the ICTR's legal narrative of gender and violence.

Other legal commentators have called for the ICTR to pay attention to both gender and ethnicity as forms of discrimination. But it was Doris Buss who took the missing step in legal scholarship of uncovering the multiple forms of discrimination that made women increasingly vulnerable to sexual violence in Rwanda. Gender, class, nationality, religion, and age are some of the factors Buss points to as having been overlooked by the single-axis construction of ethnicity as the key factor behind sexual violence against Tutsi women (2008b).

Her analysis builds on the analysis of Johan Pottier. Pottier's account provides survivor testimony so as to caution academics not to construct the Rwanda tragedy as a straightforward ethnic phenomenon. Pottier (2005: 204) argues that besides obscuring the class factor, a focus on "pure" ethnic conflict masks the deep, historically evolved rift within Rwanda's Hutu population. Pottier illustrates that gender, race, ethnicity, and class were some of the variables that influenced vulnerability and security, but also variables and identity tags that were shifting and interchangeable on a day-to-day basis during the genocide.

A genocide survivor told Pottier that "people came to tell me that I was Tutsi and not a Zairean (*zairoise* [now Congolese]). We argued for a long time until some people [among the killer mob] recognized me and said, 'Leave her alone, she is *zairoise*, and Zaireans are the friends of Rwanda'" (2005: 205). Interestingly, Pottier's survivor describes her surprise when she succeeds in escaping Rwanda and is warmly received as a Tutsi in Bukavu by Zairean soldiers. The soldiers refer to her as a Tutsi despite her protests that she is a Zairean sister. However, while her Zairean identity allowed her to disguise her Tutsi identity, it did not protect her from an attempted rape. Pottier's survivor describes how a man who once served as her house servant made sexual advances toward her, which she was able to rebuff. In her analysis of Pottier's survivor's narrative, Buss makes the plausible analysis that as the genocide erupted in Rwanda, the desire to upend perceived or actual oppressive social hierarchies (such as master and boy) may have motivated some rapists as much as or more so than ethnic hatred.[36] Pottier describes the survivor as a Tutsi, a Muslim, and a Zairean national, and this multiple identity allows her to escape Rwanda and genocide, whereas her traveling companion, a Tutsi and a Muslim of Rwandan nationality, is repeatedly raped at checkpoints and eventually killed with her baby.[37] This woman's narrative reminds us that Tutsi women occupied identities outside of their ethnicities, and this fact exaggerated vulnerability or even provided temporary immunity from violence depending on the circumstances.

It is notable that this Zairean genocide survivor is the subject of an extensive and highly individualized study by an anthropologist and not a prosecutor. When one considers the unprecedented levels of violence and upheaval accompanying a fleeing population, it is a striking feature of the survivor's narrative how much agency she demonstrated. Pottier's account reveals, however, that gender, class, race, nationality, and other dynamics at play in the individual circumstances of a perilous situation shaped the exercise of agency (in this case, the decision and ability to flee, to bribe killers, to alter identities, and to adopt and shelter persecuted children).[38]

In the following sections of this chapter, I focus on multiple forms of discrimination, particularly the intersection of ethnicity, class, and gender that appear within the ICTR case law, visible yet largely uninterrogated for their significance. Building on Buss's intersectional analysis, I present three alternative narratives but distinguish my narratives from Buss (whose focus was on Tutsi women) by focusing on a Hutu "big" woman, a Tutsi "big" man, and a Hutu "small" woman for analysis. I use the adjectives "big" and "small" to describe class status as measured by prominence in society and participation in public life, level of education, wealth, and family connections.

Alternative Narrative #1: The Rape of a "Big" Woman

The amended indictment against Bagosora describes the assassination of Hutu opposition leaders, prominent Tutsi, and Belgian peacekeepers in the earliest hours of the genocide. This indictment charges that Prime Minister Agathe Uwingiliyimana was "tracked down, arrested, sexually assaulted and killed by members of the Presidential Guard, the Para-Commando Battalion and the Reconnaissance Battalion" (31 July 1998, para. 6.9).[39] The indictment against Niyitegeka also states that: "Rape and other forms of sexual violence, including torture, degrading sexual acts and indecent exposure were integral to the genocidal policy of the conspirators . . . Not even the Prime Miniter Agathe Uwiligiyimana was spared. Her semi-nude, lifeless body was discovered on the morning of 7 April 1994 with indicia of sexual torture and sexual degradation" (25 November 2002, para. 6.61).

These and other indictments also describe the Prime Minister, the minister of information, minister of agriculture, minister of labor and communications, president of the Constitutional Court, and other politicians as having been "arrested", "brutally murdered" and killed." Clearly, these politicians were killed not only because of their moderate political affiliations but also because of their prominent status in society and their perceived wealth and superiority over ordinary Rwandans. But only Prime Minister Uwilingiyimana was sexually assaulted, which distinguishes her from her male counterparts.

However, it is notable that in the trial chamber judgments, the sexual assault of the Prime Minister is erased from the legal findings. The Bagosora judgment for example, retained the reference to the sexual assault of the prime minister after her death as a witness explicitly testified to having seen the prime minister's naked and bullet-ridden body lying in her residential compound with a bottle shoved into her vagina (para. 705). However, this aspect of her assassination did not receive legal consideration. In contrast, analogous assaults against Tutsi women received considerable legal analysis in other cases. In the Akayesu judgment, for example, the trial chamber decided that thrusting a piece of wood into the vagina of a woman as she lay dying constituted rape (2 September 1998, para. 686).[40]

The murder of the prime minister provides the backdrop to many ICTR cases, but the trial chamber erased the gender-based violence that marked

her assassination from the prosecutor's examination of witnesses and ultimately from consideration at the conviction and sentencing stages of the tribunal. This whitewash of rape was made possible because the prime minister's
Hutu identity jarred with the dominant rape narrative of the ICTR, which
states explicitly that all Tutsi women were raped and all Hutu peasants were
killers and/or rapists.

Further, the prime minister's "big" status distinguished her from the
majority of "ordinary" Rwandan women (and men) and could have contributed to the presentation by the judicial narrative of her sexual body
as (sexually) inviolable. It is not a coincidence that in the buildup to the
genocide, Hutu Power media propaganda portrayed Uwilingiyama as a sex
toy passed around by UN peacekeepers and Rwandan opposition leaders.[41]
In order to reduce her from a "big" woman to a "small" woman, her sexual
integrity was impugned, and ultimately agents of her political enemies
sexually violated her. It is a paradox that being a "big" woman made the
act of rape (which diminishes women) difficult to acknowledge for prosecutors while at the same time being "big" made rape an essential element
for Uwilingiyimana's subordination and ultimately her moral and political
assassination.

The public nature and highly sexualized violation of the prime minister's
corpse fits into the thesis that sexual violence represents an armed gender
struggle for power between men and women (Mibenge 2007b).[42] So while
conceding that Tutsi women were the primary victims of rape, the parallel
and concomitant rape of both Hutu and Tutsi women functioned as a form
of gender hegemony. Thus, the infamous propaganda tool—the Hutu Ten
Commandments—beseeched Hutu wives and sisters to ensure that their
Hutu husbands and brothers did not recruit Tutsi women as concubines and
secretaries. According to the Hutu Power ideologists, both Hutu and Tutsi
women's ambitions were restricted to serving men through roles such as mis-
tresses and secretaries.

It is impossible to ascertain from ICTR narratives whether other moderate Hutu women (whether they were as "big" as Uwilingiyimana or not)
were sexually violated as a prelude to murder, because the prosecutor never
systematically investigated the murder of Hutu moderate women.[43] The ICTR
refers to gender-based violence against Hutu moderate women in broad
strokes, as in "some Hutu moderates were also targeted for killings."

In the case of the prime minister, regional considerations that led to the
conflict between Rwanda's northerners and southerners exacerbated the con-

flation of violent conflict at the intersection of gender, ethnicity, and class. The Ntuyahaga indictment describes this political scenario:

> From 1973–1994, the government of President Habyarimana used a system of ethnicity and required quotas which was supposed to provide educational and employment opportunities for all but which was used increasingly to discriminate against both Tutsi and Hutu from regions outside of the North West. In fact, by the late 1980s persons from Gisenyi and Ruhengeri occupied many of the most important positions in the military, political, economic and administrative sectors of Rwandan society. Among the privileged elite, an inner circle of relatives and close associates of President Habyarimana and his wife Agathe Kanzinga, known as the *Akazu*, enjoyed great power. The select group almost exclusively Hutu was supplemented by individuals who shared its extremist Hutu ideology, and who came from the native region of the President and his wife. (26 September 1998, para. 1.5)

Before 1990 the great political conflict in Rwanda was the conflict between the "prosperous" North, which benefited disproportionately from the president's patronage, and the rest of the country, which was thoroughly neglected and underdeveloped.[44] In this setting, Prime Minister Agathe was a "big" woman, who overstepped and upset gender and class hierarchies, but she was also a southerner. This factor contributed to her appointment as prime minister under the power-sharing agreement of the Arusha Accords, and it should not be surprising that this factor contributed to her assassination and sexual violation. As a "big" woman and as a southerner, her status and gender must have been a particular affront to the northern Hutu Power ideologues.

The prime minister's assassination is adjudged by the trial chambers as a crime against humanity (murder) and part of a widespread and systematic attack against civilians on political and national grounds. Describing Hutus who were killed for their "moderate" politics is meant to indicate their Tutsi sympathies and opposition to Hutu Power.[45] So, while the prime minister's assassination is ostensibly not based on ethnic persecution, it is tied to her perceived empathy toward, or collusion with, the Tutsi enemy. The ICTR absolutely excludes an analysis and discussion of the significance of her gender, status, or southern identity with regard to the nature of violence and its possible wider impact on Rwandan women's security and vulnerability during the armed conflict and genocide in Rwanda.

Alternative Narrative #2: The Rape of a "Big" Man

The issue of class and other social conditions shaping sexual violence can also be seen in the Niyitegeka and Muhimana cases, where the ICTR presents a rare reference to sexual violence against a male victim.

According to witness testimony in these two cases, the killers were "tired of killing," but their zeal was reignited when they found Assiel Kabanda. "The attackers rejoiced at his capture—they had been looking for Kabanda for several days because he was an influential trader and well-liked." Kabanda was killed and then decapitated and castrated with a machete. His skull was pierced through the ears with a spike and carried away by two men, each holding one end of the spike with the skull in the middle. Kabanda's head and genitals were subsequently hung up and displayed near his shop (Niyitegeka Judgment, 16 May 2003, para. 303, 312, 417, 462, and 271; Muhimana Judgment, 28 April 2005, para. 441, 443, and 462).

The trial chamber in the Niyitegeka case treated the testimony on the killing of Kabanda as a unique and especially shocking event. Kabanda's killing was even invoked at the sentencing stage as an aggravating factor (Niyitegeka Judgment, para. 499). The case raises questions for the inquisitive gender focused legal researcher. Was the castration of men widespread and systematic? Was the castration of Tutsi men widespread and systematic? Was the castration or sexual mutilation of murdered Tutsi men a symbolic prevention of births or forced sterilization—both of which can be forms of genocide?[46] The testimony of General Romeo Dallaire suggests that the castration is another incomplete gender narrative in the ICTR case law.

Dallaire describes the state of decomposing corpses: "There were some men that were mutilated also, their genitals and the like."[47] However, his observation that men were sexually mutilated is lost in a longer testimony about the rape of women and girls. Dallaire immediately "sees sex" in the shape of women's corpses lying with their dresses over their heads, but his testimony on castrated men does not raise a hint of sexual violence against men.

The description of Kabanda's castration in the Niyitegeka case and Dallaire's account of castrated men as nonsexual attacks are in themselves the product of gender prescribed ideas of a man's body, which cannot or should not be sexually victimized, unlike the weak, sexually desirable, and vulnerable body of a Tutsi woman.[48] The Office of the Prosecutor internalized this construction in its charging of crimes. Ultimately, the trial chamber mirrored this gender blind spot, and in Dallaire's testimony in the Bagosora judgment, castration is effectively redacted, since the trial chamber only acknowledges the gender-based violence against women.[49]

When providing a gender commentary on transitional justice processes, legal researchers have largely ignored the issue of sexual violence as a form of gender-based violence against men in armed conflict. Sandesh Sivakumaran presents one of the few and most detailed legal studies on the subject. He presents evidence indicating that sexual violence takes place against men in nearly every armed conflict in which sexual violence is committed. What remains unknown is the precise extent to which this crime occurs.[50] Sivakumaran's typology of sexual violence against men challenges the legal researcher to examine the castration of Kabanda and Dallaire's cursory reference to mutilated men through a gender lens. Sivakumaran's study (2007: 265) introduces language such as "emasculation," "feminization," and "homosexualization" into the analysis of gender-based violence.[51]

The ICTR determined the killing, decapitation, and castration of Kabanda to be a crime against humanity (other inhumane acts). This conclusion was curious, considering that in a comparable testimony Niyitegeka ordered *interahamwe* to undress the body of a Tutsi woman, who had just been shot dead, and to fetch and sharpen a piece of wood, which was then forced into her vagina (Niyitegeka Judgment, 16 May 2003, para. 463). The chamber actually decided that the castration of Kabanda and the penetration of the dead woman's body were acts of seriousness comparable to other acts enumerated in Article 3 (crimes against humanity) of the statute, and would cause mental suffering to Tutsi civilians, and constitute a serious attack on the human dignity of the Tutsi community as a whole (para. 465). However, and tellingly, the ICTR refers to the attack against the woman's genitals and corpse as a sexual violation, while it describes the attack against Kabanda as "killing, decapitation and castration."[52] It glosses over the fact that castration is not merely an amputation but the amputation of a male sexual and reproductive organ and the symbolic amputation of masculinity. Dubravka Zarkov (1997: 144) explains that castration is an act of physical as much as symbolic demasculinization, of stripping man of his masculine powers symbolized by his penis. It makes a man into a non-man. It is not in itself an act of a perverted homosexual desire; it is an act of perverted desire for power. The omission in the narrative of the ICTR is clearly gendered and detrimental to male victims of sexual violence made invisible by the specter of the female rape victim.[53]

In the same vein, the killing of Belgian peacekeepers by militias provides a backdrop to the genocide in many of the ICTR cases. The Ntuyahaga indictment indicates that four Belgian soldiers were killed on the spot, while six remaining soldiers withstood several attacks for a number of hours before they too were killed. Journalists have reported that the Belgian soldiers were subjected to torture and mutilation, including castration (Peterson 2000: 292). The absence of any such reference in the charges supports a conclusion that the ICTR narrative of gender and gender-based violence precluded the militarized Western male body from sexual humiliation.[54]

Ignoring the sexual and gender construction of the crime of castration is possible because of the precedent set by the Akayesu narrative, which privileged ethnicity and essentialized sexual violence as a crime committed exclusively against Tutsi women. With respect to women, therefore, the privileging of ethnicity meant that women could be raped only if they belonged to the Tutsi group. This ethnocentric approach precluded any serious investigation, analysis, or understanding of the nature of sexual assaults against Rwandan men *or* women.

Despite the obvious difference in their sex and perceived gender roles, the desexualized description of Kabanda's assassination is analogous to that of Agathe Uwilingiyimana's described above. Both of these victims were "big," powerful, wealthy, respected, and influential. Neither fit the passive Tutsi rape-victim role. The rape of women and the castration of men are at the same end of the domination paradigm (Card 2004: 36). Sivakumaran (2007: 260) reassures the researcher focusing on violence against women that acknowledging male sexual violence will not take away from female sexual violence because ultimately it forms part of the same issue, namely, the gender dimension of conflict. There is a strong link between male sexual violence and sexual violence against women, and it is doubtful that sexual violence as a tool of warfare would target only women. Certainly, levels of sexual violence, the nature of this form of violence, and the societal meanings attaching to it and its scale would differ. Such differences would arise around gendered constructions of masculinities and femininities, and not merely around biological differences between men and women (ibid.).

Alternative Narrative #3: The Rape of a "Small" Woman

As my final alternative narrative, I introduce testimony from a "small" woman because it illustrates sexual vulnerability exacerbated by low status in society.

Muhimana was charged with genocide, complicity in genocide, and murder and rape as crimes against humanity. With respect to the rape charge, he was charged with committing rape as part of a widespread or systematic attack against Tutsi women civilians and other women perceived to be Tutsi in the Gishyita sector; Mugonero church, hospital, and nursing school; and in the Bisereso area (Muhimana Revised Amended Indictment 3 February 2004, para. 6). The particulars of this charge describe Muhimana and his cohorts committing gang rapes and multiple rapes in public spaces so as to incite spectators to rape Tutsi women. In one instance, Muhimana raped women in his home and thereafter paraded them naked before crowds of civilians and *interahamwe* (para. 6[a][i]).

At the outset of genocide, witness BJ was a house servant and, at fifteen years of age, a minor. Witness BJ's testimony leads to another alternative and marginalized narrative of gender and violence that is similar but distinct from the narratives produced by the assassinations of Uwilingiyimana, the peacekeepers, and Kabanda—and one that supports Aunt Hermien's suggestion that sexual violence against women and girls was widespread and indiscriminate—in her words, "show me a woman who wasn't raped."

On 16 April 1994, after witness BJ saw assailants killing refugees, she fled to a hospital, where she hid in a room with two other girls, Murekatete and Mukasine. Muhimana entered this room with two accomplices. The men were armed with a club, a machete, and a sharpened stick. They ordered the girls to strip and lie on their backs in order to show the men their Tutsi genitals. Witness BJ did as she was told, believing that she would be killed otherwise. Muhimana raped her as Murekatete and Mukasine were raped beside her. Muhimana then prepared to insert a sharpened stick into her vagina when one of the *interahamwe* suddenly identified her as a Hutu. Muhimana apologized to witness BJ and said he had been unaware that she was a Hutu (Muhimana Judgment, 28 April 2005, para. 284–86). She was then allowed to escape. She ran home quickly because her rapist told her that if she remained too long on the road, the *interahamwe* could mistake her for a Tutsi and kill her. The witness never saw Murekatete and Mukasine again. The fact that witness BJ was a child was considered an aggravating factor in the sentencing of Muhimana (para. 606 and 607). However, her rape and Muhimana's "apology" were treated as evidence of the genocidal intent of Muhimana and his accomplices against the Tutsi women Murekatete and Mukasine. Witness BJ's testimony was used to reinforce the prosecutor's focus on ethnic rape as opposed to rape as a form of gender-based violence that saw witness BJ and other Rwandan women preyed upon throughout the genocide and its aftermath.

Kabanda, the prominent Tutsi businessman, and Agathe Uwilingiyimana, the southern Hutu woman prime minister, occupied a completely different social plane from witness BJ. While Uwilingiyimana and Kabanda's power and privileged ethnicity collided with gender to increase their vulnerability to persecution and to sexual violence, it was witness BJ's lack of social status that exposed her to sexual violence. Unlike the *Zairoise*-Tutsi survivor Pottier described, witness BJ did not have the stature to bribe or intimidate attackers. She was unable even to speak and identify herself as a Hutu in order to spare herself from rape as a mature or more assertive Hutu woman might have attempted. She noted in her testimony that she escorted and delivered her employer's children to the church where her employer had taken refuge, and thereafter she had to seek her own sanctuary. Unlike her employer's children, witness BJ was an unaccompanied minor with no parent or guardian with whom to take shelter. Indeed, the warning she received from her rapist that she might be mistaken for a Tutsi and killed on the road is rather disingenuous. Witness BJ was raped because she was a powerless girl and not because she was mistaken for a Tutsi woman.[55]

It is feasible that Muhimana (and no doubt other men who transformed themselves into serial rapists during the genocide) did not care about BJ's ethnicity and simply preyed sexually on young women made vulnerable by displacement. Certainly, all of the other women raped by Muhimana or raped at his instigation were identified as Tutsi by the prosecutor's witnesses; however, the fact that only Tutsi rapes were investigated and charged in the indictment should not lead to the conclusion that other rapes did not take place on a widespread scale. I concur with Clara Chapdelaine Feliciati's argument (2006: 23) that the widespread victimization of the girl child is excluded from the narrative of sexual violence and genocide in Rwanda. Feliciati argues that the analysis of violence should be both "gendered" and "childered." It is unlikely that witness BJ was the only young, unaccompanied, unprotected, poor girl who was "mistaken" for a Tutsi woman during the genocide. Other "small" or vulnerable Hutu women and girls experienced violence, including sexual violence, from opportunistic predators with no overt genocidal intent (Gasana et al. 1999: 165; Adedeji 1999: 72; Amnesty International 2004: 6; and Organization for African Unity 2000: 164).[56] This claim is sustainable even without taking into account the documented widespread and systematic sexual exploitation and abuse of Hutu and Tutsi women that occurred in refugee camps in the DRC after 1994, before the repatriation of Rwandan citizens commenced (Baldwin 2006).

Pottier describes how Laetitia, a Tutsi woman who resembled a Hutu, traveled through Rwanda with a forged Hutu identification. However, her successful adoption of a Hutu identity did not stop the soldiers from raping her (Pottier 2005: 207). Hutu women fleeing violence were vulnerable to sexual violence and in many cases experienced it.

The defense challenged witness BJ's credibility on the grounds that she should have identified herself as a Hutu when Muhimana spoke specifically of the genitals of Tutsi women. Her explanation is very striking: she thought all Rwandans were the same because they had taken refuge in the same place (Muhimana Judgment, para. 290) Witness BJ's response is important when one considers her seeking refuge with Murekatete and Mukasine, young women who did not live to testify before an international criminal tribunal. At the moment Muhimana and his cohorts entered the room, the three girls were all the same. The single category of gender was the unifying characteristic of witness BJ, Murekatete, and Mukasine discerned by their rapists. They were raped because they were women, even if, ultimately, ethnicity spared witness BJ from murder, reserved in this case for Tutsi women.

Conclusion

In Chapter 1, I presented a three-tiered framework of human rights instruments and discussed the ways in which gender as a group and as an analytical tool was brought into the scope of human rights instruments in order to equitably redistribute rights to all women in their private and public lives. In particular, third tier rights instruments such as the CEDAW and CERD General Comments have situated human rights violations in situations of conflict and armed conflict and specifically called for international tribunals such as the ICTR to redress violence against women. The parameters set by human rights instruments shape the ICTR's limited interpretation of gender and violence. In the face of the historical exclusion of women from legal standing and legal protection from egregious abuse, it is admittedly difficult to challenge the application of the gender analysis predominantly on women's experience of harm. Moreover, in the face of shocking incidents of sexual violence against women in Rwanda and earlier postwar conflicts, it is difficult not to fixate on the widespread and systematic rape of women and girls at the expense of examining and analyzing issues of masculinity, sexual violence against men, and the rape of women whose vulnerability to sexual violence (on account of their class or ethnic group) is not acknowledged by policy makers and others responding to the needs of victims of violence.

I extracted my alternative narratives of Kabanda, the Belgian peace-keepers, witness BJ, and Agathe Uwilingiyimana from the case law of the ICTR. It is therefore fair to say that these "anomalies" to the dominant narrative of sexual violence are partially acknowledged, although not analyzed as evidence of gender-based persecution, by the prosecutor and the trial chambers. Gender is evident in the case law of the ICTR; however, I have used alternative narratives to illustrate that its inclusion in the narrative does not always signify a thorough or even accurate analysis of violence as experienced by men, women, and even children. While the human rights framework has encroached into the zone of armed conflict, normatively it retains a limited understanding of what gender means in the commission of war crimes, crimes against humanity, and genocide beyond the image of raped women.

My second conclusion drawn from the alternative narratives I introduced relates to the ICTR's singular focus on ethnicity to the exclusion of other factors contributing to genocide. The singular focus on ethnic persecution harks back to the widespread and systematic persecution of Jews in Europe and the decisions of the Nuremberg Trials as a model for the prosecution of crimes against humanity and war crimes. As with the Holocaust, this construction conceals men, women, and children's gendered experience of atrocity. Other conflicts were waged in Rwanda, including gender conflicts, agrarian conflicts, religious conflicts, and Hutu North and Hutu South conflicts. However, the legal framework adopted with Security Council Resolution 955 effectively erased these conflicts from reality and experience of the perpetrators as well as the victims.[57] In its alignment with the Security Council Resolutions' imagining of a purely ethnic-based conflict, the Office of the Prosecutor failed to engage in any serious investigation, analysis, or prosecution of grave breaches of humanitarian law and crimes against humanity outside of the Hutu *geno-cidaires* versus Tutsi victim paradigm.

The final outcome of the single-axis construction of discrimination produced an incomplete narrative that depends on what Martha Chamallas would call an "either/or dichotomy" (2005: 38). In this dichotomy, where "either you were raped or you are not a Tutsi," any serious analysis of gender discrimination was sacrificed to the extent that the rape of women could only be acknowledged if the victim was a Tutsi and if the Hutu perpetrator intended to commit genocide. Those social markers, such as education or lack of education, or membership in the middle class or the elite, that greatly distinguish even a universal group experience were entirely subsumed by the primary focus on ethnicity and the misdirected construction of sexual violence as only a sexual reproductive (ethnic) issue.

Understanding gender as a social construct rather than as biological functions, such as menstruation, lactation, and pregnancy, is essential to a meaningful criminal justice response to sexual violence in Rwanda and elsewhere. A broad gender analysis permits a much needed inquiry into the social, legal, and political realities that support both Aunt Hermien's assertion that "all women were raped" and the assertion made by Prosecutor Aimable's victims that "no women were raped."

Chapter 3

All Men Rape: Gender and Violence in Sierra Leone

I was sharing lunch with Chief Sesay, my host in the Sierra Leone provinces. He reminisced about his return to his chiefdom after his exile during the civil war. He recounted a conversation with Bintu, a woman who had lived under the rebel occupation of the town. This conversation made a lasting impact on the chief. According to him, the woman was disrespectful, angry, and rude: "'I [the chief] tried to tease her. I asked her, 'So, I hear you found a nice husband, didn't you have a rebel husband looking after you?' And this woman, this Bintu, she answered me: 'So what? What's the difference, Chief? Sleeping with you or sleeping with rebels? No difference. You're all just the same!'"

As the chief expected, I was visibly shocked by this anecdote. I asked him, "What did you say, Chief?" He responded, "What could I say? The lady was so angry. I mean I was only trying to joke with her. I'm the Chief; I became embarrassed, and I had to pretend I was not angry because there were people."

In the Introduction, I used another conversation with Bintu and Chief Sesay to demonstrate how gender can shape the experience of war and also the ways in which men and women remember and relate atrocity. The claim that "we women were slaves!" can be heard once again in the communication (or miscommunication) between the two survivors. Once again, Bintu and the chief provided me with thought provoking material for a narrative on gender and violence in armed conflict and the sociopolitical conflict that is its aftermath.

The chief's account disrupted my own preconceived notion of proper gender roles in Sierra Leone for a number of reasons. The first disruption was that a man, a chief my father's age, would initiate a discussion with me about sex. Until that point, I had purposefully avoided speaking to the chief about the "sex" aspect of my work. I referred to my research in his chiefdom as a study of human rights and women's participation in public life. This aversion to "sex talk" was a part of my own socialization, which made such a conversation with "my father" seem indecent or a prelude to an adulterous relationship. This particular conversation challenged my understanding of what is a respectful way for a mature man and a young woman (myself) to converse.[1] The second disrupting feature of the chief's narrative related to the first and that was that Bintu (a woman) would speak so disparagingly and frankly to a "big" man, a chief, who in my hierarchical estimation was a head of state.[2] Finally, I was surprised that the chief, unprompted, shared a story that revealed his public humiliation by a woman.[3]

Bintu's response—"what's the difference, you're all just the same"—pervades my critique of the Truth and Reconciliation Commission in Sierra Leone (Truth Commission or TRC) narrative on gender and violence before and during the armed conflict. I focus on the final report of the findings of the TRC and its analysis of gender-based discrimination and inequality in Sierra Leone as the primary source of this narrative. And just as the conversation with the chief disrupted my understanding of gender relations in Sierra Leone, my objective in this chapter is to disrupt the TRC narrative on gender hegemony in Sierra Leone.

The report presents a much needed gender critique of Sierra Leone's laws and customary law. However, I argue that the resultant narrative from this critique is an essentializing image of Sierra Leonean women and girls as perpetual victims not only of war but also of patriarchy in peacetime. At times, the report's narrative creates the impression that the subordination and the violation of the rights of Sierra Leonean women and girls are indistinguishable in war and in peace. This narrative of absolute and perpetual victimhood for women and girls in war and peace conceals the agency women exercise in their multiple responses to unequal power relations and abuse. Ultimately, the transitional justice process excludes those women survivors who are unwilling or unable to conform wholly to the victim role the TRC prescribes. Further, the narrative of absolute victimhood for women requires the absolute vilification of Sierra Leonean men as wanton abusers of women. This viewpoint marginalizes men's experience of civil, social, and economic disenfranchisement, often through violence, from the gender analysis.

While the report presents formal domestic laws as the chief political site of oppression and determines that law reform is the primary remedy for the emancipation of women, I argue that jurists have yet to investigate the meaning of formal law in a non-Western paradigm. Law in Sierra Leone is far more contested and dynamic than the report suggests, and this chapter questions the relevance or legitimacy of the formal law as the report describes.

The report produces an extensive narrative on gender inequality and discrimination in vital sociocultural and political institutions, such as the institutions of family and marriage, particularly early marriage.[4] As the report presents its gender analysis of the nature and extent of war crimes and crimes against humanity during Sierra Leone's civil war, it also establishes a link between women's experience of persecution in war and the day-to-day experience of gender inequality and discrimination against women in peacetime. However, the analysis becomes problematic when the report constructs early marriage in Sierra Leone and its related customs in terms that are indistinguishable from the formation and conditions of forced marriage in wartime, which is also referred to in the report as sexual enslavement.

Early marriage is the practice whereby families arrange the marriages of daughters who by the standard of regional human rights laws, such as the African Charter for the Rights and Welfare of the Child (African Charter for the Child), fall far below the age of majority.[5] The report describes early marriage in all its forms as a harmful social and customary practice that prejudices the health and interests of children and discriminates against girls, the primary victims of these arrangements (TRC 3:3: 116).[6] However, under the jurisdiction of the national and customary laws of Sierra Leone, early marriage is legal. The brides are recent initiates into womanhood and, therefore, by the standards of some segments of their society, are prepared for all of the privileges as well as duties that the institution of marriage implies.[7]

In this chapter, I explore competing narratives on gender and violence, particularly relating to marriage in Sierra Leone, to demonstrate the dissonance between international and regional human rights law narratives and survivors' narratives. Well before the advent of transitional justice in the mid-1990s in sub-Saharan Africa, the international human rights movement identified culture and customary law as the major cause of any discrimination African women experienced. This view of customary law has led to its exclusion as a positive frame of reference or resource in the process of remedying human rights abuses via the process of transitional justice. I argue that this approach is harmful in a society that is heavily reliant on culture and custom for political and social governance. After all, throughout decades of conflict and armed conflict, failed legislatures and judiciaries, Sierra Leonean women and men were heavily dependent on religion, culture, and customary law to negotiate and navigate everyday inequalities in their lives and relationships.

Fiounnuala Ní Aoláin challenges the ready assumption that cultural elements are the substantive barrier to postconflict recovery for women. She presses scholars to go beyond the evaluation of local culture to include a reflection on the ingrained patriarchies that international interface and oversight brings to transitional societies (2008: 8, quoting Dirlik 1987: 6). For the purposes of this chapter, I interpret these words to mean that international actors in Sierra Leone brought their own harmful culture and practices to humanitarian and other interventions to beneficiary communities. Many of these practices fall under the banner of a culture of patriarchy. It is important that international actors evaluate the harm that a patriarchal culture brings to institutional processes it oversees in Sierra Leone and elsewhere. The ingrained patriarchal culture, if left unexamined, allows international actors (such as prosecutors and defense counsel of an international ad hoc criminal tribunal) to assume power and dominance over the local beneficiary communities who enjoy little or no decision-making powers in the judicial process.

All parties to the armed conflict, including government forces, perpetrated sexual violence widely. The enslavement of girls was a particularly egregious and protracted abuse that took on different shapes and significance from one fighting force to another. It is widely attributed to the fighting coalition known as RUF-AFRC (TRC 3b:3: 298). This group, formed in 1998, included rebels of the Revolutionary United Front (RUF) and the Armed Forces Revolutionary Council (AFRC), a mutinous element of the Sierra Leone Army (SLA). Every reference to enslavement by the rebels throughout this chapter should be understood to refer to sexual violence perpetrated jointly by the RUF-AFRC and the specific manner in which they perpetrated it.[8]

Truth commissions have the power to create an authentic historical account that exposes untruths through the production of a truth that binds national, regional, and international polities. This power is granted by a parliamentary act and is therefore constitutive; it is also derived from the process of truth telling. Truth commissions are ad hoc bodies, yet their lack of institutional longevity does not preclude them from becoming from their very outset historical monuments commemorating a nation's emergence from a dark era. This status grants the process and final outcomes of commissions a sacrosanct character in the larger political process of accounting for past abuses. In the case at hand, a truth commission has the power to create an immutable history of the nature and causes of gender-based violence and even to propose recommendations for the prevention of gender inequality in Sierra Leone. This extraordinary authority demands that legal and other scholars closely review the commissioners' findings and recommendations.

The very nature of truth commissions as ad hoc, quasi-judicial, and informal mechanisms of justice gives them a broad mandate, which is most evident with respect to the very far reaching temporal jurisdiction of the Sierra Leone Truth Commission. While the TRC focused on the armed conflict, it looked additionally at the politics and history preceding that period as well as at the aftermath of violence in order to describe and define the violence in the designated time frame. So, according to the commissioners, describing gender-based violence during armed conflict required an extensive study of gender inequality and discrimination in Sierra Leone's history, dating as far back as the entry or reentry of freed slaves in the eighteenth century. This historical narrative of gender inequality and discrimination has a bearing on understanding gender-based violence in armed conflict and avoids the neat categorization of periods into peacetime and wartime. It illustrates the continuum of discrimination and its institutionalization after the conflict, and even maps the future with recommendations to the state on redressing human rights abuses committed during the civil war.

Conflicting narratives abound in the aftermath of conflict, and this is evident where gender-based violence is involved.[9] Postwar national and local narratives mistakenly refer to survivors of widespread and systematic rape as comfort women, collaborators, bush brides, war brides, prostitutes, and camp followers. These derogatory labels diminish the harm done to these women; they stigmatize women and denigrate the agency they exercised in order to survive armed conflict. I examine the report's narrative of gender and violence in order to see how well it has contributed to or challenged false representations of women's war experience.

The enacting language of the Sierra Leone Truth Commission presents it as a homegrown process that promotes an indigenous desire to restore fractured relationships through confession and forgiveness. The TRC sought to collect and propagate grassroots narratives even as it looked to international law and the case law of supranational courts to provide an overarching narrative of gross human rights violations in Sierra Leone. This double perspective creates an ambiguity in its work. The TRC was a mechanism of accountability or a process of transitional justice created with a high level of involvement and pressure from international and regional actors, including the Economic

Community of West Africa (ECOWAS) and the United Nations (Shaw 2005: 5–6). Some have argued that the government of Sierra Leone did not support the establishment or the work of the TRC but merely succumbed to the determination of the international community to establish a truth commission. Rosalind Shaw points out that although the government of Sierra Leone was unsupportive of the TRC, many Sierra Leoneans were nonetheless concerned that the national commissioners were too close to the then-ruling Sierra Leone Peoples' Party (SLPP).[10] Indeed, Shaw points out that the TRC chairman supported Sierra Leone's President Kabbah when he refused to apologize for the war on behalf of the state (ibid.).

The TRC was established in Sierra Leone, and at times it was a mobile forum as commissioners traveled and held sessions throughout the country in an effort literally to bring justice to Sierra Leoneans. On the basis of its local seat, the TRC could claim to possess knowledge of local practices and customs in ways that an ad hoc international tribunal could not. Presumably, the TRC could contextualize the civil war and better crystallize the needs of victims and perpetrators. These assumptions of belonging and knowledge are similar to that of the third tier of human rights instruments I described in Chapter 1. Such human rights instruments as the Maputo Protocol were able to criticize harmful traditional practices in Africa, such as early marriage and polygamy, without being tagged as Western mouthpieces. As we will see in this chapter, the report is indeed heavily censorious in its narrative of gender inequality and discrimination in Sierra Leone.

I question the insider status of the TRC and the legitimacy of its critique of gender inequality in Sierra Leone. I also question the extent to which the report's interchanging position at both local and international sites influences its narrative of gender roles, particularly in marriage. In the preceding chapter on the International Criminal Tribunal for Rwanda, I extracted disruptive narratives from the case law in order to challenge the dominant narrative of gender and violence found in the judgments. Here, I adopt a more ethnographic approach to disrupting the dominant narrative of the TRC report. Local gender narratives from daily life provide an important analytical tool for interrogating the report. These narratives are at times in accordance but more often in conflict with the report's narrative, which privileges international human rights law and statutory and customary law over local narratives.

Anthropologists Chris Coulter (2006) and Mariane Ferme (2001) both conducted extensive ethnographic studies in Sierra Leone. Coulter studied marriage among the Kuranko in the north of the country, particularly in the coercive context of armed conflict and its impact on young women attempting to reintegrate into their communities. Ferme studied different features of Mende society, including marriage and gender practices.[11] Their work and that of other anthropologists reminded me that my visit to Sierra Leone in 2008 as primarily a legal researcher gave me only a preliminary glimpse into the surface, or what Ferme would refer to as the "visible world" of discourses, social ties, and relations. This "visible world," however, is activated by an often ambiguous sequence of forces and meaning existing "underneath it" (Ferme 2001: 2–3). The legal framework of my research meant that my ability to understand early and forced marriage at the local level could only go as far as detecting the presence of an "underneath," even if its full meaning(s) ultimately eluded me. Carolyn Nordstrom (1997) provides the example of William Finnegan who concluded in his book on Mozambique that peasants did not understand that they lived in a political entity called Mozambique. Illiteracy, rural isolation, and tribal identity meant that peasants could not, for example, name the president of Mozambique. However, Nordstrom's own research disputed these conclusions. Nordstrom showed that peasants were perfectly aware who the president of Mozambique was but sometimes chose to feign ignorance when asked directly. They strategically employed different levels of knowledge.[12] Hers is a cautionary tale of how researchers might hear only the most superficial level of testimony from local people.

I found the "underneath of things" in Sierra Leone through the works of ethnographic researchers. An awareness of the "underneath of things" led me to apply a simple rule when analyzing human rights norms in light of the local practices revealed by ethnographers. The rule required that when an anthropologist embedded in the local shows that not all gendered institutions in a Sierra Leonean host community are degrading and enslaving and, further, that women exercise agency and power over and even against their husbands, then I had to reassess the value of the human rights narrative against these local narratives. In the same way, when a human rights law narrative condemns a local practice as harmful to individuals and their society, then I had to reassess the value and necessity of the local tradition in light of the human rights standard. This approach is necessary in order to identify the significance, if any, of the gaps between the underneath and the human rights or justice narrative.

In my own field experience, my inadvertent observation of practice often made discussions with survivors of the civil war more illuminating. I can best illustrate this informal research method with some examples drawn from my experiences of Sierra Leonean hospitality. I had the pleasure of spending some nights as a guest in several different households during my stay in Sierra Leone. I did not interview my hosts, but I was able to observe gender performances that worked in opposition to the TRC narrative of universal and/or eternal gender hegemonies.

In one household my hosts were a middle-aged widow and her very elderly mother. My sleep was disturbed by a man who banged and shouted through the windows and doors until he was allowed into the house in the early hours of the morning. In the morning, I asked the thirty-four year old son of my host about the commotion, and he explained simply: "That's my mother's friend." As I prepared to leave the house, the mother's friend, apparently in his role as the man of the house, accosted me in his boxer shorts and interrogated me about my identity and research objectives in Sierra Leone. I identified myself and my activities and thanked him for the hospitality of his home. Privately, I was shocked that a widow, particularly a mature one, would acknowledge a boyfriend publicly. According to the gender norms I was raised under, a widow that is openly sexually active would be a disgrace. This relationship also did not seem to tally with my initial understanding, supported by the TRC narrative, that marriage was the only legitimate relationship between men and women in Sierra Leone.

In another household, a career woman in her early thirties, her widowed sister, and their seven young children and dependents accommodated me. I was told that the husband was away in Freetown, and I intuited that probing further about his whereabouts would have been rude or embarrassing to the sisters. I concluded, correctly or incorrectly, that my host was a second (or third) wife and that her husband was living in Freetown with his other family.

In a third household, I asked the son of the servant the whereabouts of his father, and he informed me casually that his father lived with his "other mother" in the village and that he and his mother lived comfortably in the servants' quarters of his mother's employers. Because the little boy slept in the main house, took part in the family prayer at dawn, took meals with the family, and had his school fees paid for by my hosts (his mother's employer), I had mistakenly assumed that he was a family member and not the servant's child.

At yet another household, a successful businesswoman hosted me. Her teenaged children were studying in the United States. She had lived abroad in neighboring countries for nearly two decades with her husband, also a successful entrepreneur. She borrowed a generator from her neighbor so that we could stay up and watch the latest Nigerian dramas on her VCR. Later, her only dependent, the teenaged daughter of her servant, explained to me that "Auntie was too proud. She chased her husband and now he is with another wife." It surprised me that Auntie, who had initiated divorce proceedings, maintained the matrimonial home and property—a practice I had imagined customary law in Sierra Leone would not permit.[13] And, again, I was surprised that the servant's child was a family member.

These and other field observations reveal the presence of casual boyfriends, lovers, merry widows, cuckolds, heartsick men, adulterous wives, independent women, estranged spouses, absent husbands, and extended households. They made it difficult for me to embrace the essentialized image of the girl child and early marriage so prevalent in international human rights campaigns and the TRC report. I do not refer to these field observations as representative examples of women in Sierra Leone; rather, they hint at the underneath that is useful in challenging the TRC construction of inequality and subordination in the framework of formal law and customary law.

Gender and Violence in the TRC Report

The Republic of Sierra Leone borders Liberia to the southeast, Guinea to the north, and the Atlantic Ocean to the west.[14] The country is about 71,700 square kilometers in size and has a population of approximately five million spread across 149 chiefdoms. Seventeen ethnic groups make up the Sierra Leonean people, with the largest of the indigenous ethnic groups the Mende of the southern and eastern regions and the Temne (each about 30 percent), followed by the Limba (under 10 percent). Both the Temne and the Limba are dominant in the north (TRC 3b:3: 1–2). English is the country's official language, although the population primarily uses Krio, Mende, and Temne. Most of the population is Muslim, but there is a significant Christian population; and many followers of both Islam and Christianity respect and may even observe indigenous religions.

Sierra Leone gained independence from the British in 1961, and the country held a prestigious place in the African landscape as the land of freed slaves and as a West African center of academic excellence, boasting the oldest university on the continent.[15] As it emerges from the devastation of a civil war, Sierra Leone is one of the poorest countries in the world, despite having rich mineral resources. A dominant theory attributes the root cause and continuation of the armed conflict to the battle for "conflict diamonds."[16] Other intersecting theories on the causes of the conflict include disenfranchised youth, corrupt politicians, failed traditional institutions, agrarian crises, proxy wars fought by neighboring Liberia, an apathetic counterinsurgency by the government, and economic mismanagement and crises (Adekeye 2002; Cruise O'Brien 1996; Cook 2000; Hirsch 2005; Richards 1996).

The RUF emerged in 1991, claiming to be a social and political movement committed to rescuing the country from the corruption of the ruling party's All People's Congress (1968 to 1992 and 2007 to the present). Against the backdrop of three decades of state disintegration brought about by corruption and mismanagement, the struggle between the RUF and three successive governments raged throughout the 1990s (Keen 2005; Reno 2006). Although the RUF is consistently cited by the Truth Commission and human rights organizations as having abducted the greatest number of children for soldiering during this period, all sides in the conflict forcibly recruited large numbers of civilians (TRC 2004; Human Rights Watch 1999a; Physicians for Human Rights 2002).

A defining feature of the armed conflict was its "chameleon" character, whereby many of the belligerents changed allegiance against a background of complex military and political dynamics.[17] This feature was most clearly demonstrated in May 1997 when the SLA overthrew President Kabbah, formed the AFRC, and infamously joined forces with the RUF. Some of the conflict's most egregious human rights violations were committed during the January 1997 RUF-AFRC invasion of Freetown. There were hundreds of reports of women and girls being rounded up and raped and more than six thousand civilians killed (Keen 2005: 1). In 1999, the international community brokered a cease-fire, which led to the signing of the Lomé Peace Accord, a power-sharing agreement between the government and the RUF that granted amnesty to all combatants.[18] In spite of the Lomé Accord, political violence and pitched battles continued intermittently into 2002.

Nearly a decade after the accord, few would deny that the civilian population, including those abducted and associated with fighting forces, bore the brunt of war crimes and human rights violations. The corruption and degradation of tradition and social mores characterized atrocities during the war. TRC testimonies revealed victims' perceptions that the violence not only harmed them as individuals; it also desecrated fundamental values that defined community identities. One survivor described rebels forcing sons and mothers and sons-in-law and mothers-in-law to sing and dance together while holding the other's genitals. Her son-in-law, apparently filled with shame, was unable to obey these orders properly. The rebels slaughtered him before his mother's eyes, and they gave his decapitated head to her to hold (TRC 3:3: 205).[19]

This particular testimony speaks volumes about the rebels' desire not only to physically conquer victims but also to undermine their social underpinnings and traditions relating to relationships between elders and the youth, between men and women, between family members, between relatives by marriage, between mothers and their children.[20] This violent incident overturns a whole range of rites and relationships, including the responsibility of the living toward the dead for a proper burial and mourning rites. But, for my particular purposes, the shame of the son-in-law, which ultimately cost him his life, reminds the reader that sexualized forms of violence were also employed against men. The TRC narrative acknowledges that the men, who at the behest of rebels, carried out or simulated sexual acts with their female relatives were also victims of sexual violence.

Under the Lomé Peace Accord, the TRC was created as part of the framework for national reconciliation and the consolidation of peace. In February 2000, Sierra Leone's Parliament adopted the Truth and Reconciliation Act. It became operational after 5 July 2002, when the seven commissioners appointed by the president were formally sworn in (TRC 1:1: 4).[21]

The TRC report, the findings of the TRC commissioners, fills five volumes. In stating its objective to present a historical account of Sierra Leone's civil war, the commissioners' record of the conflict promises to depart from "popular history" and debunk certain myths and untruths about the conflict (TRC 1:1: 10). Nowhere is this desire to create an authentic history more evident than in the TRC report's narrative of gender and violence in the armed conflict and in its aftermath.

The TRC commissioners tried to respond to questions posed by Sierra Leonean survivors of the civil war: "What precipitated the wave of vengeance and mayhem that swept across the country? How was it that the people of Sierra Leone came to turn on each other with such ferocity? Why did so many abandon traditions of community and peaceful co-existence? Why were long-held and cherished customs and taboos so wantonly discarded?" (TRC 1:1: 1)." The commissioners divided their work and findings into different themes: Historical Antecedents to the Conflict; Governance; Military and Political History of the Conflict; Nature of the Conflict; Mineral Resources in the Conflict; External Actors in the Conflict; Women and the Armed Conflict; Children and the Armed Conflict; Youths and the Armed Conflict; the TRC and the Special Court for Sierra Leone; and lastly, a National Vision for Sierra Leone.

The TRC sought to create a historical record of human rights and international humanitarian law abuses from the beginning of the conflict in 1991 to the signing of the Lomé Accord (TRC 1:1: 6; TRC Act (2000), art. 6 [1]). And in the spirit of tier three instruments such as the CEDAW General Recommendations and the Maputo Protocol, the TRC objectives specifically referred to violence against women and girls as gender-based and undertook to dedicate special attention to sexual violence within armed conflict (TRC Report 1:1: 6; TRC Act (2002), art. 6 [1] [b]). It is possible that the strong criticism the South African Truth and Reconciliation Commission (1995) (South Africa TRC) had received over its marginal inclusion of women shaped the Sierra Leone TRC's commitment to a gender mandate. Yasmin Sooka, a former commissioner of South Africa's TRC, also presided over the Sierra Leone Commission, and she may have helped sensitize Sierra Leone's commissioners and ensure that they did not replicate the South African TRC's grave gender omissions.[22]

In many respects, the commissioners of South Africa's TRC perpetuated the social construction of women in conflict as merely wives and widows of men and men as freedom fighters or other political actors. As a result, many women did not testify before the South Africa TRC because their experience of apartheid did not fit the limited definition of human rights violations its commissioners had constructed. It was not, for example, necessarily considered a political crime or human rights abuse to summarily detain and torture a "wife" in order to punish or flush out her exiled husband who was a political activist against apartheid.[23]

The South Africa TRC's narrative of gross human rights violation minimized the severity of the gender-specific harms women suffered. The apartheid apparatus was particularly severe with respect to women's freedom of movement, right to work, and right to housing, which often exacerbated women's poverty and economic dependence on male guardians. Despite the daily indignities women bore under apartheid, the scope of apartheid crimes did not include forms of structural discrimination and the resultant harm that affected women, their children, and other dependents.

Another factor that may have contributed to the Sierra Leone TRC's early commitment to addressing gender-based violence was the widespread reporting, investigation, and documentation of sexual violence by local, national, and international organizations throughout the civil war and particularly during and after the RUF-AFRC invasion of Freetown (Amnesty International 2000; Physicians for Human Rights 2002).[24]

The role of international NGOs is also significant in understanding the gender policy adopted by postconflict entities such as truth commissions. International NGOs, such as Amnesty International and Human Rights Watch, are active, sending investigative missions, producing numerous reports, and providing a wide range of support for their domestic NGO counterparts, partners, and beneficiary organizations (Ní Aoláin 2008: 38). Ní Aoláin makes the important observation that previous interventions, such as those made by international NGOs, are critical to how accountability is sought, articulated, and constructed in the settlement phase of a conflict. She also points out that those international NGOs that intervene and construct previous narratives of violence and causality are often unwilling to consider their patriarchy or recognize it in an export form (Ní Aoláin 2008: 38–39, quoting Rees 2002: 51–57). Ní Aoláin's observation prompts the following questions: Who constructed the narrative of gender-based violence in Sierra Leone? Was it the TRC as a local grassroots instrument of justice, or was it the TRC as a strategic domestic forum for the international human rights community?

Sierra Leonean legislation created the TRC as a fully independent body, but the commission itself chose to be housed, for legal and administrative purposes, as a project of the UN Office of the High Commissioner for Human Rights (OHCHR) in Geneva (International Center for Transitional Justice 2004: 3). The commission entered into an important partnership with the UN Development Fund for Women (UNIFEM),[25] which led to the launching of the Initiative for the Truth and Reconciliation Commission under UNIFEM'S Peace and Security Program. This initiative made available training for commissioners, staff, and UNIFEM's NGO partners. UNIFEM also assisted the NGO community in making submissions on issues affecting women (TRC 3b:3: 31). By making submissions to the commission, assisting with the hearings, providing witnesses to the commission, and attending the hearings, UNIFEM became involved in mobilizing women's groups in Sierra Leone to participate in the commission's activities. UNIFEM also provided two international gender consultants to assist the commission both in writing the report and formulating its recommendations (TRC 3b:3: 31–32).[26] The level of intervention from international donors, particularly UNIFEM, demands a closer scrutiny by scholars of how the narrative of gender and violence in the

TRC report was "sought, articulated, and constructed." The TRC was an important mechanism of accountability for some Sierra Leoneans; however, it was also a strategic domestic forum for the articulation of those human rights interests prioritized by international human rights agencies.

The TRC report describes several procedural measures that facilitated the participation of women in the TRC process. In the *barray* phase, commissioners and staff held public meetings in local *barrays* (town halls) and reportedly reached out to women, women's groups, and agencies dealing with women, sensitizing them to the aims and objectives of the commission's work. At the outset, the commission made an effort to recruit women into senior staff positions. In addition, it ensured that more than 40 percent of the statement takers were women (TRC 3b:3: 19).

According to the report, the commission arranged for the training of all statement takers in issues of rape and sexual violence, as well as helping them cope with trauma.[27] The commission also provided guidelines on how to specifically work with women victims of sexual abuse. In summary, these guidelines directed statement takers to ensure the following basic conditions: that statement taking be done on a one-to-one basis; that the presence of husbands and fathers should be discouraged during statement taking, unless insisted on by the statement giver; and that when dealing with issues of rape and sexual violence, statement takers should be women (TRC 3b:3: 20). The commission provided trained counselors who would brief and debrief the women and girls who appeared at these special hearings (TRC 3b:3: 22–26).

The commissioners also fashioned a special hearings procedure where statements would be taken with only female commissioners and staff in attendance (TRC 3b:3: 23). The commission had expected that most women who were willing to testify would choose to do so in a closed rather than a public forum. The commission found it surprising that many women shunned secrecy, particularly in rural areas, where it was said that women who wanted the community to hear their stories had volunteered to testify in public.[28] The commissioners' misplaced assumption highlights the fact that preconceived ideas can impose silence on women. Fortunately, in the case at hand, women were able to express themselves and apparently many saw open testimony as empowering.

These provisions providing care, sensitization, training, and protection measures surpassed existing efforts by truth commissions established in earlier decades in Latin America and Africa to acknowledge the gendered nature of human rights violations and to respond with measures that would ease access to the process for victims of gender-based violence. It appears that these measures were effective. The report states that during the December 2002 pilot phase, which saw statement takers deployed to the various regions, women and girls came out in large numbers to participate in the statement taking process (TRC 3b:3: 21). Despite these encouraging accounts, the report acknowledged that the commissioners feared that many women and girls stayed away from the process; in particular, former girl combatants were underrepresented before the TRC for reasons that will become clearer in Chapter 4.

Much has been said about the ability and authority of truth commissions to bring hidden transcripts to the public forum (Blommaert et al. 2007: 37). Jan Blommaert describes testifying as a transformative process during which stories of previously voiceless victims become discourses of power and authority (ibid.). The report clearly regards Sierra Leone's women, children, and youth as belonging to a traditionally and historically voiceless segment of society. The report presents a chapter for the sole discussion of women and the armed conflict and another for the discussion of children and the armed conflict.[29] In its attempt to transform individual stories of human rights abuse into discourses of authority, the report presents Sierra Leone's civil and political, economic, and social and cultural sectors that traditionally and historically kept women voiceless. The report places special emphasis on discriminatory deprivation in the areas of education, politics, economic status, and sexuality.[30] This approach was important because it revealed that violence against women was not a random event occurring only as long as the armed conflict persisted. The TRC's broad jurisdiction, therefore, allowed it to predate gender inequality and discrimination to the prewar period.

Prominent among all these areas of exclusion is the issue of early marriage and the status and condition of women in marriage. The report identifies marriage as the central element within each sector of exclusion (education, politics, and sexuality) and also as a factor exacerbating exclusion. Thus, it links early marriage to school dropout levels for girls and early sexual activity within the marriage to the increased possibility of complications of pregnancy and childbirth (TRC 3b:3: 73, 74). This analysis is acceptable and correct; however, its limited focus creates a narrative that only partially describes marriage in Sierra Leone.[31]

So, even as the TRC report decries the Sierra Leonean veneration of marriage and all beliefs and practices surrounding it—for example, enforced virginity and female circumcision—it reproduces this veneration. The TRC primarily describes women and men in the gender roles of husbands and wives and all human rights violations against women in peacetime as arising from this inevitably oppressive relationship (for women).[32] The report specifically targets "early marriage" as a human rights violation. However, it goes too far when it suggests that early marriage precipitated and legitimized the enslavement of girls and women in armed conflict. By claiming that because of the nonconsensual nature of early marriage in peacetime, "some of the armed groups did not consider it an aberration to rape young women or use them as sex slaves" (TRC 3b:3: 85), wives and slaves become nearly interchangeable terms and experiences for women and girls. By giving slavery in armed conflict a meaning that extends beyond the limits set by the text, context, and purpose of the 1926 Slavery Convention, this crime is made banal.[33] Further, by reducing Sierra Leonean men to husbands and "enemies of mankind" and Sierra Leonean women to their victim-wives, the report also unduly stigmatizes the gendered and sociopolitical institutions of the family and marriage.[34] The TRC narrative of marriage in peacetime could raise a defense by rebels or others accused of enslaving women that forced marriage in the bush is akin to early marriage and therefore not a war crime or crime against humanity.

The TRC report impresses the dominant discourse linking marriage to gender inequality and discrimination on the reader not only through reference to international human rights instruments but also through an extensive criticism of Sierra Leone's domestic laws that enshrine gender inequality and discrimination. The commissioners present the Sierra Leone Constitution's Bill of Rights (a typical first tier human rights instrument) as illustrative of the extent to which Sierra Leone's women are left vulnerable to denials of their enjoyment of human rights. By permitting carte blanche gender- and sex-based discrimination with regard to adoption, marriage, burial, and devolution of property on death or other interests of personal law, the constitution denies women their fundamental human rights.[35]

The report's review of Sierra Leone's legal system vis-à-vis international standards was important. The review, however, was conducted in isolation from the participation of girls and women such that the historiography of women's lives before the war comes entirely from a review of international and domestic legislation and the reporting of international human rights organizations. This approach creates the impression that the laws are immutable and women's submission to the laws in the regulation of their private lives (particularly in the area of marriage) is absolute.

The commissioners' overreliance on the legislative review leads the reader to the conclusion that victims who came before the TRC related their harm to discriminatory provisions of the Constitution, the Mohammedan Marriage Act, the Civil Marriage Act, the Christian Marriage Act, the Matrimonial Causes Act, and other offending laws cited by the report.[36] Further, it assumes that legal redress is the primary avenue women and girls would take in order to seek justice at any given time. The TRC does not address the reality that this formal legal redress is highly unlikely considering that throughout the political transitions of the twentieth century the Sierra Leonean people could not rely exclusively on legislation or the courts of law as effective institutions for remedy or regulation. The institutions of the (formal) public realm, such as the judiciary, lost their authority decades before the civil war as a result of endemic corruption and other abuses of power. Nonetheless, these laws take center stage in the TRC analysis of the root causes of gender inequality and discrimination.

In its gender narrative, the report fails to note this failure of the judiciary and legislature that had preceded and to some extent provoked the outbreak of armed conflict and that had pressed Sierra Leoneans to seek other avenues for resolution and remedy. Tim Kelsall points out that English common law courts in Anglophone Africa have never been popular, in part because the language, strict adversarial protocol, and the winner-takes-all nature of the judgments are foreign to African traditions, which tend to be more inquisitive, mediatory, and restorative. Conflicts are better dealt with in local moots, informal chiefdom courts, and customary courts, which, while having their own problems, tend to be more popular and accessible (Kelsall 2005: 17).

Rather than acknowledge the failure of formal law in Sierra Leone, the report focuses on the failure of culture. It portrays women in the Third World as victims of their culture—a portrayal that both reinforces stereotyped and racist representations of that culture and privileges the culture of the West (Kapur 2002: 5). Ratna Kapur elaborates that scholars often displace the issue of culture onto a First World and Third World divide with the result that colonial assumptions about cultural differences between the West and "the Rest," and the women who inhabit these spaces, are replicated. Some cultural practices have come to preoccupy the imagination of human rights advocates in ways that are totalizing of a culture and its treatment of women but that are nearly always overly simplistic or caricatures of local practices (ibid.: 8). In this case, the TRC report is responsible for planting a totalizing image of marriage as a war crime in the imaginations of stakeholders of Sierra Leone's transitional justice process.

Indigenous responses to conflict are consigned to the category of "culture" and therefore marginalized by the TRC. However, such responses, often referred to as alternative dispute resolution mechanisms, are particularly active in regulating the entry into, conduct of, and dissolution of marriage. Some examples include interfamily mediation, faith-based counseling, counseling and training by elders, cleansing rituals, intervention and judgment by men and women's secret societies, exile from the community, witchcraft and fetish, and public shaming. It is extraordinary that these remedies (and this list is far from exhaustive) were neglected in the TRC's construction of formal law in Sierra Leone. Michael Schatzberg's argument that most studies on Africa are "out of focus" with local political realities has some resonance within my gender investigation into Sierra Leone's Truth Commission. Schatzberg warns that unless we begin to take indigenous understandings of concepts and categories more seriously than we do at present, we shall continue to miss vital and living elements of politics in Africa (Kelsall 2005: 7, quoting Schatzberg 2002: 37 and 70).

The report mistakenly speaks of customary law, norms, and practice as a formal and uniform code binding society, invariably oppressing all Sierra Leonean women and girls while presumably privileging all Sierra Leonean men. However, a more informed evaluation of this multilayered and dynamic code was called for in order to fairly criticize gender inequalities and discrimination against women.[37] The TRC's evaluation of customary law fell far below the level of a gender analysis. Such an evaluation might have been made possible if there had been more reliance on victim testimony revealing their experiences of "formal" law, as well as "informal" mechanisms of redress for injustice before, during, and after the civil war. Further, such an evaluation would have signified that the TRC used its local positioning in order to privilege the "underneath of things" with its vital and living elements that make up the political reality of Sierra Leone society (Ferme 2001; Schatzberg 2002).

In every society, there are informal rules and norms that members of society consider sufficiently important that they are legitimately treated as alternatives to the formal (encoded) ones. And informal institutions tend to become salient, especially in situations where formal ones are weak (Hyden 2008: 2–3). The informal institutions can help reinforce, complement, or undermine formal institutions (ibid.: 3). In the case of Sierra Leone, I suggest that informal judicial and legislative institutions actually override much of the authority of their formal and failed counterparts. It is only in the interest of clarity that I will continue to refer to a uniform customary code and statutory law as "formal" law and the wide ranging occurrence of customary practices and alternative mechanisms as "informal."

Customary norms resolve adoption, marriage, burial, and the devolution of property upon death and other interests of personal law. As I will explain in the final sections of this chapter detailing alternative narratives on gender and marriage, parties negotiate custom on a case-by-case and day-to-day basis. The "underneath" of the TRC's favored formal mechanism is the customary law. It is far from visible in the TRC report. This underneath of customary law relates to the "living law," or people's day-to-day application, manipulation, negotiation, and interpretation of customary law.

I recall a conversation in which a young man claimed that under custom (*de jure*), he (the man) was entitled to sole custody of his child. However, it became apparent to me that while he maintained the child financially, his former girlfriend, the mother of the child, enjoyed sole custody (*de facto*) in Freetown.[38] There must have been negotiation concerning the apparently fixed customary practice that would have discriminated against a woman's right to custody, and the extent to which other parents adapted this norm in Sierra Leone would have to be studied quantitatively and qualitatively before leaping to conclusions about its authenticity and its authority over men and women in the resolution of custody disputes.

The TRC report missed an opportunity to examine customary law as *prima facie* formal law also distinguished from statute. With respect to the enforcement of customary law, families, chiefs, and relatives who have vested interests in the dissolution of or entry into marriage replace judges and legal counsel. These vested interests may allow the actors in a divorce proceeding, for example, to circumvent or flout customary laws. The TRC report eschews any real investigation into custom as a remedy for inequality and discrimination, despite the high visibility of customary law in daily life.[39]

The scale of this omission is evident in the TRC's failure to describe women's societies as an important source of social, political and economic power for women in Sierra Leone.[40] Probably the best known of the West African women's associations is the Bundu, known locally in Sierra Leone as the Sande Society, to which roughly 95 percent of all Sierra Leonean women are said to belong (Cunningham 1996: 340, quoting MacCormack-Hoffer 1975: 173). Backed by the supernatural, the Bundu Society guarantees women respect from all members of society and plays a significant role in equalizing women's relationships with men (MacCormack-Hoffer 1975: 155).

Bundu law enhances the status of all women by protecting them, for example, from such degrading acts as male voyeurism. Should a man fail to make a warning noise as he approaches the place where women bathe, he will be charged for his offense. Should he make sexual advances to an uninitiated girl, he risks illness and death unless he goes to the Bundu leader, confesses, pays a fine, and submits to a ritual cleansing. Husbands are wary of offending their wives in marital disputes because there is always a chance that the abused wife, or her mother, will use "medicine" known to Bundu women to harm him, especially to render him impotent (MacCormack-Hoffer 1975: 162).[41] Membership in the Bundu Society can provide important benefits to women, not the least of which is the deterrence of mistreatment from husbands and other men.[42]

The exclusion of any analysis of the Bundu reveals how the human rights critique subsumes women's sources of strength.[43] The TRC justice process distorts the picture of African women's lives into a grotesque litany of subjugation by African men. Kapur describes how the British, by pointing to extreme cultural practices, such as the immolation of widows, as evidence of the barbarity of Indian society, used the position of women to legitimize colonial rule (Kapur 2002: 14).[44] This argument is relevant in the current context as the transitional justice process legitimizes itself by presenting extreme cultural practices against women as evidence of a human rights crisis in Sierra Leone and the failure of customary and formal law to deal with it—all of which prove the need for international intervention. Acknowledging the existence of a functioning and thriving customary law system could undermine calls for international criminal justice.

The TRC narrative falls into the trap set by the first tier rights I described in Chapter 1. First tier rights emphasized the private and public sphere, and the report clearly corrals Sierra Leonean women into the private sphere, first, by tagging them all as child brides and, second, by neglecting to investigate women's lives in public spaces, such as women's civil society organizations, women in military service, and Bundu societies. The Bundu Society, in particular, is a major but not the sole alternative channel through which women can acquire power in both the private and public sphere. Caroline Bledsoe makes the important observation that legal approaches tend to overemphasize the differences between men and women's official sources of authority, reserving the public sphere for men and the private sphere for women and children. By treating women as legal minors, legal advocates and legislators obscure the importance of women's political and economic ambitions and wrongly conclude that women cannot and do not acquire power and status through alternative channels (1980: 180).

The TRC report describes women's gendered experience as more than instances of sexual victimization. According to the report, women and girls assumed varied roles, including becoming armed combatants, providing medical assistance, feeding armed groups, and supplying opposing forces with intelligence information often at great risk to their lives (TRC 3b:3: 388). However, it is notable that in describing women as combatants, the TRC follows the popular humanitarian discourse that regards women as natural peacemakers and victims. The image of a soldier remains a male image, and women tend to be placed at the opposite, peaceful end of a moral continuum (Coulter 2005: 232). Therefore, the report presents women combatants as driven by "socio-economic needs, the need to protect themselves and their families or to improve the quality of their lives" (TRC 3b:3: 389). In other cases, "many women experienced personal losses, which hurt them a great deal and led them into enrolling in the Army to avenge their loved ones" (ibid.).[45] The report presents no investigation into, for example, the status of women who voluntarily enlisted, who subscribed to a political or military ideology, or who excelled at military tasks.

While a nuanced narrative of gender and violence begins to emerge at times in the report, it overwhelmingly depicts the victimization, particularly sexual victimization, of women. Although it paid some attention to the reality of women combatants, it had the effect of stripping women of agency in the same way that a narrative focusing exclusively on victimhood would have done.[46] Again, the voiceless are granted an audience only for selected narratives and to emphasize the human rights law framework laid out at the outset of the Truth Commission's process. Even as the commission attempts to put violence against women into a political and authoritative framework, it depoliticizes women, their experience, and their agency (Shepler 2005: 205–206). The rigidity with which this framework is observed creates risks for losing the importance of women strategically manipulating this framework (ibid.: 206). Allowing for an inquiry into women's battle experience would have allowed room for fuller testimonies that show that victimhood and active political roles are not mutually exclusive but, in fact, overlap and intersect with some frequency in Sierra Leone.

Marriage as Violence

As a transitional justice mechanism with no legal authority, the TRC is not constrained by strict legal definitions. This freedom can be seen in its definitions of sexual slavery and forced marriage, which overlap significantly. According to the report, sexual slavery occurred when women and girls were captured and abducted. They became part of the entourage of an armed group to which their captors belonged and then moved along with them in a type of roaming detention that could last from one or two days to several months and years (TRC 3b:3: 299 and 304). The arrangement of forced marriage arose when abducted women were handed over to individual combatants and became their "bush wives" for the purpose of satisfying not only their sexual needs but also to perform a host of different duties, including domestic chores (TRC 3b:3: 301). With this account by the TRC, what distinguished sex slaves from bush brides was that bush brides performed domestic chores, such as cooking and cleaning, and had an exclusive sexual relationship with a male combatant. The definition is simplistic, and the commissioners themselves point out that "while some of the girls were assigned and attached to one partner, such attachment did not prevent other perpetrators from using them, particularly if the combatant they were attached to was not a senior commander. In some cases, husbands willingly offered their wives out to other fighters" (TRC 3b:3: 302). The following testimony illustrates the ambiguity of a monogamous bush union: "I lost my virginity to this C. O. Koroma, who was 45 years old. I was kept in a locked room always ready for him to sex me. Sometimes when he is away, his junior boys will come and open the door, sometimes three, sometimes four men. They will force me, telling me I refuse them they will kill me. As a small girl I will allow them to satisfy themselves" (TRC 3b:4: 172). Despite the attempt to provide legal definitions that distinguish sexual slavery from forced marriage, the TRC commissioners describe the experience of girls and women abducted by rebels interchangeably as sexual slavery or forced marriage throughout chapter 3 of the report. The commissioners note that enslavement becomes a gendered form of persecution—that is, sexual enslavement—when an individual is enslaved because of his or her particular function in society, as when women are used for cooking and cleaning or for sex and reproduction. They describe enslavement as the nonsexual form of sexual slavery, which includes forced domestic labor or mining (TRC 3b:3: 194). When referring to women and girls, the term *enslavement* is discarded in favor of *sexual enslavement* because, as the report says, "bush brides are not slaves but sex slaves because every relationship of forced marriage involved forced sex or the inability to control sexual access or exercise sexual autonomy" (TRC 3b:3: 184).

The ill demarcated categories of forced marriage and sexual slavery reduce boys' and girls' gendered experience of abduction or forced conscription to a rape experience for girls. This is the narrowest application of a gender analysis and does little to advance any understanding of women's and men's full experience of surviving war. In demonstrating the link between structural inequalities in Sierra Leone's society and gross human rights violations against women during the armed conflict, the narrative of the TRC collapses the distinction between the institution of early marriage and the relationship of forced marriage. As I mentioned earlier, the commissioners and NGOs operating at the local level have suggested that bush marriages in wartime mirrored arranged or early marriages in peacetime. This approach is useful to international NGOs as a tool to strengthen the ongoing human rights campaign against early marriage in Sierra Leone and throughout Africa. It produces an advocacy narrative against early marriage and its attendant harms. The mandate of the TRC did not envisage this outcome.

References in the TRC report to initiation and other rituals and the award of social status and power to bush wives in forced marriage have been used inappropriately to support the claim that bush marriage and early marriage are similarly situated as human rights violations.[47] I discuss these elements of bush marriage below (marriage rituals and privileges) and dispute the argument that they somehow validated forced marriage in war as an institution comparable to early marriage in peacetime.

Ethnographers have described traditional institutions, ceremonies, and mechanisms governing relationships in the bush, including bush marriage. Chris Coulter's informants, many of whom had escaped bush marriage, spoke of the presence of a senior woman or Mammy Queen in the bush and the elevated status of girls married to commanders who acted as mediators in disputes between or affecting girls in camps.[48] Her interviews revealed that Mammy Queens in the bush conflict were actually called upon to "do the marriage," which presumably meant that they could conduct some form of marriage ceremony. This is the only account I have encountered suggesting that marriage ceremonies or imitations of marriage ceremonies were conducted in the bush. Coulter cautions that despite the high esteem a Mammy Queen enjoyed in the bush, there was little a Mammy Queen could do to protect women from their own bush husbands. An informant revealed that despite the presence of a well-known broker, such as a Mammy Queen, disputes were not settled in a customary way. "There was no one to report to if your husband abused you. . . . There my husband was a big man, where will I report him? Nowhere! When he do me I only hold God and sit" (Coulter 2006: 188–89). Coulter concluded that the presence of Mammy Queens testified to the continuity between the organization of ordinary and wartime life and suggests that women's submission and lack of recourse to justice in the face of abuse from bush husbands "was no different from life in peacetime" (2006: 188). At best, this parallel is tenuous and understates the alternative dispute resolution mechanisms available through religious channels, indigenous courts, secret societies, and so on. At worst, the parallel compares Sierra Leonean husbands and men to drug fueled rebels who had the power of life and death over girls and women. Rape, summary beatings, and the fear of execution were inherent to enslavement; however, it is far from accurate to suggest that rape, beatings, and the fear of execution are inherent features of marriage in Sierra Leone, even early marriage. It is highly questionable that women's subordinate position had resulted in widespread impunity for men who mistreated their wives and otherwise failed to fulfill their obligations toward their families. I will explore this question more deeply with my selection of alternative narratives below.

Finally, considering the protracted process that leads to early marriage, the role of the Mammy Queen or even suggestions that a marriage ceremony was conducted are insufficient evidence that bush marriages were legitimate. In some cases, initial agreements between families and betrothals have been made before or at the birth of a child. Irrespective of its obvious contravention of international human rights standards, the complex process of early marriage cannot be compared to the summary allocation of girls to commanders and other fighters. Child betrothal is a harmful practice that should be challenged but with more considered strategies.

The sentiment that bush marriage elevated the status of abducted girls and the picture of the "happy" bush wife stems from privileges and wealth said to have been enjoyed by bush wives compared to the villagers who were victims of rebels' wanton looting and attacks. Coulter recounts, for example, that favored wives of senior commanders held authority in rebel social life. Apparently many had several people, young and old, both men and women, working for them, preparing food, laundering, and taking care of their children. Often, senior wives were in charge of the distribution of arms and ammunition before an attack (2006: 194). Further, commanders' wives had the power to punish or reward and were often in a position to get everything they asked for, including jewelry, music, and clothing, either by looting it themselves or having it done for them. Coulter shows that these girls were often envied and revered by girls in the lower rebel social hierarchy, and some of her informants admitted that they had feared violent reprisals from commanders' wives more than they feared the actual commanders (ibid.).

Discussing privilege and protection in the bush must be done with caution and with an understanding of the violence and potential for violence in the context of confinement and coercion in the bush in the midst of armed conflict. The following testimony indicates that sexual slaves, even those bearing the title of bush wife, were potentially available to a wide range of men and, further, that such factors as the age of the "wife" or the military rank of a bush "husband" also had an impact on the vulnerability of abducted girls to sexual violence. "On our arrival we were assigned to the wives of commanders and later given to commanders or fighters to be their bush wives. As a bush wife, my duties were to provide for him anything he requested, including sex any time of the day. I was used as a sex slave for each commander when they came to our camp, especially because my bush husband was not a senior commander" (TRC 3b:3: 171). Access to privileges such as looted goods was highly dependent on various factors, including the status of the commander or fighter "husband." And it should be noted that these privileges (of bush wives) had no comparison with privileges and status women were awarded once they were wed in peacetime. Much of this privilege in peacetime was associated with initiation, which includes but is not limited to circumcision, as well as induction into a secret society through the medium of the bush.

Before attempting to explain the phenomenon of bush marriage, I should provide some insight into the term *bush*. It is a gendered site as well as an adjective that when attached to the institution of marriage, provides much symbolic meaning and power. The word *bush* can connote the wildness of nature, the taming of the untamable, familiarity with nature, and the anti-social as well as the undomesticated individual (Coulter 2006: 182, quoting Jackson 1977: 34). It can be a derogatory adjective attaching, for example, to a rustic person.[49] During Sierra Leone's eleven-year war, the bush was a site where people were transformed from civilians into deadly and even invincible fighters, through harsh military training but also through magic rituals and seemingly bizarre but carefully choreographed physical and psychological initiation processes. In this sense, *bush* was used as the opposite of life in the village. The village was domesticated and restrained, and the bush wild and unbridled (Coulter 2006: 182). Rebels returning from combat to their villages, whether as escapees during the war or as demobilized fighters after the peace, were described as "returning from the bush," and abducted women referred to their wartime experience as when they were "in the bush" (ibid.).[50]

Outside of the war context, women and girls also conquered the bush. The bush has been described as the site of a girl's greatest journey, that is to say, the journey from childhood to womanhood (Coulter 2006: 44). Initiation requires that girls be separated from their community and taken into the bush where they are trained in a wide range of subjects, including the ways of womanhood, marriage, and matrimonial sex.[51] In this context, the bush, which can be seen as a male or animal figure, becomes the site of a highly gendered psychological and physical conquest for women as well as a transformation through excision in preparation for penetration through sexual intercourse, gestation, and, ultimately, childbearing.

The bush was wild but could be mastered by hunters, by rebels, and by women who set aside their fear of the bush and entered it in order to domesticate the passions of young, uninitiated girls in preparation for the rigors of womanhood.[52] For many girls, marriage followed within a few weeks or months after returning from the bush as a woman, and indeed many suitors funded the costly initiation process on behalf of their in-laws and as a condition of marriage (Coulter 2006: 144). This great journey and the privileges it bestows, including the status of a woman and entry into the institution of marriage, is a far cry from the bush capture, abuse, and lingering stigma bush wives endure after reunification with their families.

It is noteworthy that even in the oppressive conditions that marked relations in the bush, a tone of moral righteousness sneaks into Coulter's informants' distinction between the status of attached and unattached women (2006: 223). Those girls and women who did not become wives were forced to work far more strenuously than wives, and any number of men continuously sexually abused them (ibid.: 196). As one informant put it, those who were selected by commanders and brigadiers for marriage were "free" from being used for gang rapes and became "good women." One informant referred to the unmarried women as "riff-raff women" who were used all day and all night by every man (ibid.: 223). The disdain for riff-raff women is clear, and the multiple rapes are treated as promiscuity on the part of the victim.

However, security and status for the "good women" could also be no more than an illusory state since a commander's protection could be withdrawn at a whim. As Coulter relates, "Musu was one of six bush wives to a commander.

She became pregnant but miscarried, and thinks this was because of frequent beatings from her husband. The reason for the beatings, she believed, was that her bush husband usually took drugs which made him wicked" (ibid: 189). Husbands provided a measure of security for some girls; however, these husbands were often heavy substance users, brutal, brutalized themselves, and likely to be suffering from the traumas of rebel life and atrocities regularly committed against others. The husband's ownership over his wife included the power to kill her summarily for any hint of disobedience.

It should be noted that even as security is shown to be very subjective in the context of abduction in armed conflict, women's attempts at negotiating their own safety should not be underestimated. Doing so involved a variety of means, including acquiring and mastering small arms, aligning themselves with a powerful male commander, perpetuating impressive acts of violence, and engaging in subtle acts of acquiescence as well as bold acts of resistance. These mechanisms, which carried varying degrees of success, highlight the girls' capacity for negotiation and agency as well as resourcefulness, resistance, and mutual forms of support (Denov and Gervais 2007: 895).[53]

So some highly tenuous parallels could be drawn between life in the bush and life in the village: In the bush, marriages were entered into, polygyny was practiced, Mammy Queens were apparently appointed, and rebel camps, hierarchies, and the gendered division of labor were organized. There was a perceived superiority of bush wives over unattached women, and, clearly, abducted women and rebels themselves used the language of "marriage" to describe their bush relationships. However, it would be careless for the legal scholar to accept these terms without investigating the motives men and women would have for describing violence and subordination in conjugal terms. An obvious motive would relate to protection, which I have discussed at length above. Describing oneself as a wife could have also reflected attempts to legitimize these relationships in order to minimize stigma or possibly to maximize profits that could be gained as a "wife" or indeed as a "husband." While few scholars have ventured into a gender analysis of men and wartime masculinities in the construction of bush marriage, I speculate, considering the improved status of men upon marriage in peacetime (in Sierra Leone and elsewhere), that acquiring a wife and being able to claim her as an exclusive possession depended on one's rank and power over other men.[54] Conversely for women, while bush marriage may have improved their status in the bush, it proved to be a damaging label in peacetime. Women who escaped rebel control after shorter periods of enslavement were welcomed back by their communities more readily than women regarded as having entered into rebel marriages.

Brenda V. Smith (2006: 580–81) describes complicated relationships that sometimes emerge between captive and captor. The roles of the oppressed and the oppressor can become confused, sometimes resulting in relationships that stretch traditional boundaries of captor and captive. These relationships were often motivated by need. The oppressor might have had access to items that would make slavery or imprisonment more bearable: better food, clothing, better work assignments, protection from other oppressors, and increased status within the framework. A psychiatric analysis also raises the issue of chronic traumatic stress experienced during captivity. Abusers may alternate between kindness and viciousness; for psychological survival, the victim may form positive feelings for that part of the perpetrator that is kind and ignore the vicious side. This "traumatic attachment" can result in seemingly illogical behavior, such as the victim becoming protective of the perpetrator or evading law enforcement assistance (Srikantiah 2007: 200–201, quoting Hidalgo et al. 2005: 404).[55] Claiming one's torturer as one's husband could be viewed as "traumatic attachment" under the banner of "seemingly illogical behavior."

The implication that bush wives were lucky or better off than those who were not selected belittles the suffering girls and women experienced irrespective of marital status. It creates a "false universalism" between wives in peacetime and girls enslaved by rebels in Sierra Leone; it unduly stigmatizes Sierra Leonean marriage and creates a contest that is not worth entering into, namely, the "who suffered the grossest human rights violation" contest.[56]

Alternative Narratives of Marriage

The following narratives offer a small sample of divergent experiences and voices, which hint at the underneath of dominant narratives of gender inequality and discrimination in the human rights discourse in Sierra Leone. I use these narratives of marriage as an analytical tool that can force a reevaluation of the human rights discourse on the subordination of women under law and customary law in Sierra Leone.

A rights-based narrative presents this analysis of customary law: customary laws discriminate against women in Sierra Leone and prescribe no minimum marriage age. Further, the consent of the husband is sought but that of the woman is in many cases not necessary (Sierra Leone Lawyer's Center for

Legal Assistance 2004: 21). A woman is considered the property of her husband and can be inherited by other male family members on the death of her husband (ibid.: 22). Married and single women alike have no right to refuse sex with their husbands or other men (TRC 3b:3:74).

This account of customary law is accurate if, as human rights lawyers, we seek only to shock, shame, and condemn. However, this account is far from adequate if we want to work toward systematic engagement in a "cultural negotiation" that would emphasize the positive cultural elements and demystify the oppressive elements in culture-based discourses.[57] I would add that the human rights lawyer must also seek to demystify the oppressive elements of rights-based discourses before attempting an analysis of culture.

Culture is not applied uniformly by its constituents, and variations in practice within apparently homogenous communities can be attributed to the fact that people may and do pick and choose to emphasize those aspects that apply and appeal to their situations. Shock tactics obscure and mystify customary law and the different ways in which it is observed. My fieldwork experience revealed that despite the failure of the Constitution, legislation, and customary laws to protect the rights of women and girls, many Sierra Leoneans, men and women, are indeed engaged in cultural negotiation that has transformed or is transforming hegemonic models of gender. Furthermore, reaching beyond the human rights law discipline is essential but only if the human rights lawyer is willing to confront or negotiate with narratives of gender at the local level that challenge the authoritative narrative emerging from transitional justice processes, in this case, Sierra Leone's TRC.

In Chapter 1, I discussed the human rights law discourse categorizing the division of the public and the private into gendered and binary spaces. Men ostensibly occupy the public spaces of society, such as political platforms, while women inhabit the private spaces, such as the household. Deconstructing the public-private divide has been an important centerpiece in the feminist battle against gender inequality and discrimination. In such areas as criminal law, for example, eroding the divide between public and private spaces has contributed to the criminalization of "private abuses," such as spousal abuse, stalking, and date rape (Pateman 1983: 281–303). However, as the work of ethnographers reveals, it is a model that is regularly deconstructed at the grassroots level in Sierra Leone as men and women distribute and redistribute power in gender relations.

Ferme's experience with the Mende people reveals a multitude of ambiguities and transgressions in appropriate gender roles and practices (2001). She acknowledges the visible gendered division of public and private spaces into certain objects and spaces "owned" by men and others "owned" by women. However, she also describes an "underneath of things" where women arbitrarily seize public spaces from men. She provides the example of Kpuawala women's ceremonial occupation of the male public domain for several days "visibly, in large numbers and while explicitly declaring them off limits to men" (ibid: 62–63). She also describes women known as the *Mabolesia*, who can be initiated as high ranking female officials within the men's Poro Society and appropriate seemingly male domains. The *Mabole* woman hunts with men, fishes with women, but is perceived as a marginal member of both the fishing community of women and the hunting community of men (ibid.: 74–75). It is impossible to clearly identify the gender roles of the *Mabolesia*, for they possess male and female attributes and overlapping gender qualities (ibid.: 78). The *Mabole* is an important figure demonstrating that disruptions of gender roles do occur in Sierra Leone, sometimes in a spectacular fashion. Ferme's analysis also reveals that African women's disruptions of the public and the private may not resemble disruptions by Western feminists through legal theorizing and advocacy; however, they merit our serious attention and acknowledgment.

The limitation of the TRC report is that it does not note the fluidity of gender hegemonies throughout Sierra Leone's rapidly changing political landscape and that individually and collectively there can be room for women and men to navigate gender identities and spaces. And this limited representation of gender hegemonies makes it entirely possible to construct bush marriage as emblematic of inequality and discrimination in Sierra Leonean society, culture, and laws.

In this section, I am interested in the question of power (a word associated with the public) in marriage (a word associated with the private). By power in marriage, I mean the ability of married persons to exert influence over the other parties to the marriage (the husband, co-wives, children, stepchildren, in-laws, parents, clan, etc.) in order to negotiate the terms and conditions of the matrimonial contract. Parties to a marriage exercise power when they are able to enforce or partially enforce the duties they believe they are owed by the other parties to the marriage and exploit those privileges they believe they are owed by virtue of the union. Power in marriage is also linked to the ability to enter into and extract oneself from marriage at advantageous moments.

Ferme's research is useful for human rights law scholars because her description of marriage and forms of dependence in her host community reveals that marriage is a gendered institution that can bestow as well as wrest power from both men and women. She describes, for example, the different ways that men and women in marriage and through marriage could alternate between the role of slave or dependent and the positions of patronage, such as "big" man and "big" woman.[58] She describes slave and master relationships in the idiom of marital and kin relations: for example, a maternal uncle is the master of his "slave" nephew (2001: 82). The matrilateral uncle owns the nephew and in the past would have possessed a right to sell the nephew into slavery (ibid.: 87). Thus, by arranging a strategic marriage, "enslaved" men and women and even families could free themselves from relationships of dependence and even increase their own control over other individuals or families.[59]

Ferme's analysis not only focuses on women's dependency, as the TRC human rights discourse is wont to do, but also describes male privilege at times weakened or reinforced by strategic marriages. Rather than attempt to repeat Ferme's analysis, this section only presents certain studies of marriage types represented in her work that emphasize that gender hegemonies are not as clear cut as the human rights discourse supposes.

In contrast with the TRC report, Ferme identifies several types of marriage. One category includes variations of early marriage: for example, the betrothal of girls to a suitor and the courtship by a suitor of a newly matured woman preparing for initiation or recently initiated (ibid.: 89–91). A second category is the marriage of mature women, for example, widowed women or women who separated from or deserted earlier unions and wish to remarry, often a lover who may have contributed to the demise of the earlier marriage. These women, whether widowed or separated, may well have experienced early marriage and may indeed be child brides under the international and African regional law framework, but the significance of their narratives for the purposes of this study is that they illustrate that power is not necessarily extinguished when girls/young women enter into (and leave) marriage. What is emphasized is that in Sierra Leone, as in many sub-Saharan African countries, marriage is often less a discrete event than an ambiguous process sometimes lasting years: a process involving the transfer of wealth, the inception of sexual relations, the birth of children, the establishment of a joint residence, and the exchange of symbolic tokens (Bledsoe and Gage 1994: 2 and 4).

The following examples illustrate that customary law and custom cannot be easily written off as perpetuating the inequality and disempowerment of women. They also highlight that marriage cannot be reduced to a single, undifferentiated category, wherein people were married or unmarried, and all marriages had the same significance (ibid.: 4).[60] And last, they emphasize that women as well as men are social actors with needs and goals of their own. Like men, women use marriage and divorce as tools for their own purposes and often disrupt male ambitions and strategies of advancement (Bledsoe 1980: 179). The following narratives describe the case of a litigious wife and cases of deserted husbands and cuckolds.

Ferme describes a respected headman who showed up at his friend's home to be fed because his own wife had refused to cook for him since he had slapped her in an argument. Subsequently, his wife sued him in the chief's court, which found him guilty and demanded that he apologize and pay her a punitive fine.

In another case, Ferme returned to Kpuawala after an absence and found that three wives had deserted a "big man," the head of the two towns. One was pregnant at the time she instituted divorce proceedings. Ferme also observed that other women she knew who had left husbands did not even bother with official (customary law) divorce proceedings. Ferme describes how one husband appeared desolate and confessed that it was due to his suspicion that his wife was having an affair: "He was so worried that she would leave him for her lover that he did not have the courage to confront her with his suspicions" (2001: 103).

In another case of suspected adultery, Alimatu lived as Momoh's wife, although no formal customary marriage ceremony had been conducted by their kin. She met Momoh after leaving a previous husband. Annually, Alimatu left Momoh to visit her relatives in a distant hometown, but one year her visit extended beyond two months. Momoh followed Alimatu to her hometown, but she refused to return to their home. It transpired that she was cohabiting with another man, so Momoh, lacking the means to force her to return against her will, returned to Kpuawala alone (ibid.).[61]

And, finally, Ferme describes Moinana, a man who had only one wife. When he suspected she was pregnant as a result of an extramarital affair, he forced her to confess her lover's name in court. She did so, but then declared that she no longer wanted to return to her husband. Instead she asked to stay with the younger lover whose baby she was expecting. Her lover was fined, but he also helped her raise the money to obtain a divorce and later he married her. Ferme notes that the outcome of this case depended in part on the willingness of the woman's relatives—particularly, her parents—to support her bid for a divorce because the union with the lover was more profitable as he shared a lineage with the family (ibid.: 104).

Narratives such as these gleaned from ethnographic research allow for a multiple layered and complex picture of women, men, and gender roles in marriage in Sierra Leone to emerge. The narratives show that girls and women may exercise forms of agency in the selection of partners, terminating marriages through strategizing, and building alliances that allow for a negotiation of customary law modes of justice. The narratives also introduce the idea that marriage itself is a process and not a final destination. These examples suggest a winding trajectory of marriage, negotiated separations, remarriage that has implications on dependence, mobility, and independence that are as yet unexplored and unacknowledged by the human rights discourse around marriage in Sierra Leone.[62]

The narratives are discordant with the human rights discourse of the TRC, which presents an essentialized view of marriage as undissolvable and pervaded by violence, forced labor, and forced sex. Most important, these alternative narratives permit a gap to develop and widen between the practice of marriage in Sierra Leone, in all its forms, and rebels' sexual enslavement of abducted women and girls in wartime.

Conclusion

The TRC report presents a skewed and incomplete image of marriage and gender hegemonies in Sierra Leone. However, my conclusion is not that the TRC is a colonial expedition or an illegitimate humanitarian intervention violating Sierra Leone's fundamental laws or ideas of natural justice. I believe that it is the case that the reduction of women's lives to an essentialized position of subjugation effectively serves to legitimize a postconflict justice response. The TRC was for all intents and purposes imposed on the government and the people of Sierra Leone. This imposition manifests itself in an elitist urge to devalue indigenous institutions' norms and processes in order to legitimize the power of elite institutions such as commissions and courts.

The TRC process of creating a historical, legal, and political narrative was necessary in order to define sexual violence as a weapon of war and part of the political economy of the armed conflict. However, this narrative leaves no room for any inquiry into individual stories such as Bintu's. At the beginning of this chapter, Bintu asks the chief, "What's the difference? You (rebel husbands and civilian husbands) are all the same." The significance of this statement occurred to me more than a year after I left Sierra Leone. Although

Bintu's claim appeared to be that rebel marriage was as exploitative and cruel as marriage to the chief or other men in peacetime, I concluded that Bintu was not equating herself with a bush bride or sex slave. My understanding is that Bintu and many women I spoke with regarded marriage as a failed institution. These women seemed to agree equivocally that husbands did not protect wives from rape by rebels and marriage failed to protect bush wives from constant violence in the bush and stigmatization on returning to their communities. Bintu's statement was an assertion of her postconflict transformation into an elected councillor and political figure and not her submission to enslavement as an element of her conjugal relationship.

The parallels made by the TRC between bush marriage and early marriage are superficial to say the least. The differences between life in the bush and life in peacetime were profoundly transgressive: people were killed, age hierarchies were reversed, traditional relations of reciprocity were severed, kinship and language ties were obliterated, and consciousness was altered through the massive use of drugs (Coulter 2006: 174). Coulter describes bush life as a radically transformed organization of social relationships, a violent exaggeration of regular life (ibid: 193). If in fact the violence of bush marriage became normalized in armed conflict, it does not mean that in the aftermath of armed conflict, in the narrative of transitional justice, bush marriage should be normalized and affirmed by judges, commissioners, prosecutors, and defense counsel. Sierra Leonean people do not form a homogenous culture that condones forced marriage as a type of marriage. Adopting the term *forced marriage* legitimizes the criminal acts of rebels and pushes an international crime into the area of conjugal and coital relationships.

The commissioners put the idea forward that the abduction of girls as bush wives and sex slaves during the war could partly be attributed to the traditional beliefs that governed the issue before the war. It is a harmful sentiment that ignores the evidence that the RUF sought to degrade culture and traditional institutions. This desire to degrade explains why chiefs, prominent members of the Poro Society, and other cultural leaders were attacked in the most degrading ways.[63] And marriage as a venerated institution steeped in culture and tradition was not exempt from attack. Rebels, by abducting and enslaving girls, were breaking, not making, vows of marriage.

Life in the bush was less of a "radicalised form of peacetime social life" than a "perverse universe," "an inverted morality," or an "upside-down world" (Keen 2005: 76 and 233). Social life and mores in the bush were impossible to navigate and contrary to anything known in peacetime. In effect, the rebels turned law and morality on their heads: what was immoral became not only justifiable but even heroic. Slavery was the antithesis of the matrimonial union: the selection of virgins from among captive girls was not a prerequisite to initiation and marriage but rather a prelude to multiple rapes. The questionable privileges of bush marriage, such as control over other abducted children and access to drugs and looted goods, have no relation to what is perceived by many to be the primary privilege of early marriage for daughters: they are protected from exposure to predatory men and the dishonor of premarital sex and illegitimate children. Further, they gain the social status that only married women can hold (World Vision 2008: 8, citing Hyun 2007: 1). The TRC report's narrative of gender and violence legitimizes rebel acts and stigmatizes marriage in Sierra Leone. It relies on an overzealous human rights discourse and does not engender the necessary investigation into the institution of marriage, gender, inequality, and discrimination in Sierra Leone in the aftermath of armed conflict and a transition from civil war to democracy.

Chapter 4

All Women Are Slaves: Insiders and Outsiders to Gender and Violence

In February 2007, I conducted an interview with Lars Sven, a development worker in Sierra Leone. In the course of the interview, he explained that he was not at all surprised by the cruelty women and girls suffered in war because Sierra Leonean women were no more than slaves in peacetime too. According to Lars, "It's the same in war and peace; these little girls are sold into marriage by their parents; they are slaves in marriage. They are no more than slaves to their husbands." In January 2009, I shared Lars's observation with Papa, a Sierra Leonean colleague in the United States. Papa responded that actually he was not at all surprised by Lars's comments because "that's what white people think about us [Africans]." I countered: "I don't know if that's fair. This man has lived and worked in Sierra Leone for many years. His wife is Sierra Leonean. He loves the country." Papa replied, "Those are the worst kind. They tell lies about our culture and tradition, and we applaud them. He doesn't know a thing about Sierra Leone or Sierra Leonean women or the way we marry. And neither does his wife."

My conversation with Lars and Papa's reaction to it support my argument in the previous chapter against a totalizing narrative that rhetorically enslaves all Sierra Leonean women. However, in this chapter, my focus is on locality and the contest it can raise at the individual and institutional level. Those who possess or claim to possess insider status often compete over whose knowledge of the local is legitimate. These claims and assumptions are difficult to sustain when one's identity is part insider, part outsider. Indeed, one's identity is rarely monochromatic. Thus, a local resident might also be an expatriate, while a citizen may be separated from his motherland by an ocean and a foreign passport. Is it possible that an expatriate in Sierra Leone may be better versed in the harsh realities of local culture than a Sierra Leonean in the diaspora?

As my earlier discussions on transitional justice processes revealed, models of justice do not fall neatly into such categories as "grassroots" or "international." And it should not be taken for granted that a tribunal, even an international one, is impartial, legitimate, and knowledgeable. Could the case law of an international tribunal make a greater contribution to enforcing the rights of women than that of an indigenous tribunal? Does a court with a local seat co-opt local culture and sensibilities in its decisions more effectively than an international court? Does a local seat ensure civil society's support for the transitional justice system? My review in this chapter of the Sierra Leone Special Court's narratives about forced marriage and sexual enslavement will show how the court's multiple locations, as both a local and international tribunal, affected its construction and definition of gender-based violence.

Rather than conducting a traditional case law review and producing a detailed review of the judgments in the completed trials before the Sierra Leone Special Court, I focus my gender review on the material jurisdiction of the statute of the Special Court, the selection of reliable witnesses and victims by the prosecutor, and the prosecutor's inclusion of charges in the indictment. And in order to reveal individual agency behind the often opaque façade of international institutions, my focus is largely on the prosecutor and the ways in which gender is a factor in the exercise of his extensive discretionary powers. I base my analysis of the prosecutor's gender biases not on empirical research but rather on hypotheses based on gendered outcomes of the transitional justice process.[1] Hilary Charlesworth describes feminist method as exposing and questioning the limited basis of international law's claim to objectivity and impartiality. Feminist method insists on the importance of gender relations as a category of analysis. She warns that observing this method will not produce neat "legal" answers but will challenge the very categories of "law" and "non-law" (Charlesworth: 1999: 379). My intention in this chapter, as it was in Chapters 2 and 3, is to disrupt legal practitioners' standard categorization of violence against women into an incomplete and/ or inaccurate legal category.

My gender critique in this chapter arises from the statute of the Special

Court's focus on widespread and systematic acts of sexual violence as definitive crimes against humanity or war crimes committed against women during Sierra Leone's civil war. My critique is of decisions made by the prosecutor and trial chambers at the pretrial and trial stages of the criminal proceedings. In Chapter 3, I argued that the TRC's analogy between forced marriage and early marriage used the egregious crime of slavery to stigmatize the institution of marriage in Sierra Leone. In this chapter, I continue this argument by elaborating on the definition of slavery in international law and the narrative of gender and enslavement as told by international courts, including the Special Court. I argue that the crimes of forced marriage and sexual slavery are legal fictions erroneously pursued by the prosecutor. Enslavement was a sufficient term under which to prosecute and do justice to the experience of Sierra Leone's abducted girls and women. I interrogate the reasons that moved the Special Court toward "sex" slavery as well as the experience of abducted or conscripted women and girls, and I conclude that besides defeating efforts to conduct a thorough gender analysis of enslavement, "sexing" slavery has had a negative impact on the girls as well as boys enslaved by rebel forces.

I take a long look back to transatlantic slavery and colonial slavery as sites that can inform our present understanding of gender and the ways in which it shapes enslavement. This retrospection, in turn, informs my review of contemporary constructions of the elements of enslavement in the decisions of the International Criminal Tribunal for the Former Yugoslavia, the Women's International War Crimes Tribunal 2000 for the Trial of Japanese Military Sexual Slavery, the Rome Statute for the International Criminal Court, and, finally, the decisions of the Sierra Leone Special Court. As in the preceding chapter, I use the work of anthropologists who have lived and worked closely with communities struggling to reintegrate child soldiers in order to enrich legal research. Their work demonstrates the historical continuities and cultural underpinnings in the use of child soldiers for enslavement and other abuses and exploitations (Shepler 2005: 2–3).

Establishing the Special Court

The Sierra Leone peace process initially called for a full amnesty for combatants from criminal prosecution but later demanded the establishment of individual criminal responsibility for those most responsible for gross violations of human rights in Sierra Leone. The Lomé Peace Accord granted the leader of the Revolutionary United Front (RUF, or "the rebels"), Corporal Foday Sankoh, an absolute and free pardon.[2] A blanket amnesty was also adopted in the earlier Abidjan Peace Accord of 30 November 1996 and the Conakry Agreement of 23 October 1997. Under this and the past agreements, the government of Sierra Leone was prohibited from taking any official or judicial action against any member of the RUF or other fighting forces in respect to anything done by them in pursuit of their military and political objectives. In addition, the government was required to adopt legislative measures necessary to guarantee immunity to former combatants, exiles, and other persons outside the country for reasons related to the armed conflict and to protect the full exercise of their civil and political rights (Lomé accord, art. 9 [1] [2], and [3]).

The Lomé accord appointed Foday Sankoh head of a new Mineral Resources Commission and granted him the status of vice president (Keen 2005: 251). Despite the generous amnesty and award of political legitimacy, Sankoh's RUF and the Armed Forces Revolutionary Council (AFRC) repeatedly violated the accord. The RUF continued to fight the AFRC and Civil Defense Force (CDF) in the countryside, prevented the deployment of UN peacekeepers to the diamond rich eastern provinces, and, in one infamous incident, held more than five hundred peacekeepers hostage, confiscating their heavy weapons and vehicles. Reports of rebels raping, looting, and abducting children in the countryside escalated (Adekeye 2002: 101). Public resentment of Sankoh and his apparent impunity intensified and calls for a waiver of the amnesty provisions were heard in Sierra Leone and internationally. It was evident that repetitive awards of amnesty and impunity only fueled the rebel's desire for war and did nothing to promote peace and reconciliation in Sierra Leone.[3] Following a public demonstration by civilians, Sankoh was arrested on 17 May 2000. By the close of 2000, it seemed possible that security could be restored to the nation as the UN Mission in Sierra Leone swelled to more than twenty thousand peacekeepers, the largest peacekeeping operation in the world at that time (Keen 2005: 206, quoting Patel 2002: 37).

The permanent representative of Sierra Leone to the United Nations initiated a request to the president of the Security Council for the establishment of a criminal tribunal to prosecute leaders of the RUF (Kunowah-Tinu Kiellow 2008). This request led to the establishment of the Special Court for Sierra Leone jointly by the government of Sierra Leone and the United Nations pursuant to Security Council Resolution 1315. The Resolution and the Statute of the Special Court for Sierra Leone mandated the court to try not only the rebels, as the government intended, but all those who bore the greatest responsibility for serious violations of international humanitarian law and Sierra Leonean law in the territory of Sierra Leone from 30 November 1996 onward (Statute, art. 1).

The statute of the Special Court unequivocally waives amnesty for any person who planned, instigated, ordered, committed, or otherwise aided and abetted in the planning, preparation, or execution of a crime against humanity or a violation of the laws of war (art. 10). Further, it excludes perpetrators under the age of fifteen at the time they committed crimes against humanity or war crimes from its jurisdiction (art. 7 [1] and [2]).[4]

The prosecutor has indicted a total of fourteen individuals, three of whom—Sam Bockarie, Foday Sankoh, and Samuel Hinga Norman—subsequently died.[5] The trials of three former leaders of the AFRC, two members of the CDF (or "Kamajors"), and three RUF leaders have been completed, including appeals. A trial judgment for Charles Taylor was delivered in March 2011. The trial judgments in the AFRC and RUF cases are the first to result in convictions for sexual violence and other forms of gender-based violence.

The Special Court is widely regarded as representing a new wave of mechanisms of accountability incorporating both domestic and international features. For this reason, it has been described by scholars as a "hybrid" court. In my view, this classification is unwarranted because apart from its geographical location in Freetown, the Special Court's core prosecutorial features are international and absent of any significant influences from Sierra Leone's legal system.[6] Despite its local presence, many argue that the court remains remote from local people (International Crisis Group 2003: 11).[7] "Local" in this sense refers not to a geographic location since both the Special Court and the TRC were situated in Sierra Leone. Rather, it refers to the real or imagined proximity to the social and cultural context underlying the formal transitional justice process. "Local" also presumes an independence from outside pressures exerted by international donors or third party states.

The Special Court's Statute and Rules of Evidence and Procedure reveal its international origins. The rules of the Special Court replicate the Rules of Evidence and Procedure of the International Criminal Tribunal for Rwanda (ICTR). It overlooks Sierra Leonean national rules of evidence and procedure, which further discredits the "hybrid" tag.

The material jurisdiction provided by the Special Court statute covers crimes against humanity and war crimes. The statute attempts to enhance the role of domestic laws by giving the Special Court the jurisdiction to prosecute crimes falling under the Prevention of Cruelty to Children Act (PCCA), an archaic statute that manifestly discriminates against the rights of the girl child.[8] The PCCA is replete with defenses that are backward in the face of contemporary developments in the rules of evidence and procedure at the level of international criminal law. For example, the rules of the ad hoc criminal tribunals for Rwanda and the former Yugoslavia and the Sierra Leone Special Court specify that corroboration of the testimony of victims of sexual violence is not necessary. In contrast, the PCCA provides that the evidence of girl witnesses must be corroborated, particularly if the child was a common prostitute or of low morality.[9] The two positions are irreconcilable.

This attempt at incorporating national law into the statute in order to enhance the appearance of the "hybrid" nature of the transitional justice model reveals the international community's desire to show their respect for and recognition of Sierra Leone's legal system. However, this inclusion also reflects the drafter's failure to investigate the legitimacy of local laws vis-à-vis the international duty to protect and promote the rights of women and girls in Sierra Leone. The prosecutor for the Special Court wisely ignored the PCCA when framing the charges against accused persons in the indictments, and its inclusion remained a dead letter.

Arguably, the Special Court's hybrid personality would be enhanced by the fact that a significant number of its staff members were Sierra Leonean. The deputy registrar was Sierra Leonean, as were two of the four appeals chamber judges.[10] At the same time, a significant number of its senior staff members were recruited from the ICTR and the International Criminal Tribunal for the Former Yugoslavia (ICTY), including the registrar, deputy registrar, prosecutor, and chief of the Victims and Witnesses Unit. It is safe to assume that these appointees brought the institutional culture of international criminal tribunals to the Special Court. A head count of local versus foreign staff is, however, a formulaic approach and does not ensure that a tribunal is "hybrid."[11] Even if Sierra Leonean senior staff were to outnumber foreign senior and core staff, this factor would not of itself make the court a "hybrid" or even a "local" court.

The Special Court is an ad hoc international criminal tribunal in the nature of the ICTR and ICTY. Unlike these two bodies, however, the Special Court was not the result of a Security Council Resolution. This difference did not reduce its power to indict the former president of Liberia Charles Taylor, to exert pressure on Nigeria to extradite him to Sierra Leone, and subsequently to effect the transfer of his trial to The Hague. The Special Court exerted political clout commensurate with its status as an international court. The Special Court's primacy over Sierra Leone's domestic laws and its power to override decisions of domestic courts are other demonstrations of its supremacy over local institutions.[12] If the drafters of the statute, namely, the international community (which includes the Sierra Leonean government), intended the national laws and procedures to play a meaningful role in the prosecution process of the "hybrid" court, the statute would have specifically stated so. The term *hybrid* is not a creation of the statute but that of the international actors seeking to emphasize a "home-grown" or "grassroots" institution in order to legitimize transitional justice. Clarifying at this stage that its international identity trumps any genuinely hybrid elements, I lay the groundwork for an analysis of the ways in which the "international" identity of the Special Court influenced decision making relating to gender and relationships with victims, witnesses, and other stakeholders, such as the government.

Gender, Violence, and the Prosecutor

In Chapter 1, I described the Beijing Declaration and Platform for Action as progressive third tier instruments that called on states to integrate a gender perspective in the resolution of armed conflicts and to aim for a gender balance when nominating or promoting candidates for judicial and other positions in all relevant international bodies, such as the ad hoc tribunals for the former Yugoslavia and for Rwanda, as well as in other bodies related to the peaceful settlement of disputes (Beijing Declaration, para. 144 [c]). Such instruments also called upon states to ensure that these judicial bodies are able to address gender issues properly by providing appropriate training to prosecutors, judges, and other officials in handling cases involving rape, forced pregnancy, indecent assault, and other forms of violence against women in situations of armed conflict, including terrorism (ibid., para. 144 [d]).

The Sierra Leone Special Court is the ad hoc tribunal that best reflects the gender considerations of the Beijing Declaration and Platform. And, indeed, observers of processes of transitional justice have lauded the statute of the Sierra Leone Special Court for extending the list of crimes provided by the ICTR and ICTY statutes with respect to the crime of rape.[13] The Special Court statute lists rape as a crime against humanity but also includes sexual slavery, enforced prostitution, forced pregnancy, and any other form of sexual violence as crimes against humanity.[14] In addition to crimes against humanity, the Special Court has the power to prosecute persons who committed or ordered the commission of serious violations of Article 3 common to the Geneva Conventions and of Additional Protocol II. The war crimes listed are extensive and include outrages upon personal dignity, in particular, humiliating and degrading treatment, rape, enforced prostitution, and any form of indecent assault.[15] The statute provides a list of other serious violations of international humanitarian law, most notably, conscripting or enlisting children under the age of fifteen into armed forces or using them to participate actively in hostilities (art. 4 [c]).

The prosecutor was to be responsible for the investigation and prosecution of persons bearing the greatest responsibility for serious violations of international humanitarian law committed in Sierra Leone after 30 November 1996 (art. 15 [1]). The statute provided that, given the nature of the crimes committed and the particular sensitivities of girls, young women, and children victims of rape, sexual assault, abduction, and slavery of all kinds, due consideration should be given to the appointment of prosecutors and investigators experienced in gender related crimes and juvenile justice (art. 15 [3] and [4]). This provision demanded gender competence as a professional requirement not only of the specialist investigators focusing on gender-based violence but also of the entire staff of the Office of the Prosecutor. This requirement revealed that the drafters of the statute and architects of justice had recognized the widespread and systematic nature of sexual violence perpetrated throughout the civil war. Furthermore, the specific reference to gender was a strong mandate for the prosecutor to investigate not just the rape of women but all manner of gender-based crimes committed against civilians.[16]

The statute also mandated the Special Court's Registry to establish a Witness and Victims Unit (WVU) to provide protective measures and security arrangements, counseling, and other assistance for witnesses and victims appearing before the court. The statute specifically laid down the requirement that the unit personnel would have experience in trauma, including trauma related to crimes of sexual violence and violence against children.[17] The psychosocial unit consists of staff trained in counseling, plus two medically trained staff members and one psychologist (Vahidy et al. 2009: 137). The makeup of the personnel was another demonstration that the architects of transitional criminal justice in Sierra Leone had placed justice for women and children at the forefront of their prosecutorial objectives. Witnesses and victims of the fighting forces or the government were not just an indistinguishable mass but were to be seen as men, women, and children who survived the brutalities of an armed conflict. At the same time, the provisions of the statute described above show that women suffered harms that were specific to their gender, age, and other intersecting factors.

The provisions of the statute for the Sierra Leone Special Court present a narrative that takes it for granted that gender affects victims' experience of armed conflict. However, the intersection of gender and violence before the tribunal was overwhelmingly interpreted as violence against women: the statute presented crimes against humanity and war crimes as crimes against civilian populations that may take specific shapes and forms when committed against women. It is the "add women and stir" approach, but it remains an important justice narrative for the purposes of academic critique and analysis in a world where transitional justice processes are an inherent part of the postwar reconstruction process.

The statute clearly spelled out the gender mandate of the prosecutor, but did the prosecutor fulfill his obligation toward victims of gender-based violence? A report by Kyra Sanin and Anna Stirnemann for the War Crimes Studies Center at the University of California, Berkeley (known as the Berkeley Report) concluded that contrary to the statute's requirements for gender competency, most prosecution investigators and attorneys responsible for determining the most resilient witnesses were not trained to incorporate gender into their work (Sanin and Stirnemann 2006). The Berkeley Report indicates a prosecutorial strategy that discriminated against child witnesses, specifically girl witnesses. A review of the CDF, RUF, and AFRC cases showed that the number of child witnesses was kept to a minimum. Further, it revealed that as of 2006, all the witnesses categorized as child witnesses who had testified at the court were boys (ibid.: 15). This revelation was startling considering that up to 25 percent of children in the fighting forces were girls (ibid.). As of December 2005, only one female former combatant had testified before the Special Court. Other female witnesses testified about crimes they were forced to commit after abduction into the fighting forces, but generally the prosecution did not categorize these witnesses as former combatants (ibid.).

The prosecution's principal criterion for determining when it would hear a child witness was whether or not the witness was a child combatant; the individual's actual age did not figure in the calculus (ibid.: 11). As girl witnesses were not considered to be combatants, it seems the issue of gauging whether they were children (under eighteen, according to international standards) was not raised (ibid.: 15). The disproportionate representation of boy fighters as witnesses leads to the conclusion that investigators did not recognize girls as combatants.

The prosecutor's omissions with respect to girl combatants mirror the development of the laws of war with respect to child combatants. The four Geneva Conventions omitted any regulation of the participation of children in armed conflicts, and their protection as children qua children came later with the two Additional Protocols of 1977 (Happold 2000: 31). The protocols impose an obligation on states not to recruit children under fifteen into the armed forces and to ensure that children under fifteen do not take part in active hostilities. A direct part in hostilities, when narrowly defined, means that "the person in question performs warlike acts which by their nature or purpose are designed to strike enemy combatants or material; acts therefore such as firing at enemy soldiers, throwing a Molotov cocktail at an enemy tank, blowing up a bridge carrying enemy war *matériel*, and so on" (Happold 2000: 36, quoting Kalshoven 1987: 91).

The prosecutor clearly followed the narrow international humanitarian law definition of "active hostilities" and consequently excluded former girl combatants from participation as witnesses in the transitional justice process. The prosecutor's position undermined the multiple roles Sierra Leonean girls filled during the armed conflict, serving simultaneously as fighters, porters, cooks, food producers, messengers between camps, communication technicians, workers in diamond mines, assistants to the sick and wounded, wives, slaves, launderers, child-care providers, spies, and laborers (Sanin and Stirnemann 2006: 15; Mazurana and Carlson 2004: 1). If indeed they were sent to the front lines less frequently, it is due to the fact that they were so crucial to the war effort. In many cases, they were regarded as less expendable than boy combatants (Sanin and Stirnemann 2006: 15).[18] And yet this very reality is what disqualified girl former combatants from combatant status by the prosecution through its witness selection process that boxed girls and women into the gender roles of "child brides" and "rape victims."[19]

The statute gives the prosecutor the power to prosecute persons who conscripted children under the age of fifteen into armed groups or used them to participate actively in hostilities (art. 4 [a]). The statute provides that the mere act of conscripting children into an armed group is in itself a serious violation of international humanitarian law. Thus, the perception that only boys were conscripted for participation in active hostilities violates the spirit and intent of the statute. The statute required that the prosecution would provide testimony from children (both boys and girls) conscripted by armed forces.

Participation in active hostilities was not conditional to a prosecution for conscription of children into armed groups. Beyond the letter of the statute, what was required was gender competence that allowed for an understanding of the context and nature of girl soldiering as a core contribution to active hostilities. This contextual analysis is found in the scholarship of social scientists but still eludes inclusion within legal scholarship and justice processes. And this analysis is crucial in shaping a gender competence that would recognize women's and girls' war experience beyond one of sexual victimization.[20]

Several factors could be applied to mitigate the prosecutor's exclusion of girl combatants from the witness stand: first is the claim that girls fear stigmatization more than boys for their association with fighting forces and are more likely to evade investigators and avoid participation in a criminal justice process that would expose their association with fighters; second, it is possible that girls more than boys remained under the control of former commanders after the demobilization, demilitarization, and repatriation process and feared reprisals if they cooperated with the prosecutor;[21] and, third, girls may have been more likely than boys to be traumatized under examination and cross-examination considering the combined experience of armed violence and sexual violence.

None of the arguments put forward is tenable in light of the strong gender mandate vested in the prosecutor by the statute combined with the special gender sensitive measures required of the WVU (Statute, art. 16). Manned by psychologists and social workers responsive to symptoms of traumatic stress disorders, a WVU would guarantee a vigilant response to the needs of girl combatants. And, finally, the possible retraumatization of victims of gross violations of human rights is a reality for any international court seeking justice for survivors of civil war. The response to this high probability of trauma is not to limit witness testimony and participation but to ensure that tribunal staff members are capable of supporting witnesses before, during, and after their testimony.[22]

While issues of stigma, trauma, and security fears are valid concerns for girl fighters, they can and do apply to many boy fighters. Obstacles, such as the fear of reprisals from commanders and negative reactions from family members, are common to witnesses irrespective of gender. It would appear that in the case of boy soldiers they have been overcome, not easily, but with the Office of the Prosecutor's careful pretrial assessment and the WVU's counseling, protection services, and follow-up care.[23] The failure to extend this response to girls supports the claim that the prosecutor's disproportionate representation of boy witnesses is a form of gender discrimination against girl combatants. The gender mandate prescribed by the statute was unfulfilled, and girls were denied equal access to justice.

The Berkeley Report on child witnesses at the Special Court details the case of Aisha, the only girl combatant called as a witness. Her story confirms that with political will, the special and gendered needs of girl witnesses, such as child care and protection from intimidation by an unsupportive family, can be realized and their participation in the process successfully facilitated.[24]

> Aisha was 17 at the time of demobilization and she already had three children with her bush husband. At the time of testifying she was still married to her bush husband and was raising her children with him. The Report reveals that she successfully concealed the fact that she was cooperating with the Court from her husband, because she feared that as a former RUF combatant himself, he would not support the prosecution of the alleged RUF leaders. She worked closely with the Witnesses and Victims Services and the prosecution to devise explanations for her frequent travel to Freetown and prolonged absences from her family. (Sanin and Stirnemann 2006: 16)

The prosecutor's relationship to the process that defines victims in terms of eligibility for participation in a trial is far from impartial, and it has been discussed by feminist scholars at the domestic level with respect to such gender-based crimes as trafficking of women and domestic violence. Jayashri Srikantiah provides a review of U.S. federal immigration agencies' construction of an iconic victim in the antitrafficking discourse. Prosecutors and agents investigating traffickers construct this iconic victim. Srikantiah (2007: 160) points out the fact that the same prosecutor who decides whether a victim would be a good witness also decides whether the victim is a victim for the purposes of the relevant remedy (a special U.S. humanitarian visa). Her analysis illustrates the conflict inherent in placing the victim identification function in prosecution hands as each prosecutor determines subjectively who is a "deserving" victim (ibid.). In the U.S. case, lawmakers successfully used an image of the traffic victim as meek, passive, sexualized objects in order to pass protecting legislation. They ignored victims of trafficking for forced labor and emphasized the sexual exploitation of women and girls in their advocacy campaign. Srikantiah argues that this political rhetoric has an impact on the prosecutor's identification of actual trafficking victims, with tragic consequences for victims of labor or sex trafficking who do not tell stories consistent with it (ibid.).

I find parallels between the sex traffic narrative and the sex slavery narrative. Srikantiah traces the need for an iconic victim back to two sources. First is the need to distinguish between trafficking victims and unlawful economic migrants. The latter are categorically denied victim status as this might legitimate their "willful" illegal entry and residence in the United States. The former are thought to enter under the complete physical and psychological control of the trafficker. Second, the stereotypical victim story of the passive and paralyzed (with fear) sex worker is a highly effective prosecutorial strategy allowing prosecutors to describe the trafficker as maximally culpable (2007: 160–61). Similarly, in the case of the Special Court, the prosecutor's strategy required a distinction between "paralyzed" female victims of sexual violence who had taken no part in active hostilities and active combatants.

Apart from denying women and girls their own narratives of armed conflict, the prosecution's strategy regarding the selection of witnesses reveals some damaging gender assumptions and outcomes. The first is that the testimony of boy combatants is more reliable than that of girls. The Special Court established guiding principles for working with child witnesses. With regard to witness selection, the rules specify that the prosecution should approach only the most resilient child witnesses and only those who are already resettled with their families or communities. In identifying potential child witnesses, only children in the care of their families or legal guardians should be considered (Sanin and Stirnemann 2006: 18 and 20).

This policy showed a disregard for the gendered realities of abducted girls, who for the most part experienced greater challenges to demobilization, rehabilitation, and family reunification than boys. Many girls experienced discrimination and exclusion from a demobilization, demilitarization, and repatriation program that was designed to address the needs of men and boys (who were perceived as combatants) (Mazurana and Carlson 2004: 21).[25] Thus, girls were more likely than boys to face rejection when they returned to their families with no money earned and no vocational skills acquired from participation in demobilization, demilitarization, and repatriation processes. Many girls returned home having had a child or children and with low prospects for marriage. Girls formerly associated with fighting forces were more likely to be branded "bad apples" than boys. The prosecutor's exclusion of their narrative from the justice process reinforces this social narrative. The narrative of girl soldiers would have contributed greatly to sensitizing Sierra

Leoneans about the coercive and violent society girls inhabited and navigated during their captivity. Instead, the prosecution strategy perpetuated society's stigmatization of abducted girls.

An intersecting assumption arising from the discriminatory exclusion of girl combatants from participation as witnesses is that girls were less innocent than boys. Laura Suski's critique of development organizations' discourse that positions children of the South as deprived versions of children of the North is useful to my discussion.[26] This geopolitical (North and South) binary distracts us from seeing the social and economic deprivations that prevent some children in the South from being considered priceless or worthy of protection. Suski argues that the imposition of a Northern version of child rearing, family life, and early education not only neglects alternate versions of childhood but also fails to address the complexities that children face when economic pressures take them far from the "ideal" and "normal" model of childhood (2009: 206, quoting Penn 2002: 118–32, and Penn 2005).[27]

Adopting Suski's (the model child) and Srikantiah's (the iconic victim) analysis in the area of transitional justice, it is not unreasonable to speculate that the Special Court with its international positioning would struggle to place the experience of the Sierra Leonean child soldier within the dominant construction of childhood in the Western/international world.[28] The child soldier is a victim but also an active and in some cases a zealous perpetrator of human rights abuses. He/she is susceptible to substance abuse and other vices. Serious breaches of accepted or expected gender roles only make it more difficult for the Western gaze to assume the innocence of a child soldier. Thus, the image of a child soldier pregnant with a child, carrying her child on her back, strategically and aggressively initiating a sexual relationship with commanders in exchange for security, or engaging in sex work after demobilization is so transgressive an image of childhood that the transitional justice process could not reconcile itself to it.[29] Girl soldiers more than boys became "deviants from modern childhood," and the narrative they would contribute from the witness stand cannot possibly be one that "pleads for the restoration of their childhoods."[30] It would be impossible to undo or conceal that they are not virgins, that they are mothers, sex workers, and wives. The excluding outcome of the prosecutor's strategy in witness selection indicates a failure to concede that while victims may be able to exercise some free will within exploitative relationships, this ability or agency should not negate the physical and psychological control of the exploiter (Srikantiah 2007: 161).

Further, Suski makes the observation that development campaigns often voice the narrative of children of the South visually, through tears or vacant looks (2009). In conclusion, I am inclined to concur with the sentiment that the narrative of girl soldiers "does not fundamentally require a voice." This view has some resonance with the prosecutor's application of the mass abduction and mass rape of girl soldiers as a backdrop to the justice process without actively seeking participation through the testimony of girl combatants in the courtroom.

The TRC report associated the crimes committed by the CDF, the Sierra Leone Army, and the RUF-AFRC rebels as grave violations of international humanitarian law and crimes against humanity. The report rejected the argument from some quarters of Sierra Leonean society that crimes committed by the government and its agents (including the CDF) fighting an insurgency should be judged less harshly than acts of the rebels. The TRC narrative is particularly clear with regard to violence against women that sexual violence was not limited to rebel factions (TRC 3:3: 6 and 200).[31]

Therefore, it is striking that the prosecutor's indictment issued against CDF leaders did not include a single charge of sexual violence. This omission makes the CDF defendants an anomaly as the other nine defendants were charged with sexual violence against women. In the following paragraphs, I will discuss the factors that contributed to the omission and also present a comparative overview of the TRC report and its inclusion of the narrative of sexual violence committed by the CDF with the Special Court's exclusion of the narrative on sexual violence from the CDF case.

The report made a careful distinction between the CDF as a militarized agent and ally or even an arm of the government of President Kabbah and the CDF as a unit that traced its roots to a traditional hunting society.[32] The CDF was a network of civil militiamen created in 1996 from several different units, including Kamajors, Gbethes, Donsos, Tamaboros, and Kapras, organized according to ethnicity and their district of origin (TRC 3b:3: 347). This distinction allowed the TRC to vigorously investigate allegations of sexual violence against women by certain elements of the CDF.[33]

The report found that the traditional initiates of the hunters' secret societies tended to respect and uphold the rules and regulations that governed their society membership, and breaking any of the rules was taboo (TRC 3a: 558–62, 571; and TRC 3b:3: 349). Secret society rules apparently prohibited men from having sexual intercourse with women while performing their society duties, as they believed that sexual contact with women before a battle would diminish their supernatural powers of immunity in battle. The commissioners of the Sierra Leone truth commission detected scarcely any sexual violations attributed to the CDF in Sierra Leone the years before 1996 and concluded that the predecessors of the CDF, most of whom were vigilantes and hunters, did not commit sexual violations or rape systematically (Keen 2005: 91).

While many CDF combatants laid claim to being traditional hunters with origins in their secret societies that predated the conflict, the report clarified that the overwhelming bulk of the fighters, particularly Kamajors, were in fact disaffected youths who were crudely enlisted into combat through illusory ceremonies of initiation (TRC 3a:3: 558–64).[34] This situation arose as the armed conflict escalated, and the CDF was compelled to increase the number of recruits in its fighting forces. According to the report, the rapidity with which this expansion occurred meant that recruitment standards lapsed, numbers became unmanageably large, and the purported code of ethics was overlooked. The effect of lax enrollment procedures was that newer "initiates" into the CDF did not feel bound by age-old traditions and practices. Indeed, the new generation of CDF adopted a different ethos that was entirely geared toward war and the perceived benefits it could yield (TRC 3b:3: 352).

The report does not shy away from describing the CDF's sexual exploitation and abuse of women and girls. It explains that because CDF units were usually attached to a specific town or village for a specific period, they were not as mobile as the RUF-AFRC. Therefore, in contrast to the "roaming detentions" of the rebels, the preferred modus operandi of the CDF was to abduct women and girls, taking them prisoner. Women would then be confined to a single secure location, usually in a village or town under the complete control of the CDF. They would often be held naked and were freely available to be raped or gang raped (TRC 3b:3: 353 and 345).

Human rights observers and scholars gathered survivor testimony describing sexual violence committed by the CDF, and these local narratives corroborate the TRC's narrative on the gender violence and the CDF.[35] Many of these testimonies reveal the widely held belief among civilians and CDF members themselves that the CDF was an arm of the government or an extension of the Sierra Leone Army, thereby immune from punishment for civilian abuse. "Twenty CDF came to the guardroom and told us, the women, that we could choose between [being raped] or killed. I was raped by a young CDF on the ground of the guardroom. I told him that I was a suckling mother, but he did not care. My baby was in the room when he raped me. He made me stoop like an animal. He said, 'I am a government man, so no one will ask me anything about this'" (Human Rights Watch 2003: 47). In the latter period of the conflict, from 1997 onward, the commission noted a marked increase in the number of violations attributed to the CDF. The report refers to the commission's database of violations, which revealed that sexual violence was not a random act by CDF members but rather a defining act by the group committed on a widespread and systematic scale. Rape was one of their weapons of war (TRC 3b:3: 355). The conclusion is drawn by the report that CDF perpetrators demonstrated twice as high a propensity to commit rape than their propensity to commit other violations overall. CDF forces acted with a savagery comparable to the RUF toward women and girls (TRC 3b:3: 351–55).

The prosecutor's 2004 indictment issued against CDF leaders Samuel Hinga Norman, Moinina Fofana, and Allieu Kondewa is at odds with the TRC's charge that the CDF used sexual violence as a weapon of war. The accused were jointly charged with crimes against humanity, violations of Article 3 Common to the Geneva Conventions and of Additional Protocol II (war crimes), and other serious violations of international humanitarian law.

A vigorous legal conflict between the prosecutor and the appeal chamber erupted four months before the beginning of the CDF trial when the prosecutor attempted to amend the indictment in order to include four new counts of gender-based crimes, namely, rape as a crime against humanity under Article 2 (g) of the statute; sexual slavery and any other forms of sexual violence as crimes against humanity under Article 2 (g) of the statute; other inhumane acts as a crime against humanity under Article 2 (i) of the statute; and outrages upon personal dignity as a war crime under Article 3 (e) of the statute. The prosecutor pleaded that women's reluctance to come forward and testify as to sexual violence caused the delay.[36]

The majority of the judges held that the prosecutor was aware of gender-based crimes as early as June 2003 and that it was not timely to wait until February 2004 to request the amendment. The majority judges opined that the proposed charges relating to sexual violence did not merit an exception to the general rules on timeliness (Norman et al. Prosecution Request to Amend Indictment, 9 February 2004, para. 84). The majority denied the application.[37] This denial brought the gender competence of the Office of the Prosecutor into disrepute. The judges chastised the prosecutor, "who is at the helm of the investigation process," for neglecting to "exercise extraordinary vigilance, diligence and attention so as to immediately and without any undue delay, as stipulated by Article 17 (4) (c) of the Statute of the Court, bring before justice for trial, all those suspected of having committed gender offences and other categories of offences within this competence."[38] The majority judges also considered the consequences for the accused's right to a fair trial should new charges to the indictment be allowed. They expressed their concern that such an amendment would present a potential delay as the defense counsel would have to respond to the charges.

The prosecutor subsequently sought leave from the trial chamber to appeal the chamber's decision. The trial chamber soundly rejected his application.[39] The prosecutor subsequently appealed to the appeals chamber, but that chamber ruled that it did not have jurisdiction to consider the appeal.[40] What followed the trial chamber decision of May 2004 was a trial that in many key moments relied on the testimony of women victims as witnesses but that muzzled any attempt by the prosecutor or witnesses to refer to sexual violence.[41] Indeed, throughout the trial, the majority judges made several rulings precluding the admission of evidence of gender-based violence. In these rulings, the majority judges prohibited the introduction of or expunged from the record a wide range of evidence: actual evidence of forced marriage and sexual violence, evidence that might concern forced marriage or sexual violence, and evidence that was potentially linked to forced marriage or sexual slavery (Oosterveld 2009). Shannee Stepakoff and Michelle Staggs Kelsall confirm, through interviews with women who were called as witnesses but were not permitted to speak of sexual violence they experienced or witnessed, the psychological harm they suffered from this silencing (2007: 373).[42]

The testimony of women victims and witnesses in the CDF case was appropriated and misrepresented in the official court transcripts (Muddell 2007: 98). Women who had been "bush wives" were unable to testify about being abducted and forced into marriage. Instead, their testimony had to begin at the point in their story where they were "married." And the official record did not indicate that this "marriage" was forced on them and actually a crime against humanity under the statute of the Special Court (ibid.).

The prosecutor put different reasons forward for the initial omission of sexual violence from the CDF indictment. Apart from the alleged reticence of witnesses to cooperate with the prosecution, the prosecutor argued that despite the availability of evidence of sexual violence as early as June 2003, initial investigations had not uncovered sufficient evidence to support counts of sexual violence against the CDF beyond a reasonable burden of proof (Stepakoff and Staggs Kelsall 2007: 360). In seeking leave to appeal against the decision of the trial chamber, the prosecutor also argued that evidence of gender-based violence in the CDF case was not comparable to other Special Court cases. The CDF case raised special difficulties for investigation because many survivors of sexual violence were supporters of the CDF and continued to live in the same communities as their abusers. Further, many Sierra Leoneans regarded the CDF in the aftermath of the conflict as heroes who rescued Sierra Leone from defeat by rebels (Norman et al. 2 August 2004, para. 8).

In an attempt to mitigate the prosecutor's alleged negligence, Stepakoff and Staggs Kelsall recommend that special measures relating to sexual violence could have resolved the impasse between the prosecutor and the judges. For example, a provision in the rules could have extended the period during which evidence of sexual violence could be admitted due to the specific challenges involved at the investigative stage. This argument might have been appropriate in the case of the novel international ad hoc tribunals for Rwanda and the former Yugoslavia where prosecutors had no precedent for investigating and prosecuting rape committed on a widespread and systematic scale.[43] Such an extension is unnecessary, however, when the court's statute provided extensive impetus for the prosecutor to investigate thoroughly. What was needed was a prosecution strategy that put gender at the core of its investigation and prosecution strategy as called for by the Beijing Declaration and Platform for Action, Security Council Resolution 1820, and other human rights instruments.

Sierra Leone is a small country with a small population. It could be said broadly that the armed conflict affected all Sierra Leoneans as primary or secondary victims, or both. And in many cases, the line between victim and perpetrator is blurry.[44] Victims often experienced abuse at the hands of acquaintances, neighbors, relatives, tribesmen, and other intimates. This interpersonal feature of the conflict was obvious to human rights observers, to truth commissioners, and to the prosecutor. Local and international human rights observers and truth commissioners were able to elicit reliable and timely testimony from victims and witnesses of sexual violence by the CDF, while the prosecutor failed in his responsibility to do the same.

While the prosecutor has borne the greatest scrutiny for the omission of gender-based violence from the narrative of the CDF trial, many have also criticized the trial chamber for its arguments rejecting the prosecutor's application (Mibenge 2007a; Oosterveld 2009; Shaw 2007). In its concern for an expedient trial, the trial chamber failed to seriously consider the issue of the consequences of its decision for victims of gender-based violence at the hands of the CDF (Mibenge 2007a). The prosecutor described the consequences of his omission and the trial chamber's denial of an amendment quite accurately as precluding the victims from having their crimes characterized as gender-based crimes; impairing the remedies to which they are entitled; and establishing impunity with respect to gender crimes, as the prospect of prosecution under domestic jurisdiction for sexual violence was highly improbable (Norman et al. 2 August 2004, para. 6). The prosecutor also argued that he could not establish a complete and accurate historical record of the crimes committed during the armed conflict in Sierra Leone and could not acknowledge the right of the victims to have crimes committed against them characterized as gender-based crimes (ibid., para. 4).

Dissent, however, did arise from within the trial chamber. Justice Boutet showed that he believed the prosecutor's request was made in a timely manner and decried the trial chamber's failure to acknowledge the difficult nature of collecting evidence of gender-based violence.[45] In his dissenting opinion, Justice Boutet wrote that the trial chamber's refusal to grant leave to appeal threatened to undermine the mandate of the court outlined in article 1 (1) of the statute, namely, "to prosecute persons who bear the greatest responsibility for serious violations of international humanitarian law." He stressed that this mandate was founded on recognition by the secretary-general that sexual violence committed against girls and women was one of the most egregious practices committed during the armed conflict in Sierra Leone (Fofana and Allieu Kondewa Dissenting Opinion of Boutet, 28 May 2008, para. 18).

A judgment was passed in the CDF case by the trial chamber on 2 August 2007 and included no reference to sexual violence. Nine months later, an appeals chamber judgment attempted to remedy this omission without actually introducing evidence of crimes of gender-based violence against women into the CDF judgments, effectively excluding evidence of sexual slavery and rape from the narrative.[46] Justice Winter also added her dissenting voice. She criticized the trial chamber majority for failing to correctly balance the rights of the accused with the prosecution's duty to prove guilt beyond a reasonable doubt and the mandate of the Special Court to prosecute gender-based violence and the ability of victims to access justice.[47]

The question of positionality raised afresh by Lars and Papa in this chapter's introductory narrative is salient. As we recall, I could not conclusively state the insider-outsider status of either of these men based on their political, spatial proximity to the conflict and postconflict society. The ambiguity raised by Lars's and Papa's status as experts on gender and violence reminds us that well before the establishment of the Special Court, there was what Fiounnuala Ní Aoláin refers to as a previous narrative of violence and causality. The ever watchful and deeply involved international community constructs this narrative (2008: 39). According to this narrative, the CDF was indistinguishable from the democratically elected government of President Kabbah (1996–97 and 1998–2007), a rare emblem of democratization and good governance in the troubled West African nation after a brutal civil war. The international community's heavy involvement in and commitment to the physical and political reconstruction of Sierra Leone depends on the presence of a government perceived, both locally and internationally, to be of high integrity and responsible for the security of its citizens. "Defaming" the government and its allies or agents with an overtly heinous charge sheet would have gone against such interests. The glaring absence of sexual violence as a form of gender-based violence from the CDF judgment has caused many in Sierra Leone to believe that political considerations trumped the rights of women to justice and an effective remedy.

Gender and Enslavement

The proper naming of crimes is a key objective of the international criminal justice process. Naming has many implications for the development of law and the dispensation of justice, but it also contributes to the war narrative as a legacy of the justice process. This narrative also constructs a typology of crime that marks any given conflict and contributes to the formation of a collective historical memory of armed conflict. For example, at the International Military Trials after World War II, the crime of aggression (charged by the prosecutor) figured prominently in the case law, subsequent media reporting, and historical record, whereas the crime of enslavement did not.

In this section, I invoke a different past, that of transatlantic slavery and colonial slavery. The leading literature on the subject reveals that historically the ownership of another human being through slavery has been connected to sexual and reproductive exploitation of peoples. This thesis informs my analysis of the construction of gender and enslavement in contemporary processes of justice.

The preamble to the 1926 Slavery Convention repeated the declaration adopted by the General Act of the Brussels conference of 1889–1890 to put an end to trafficking in African slaves and to secure the complete suppression of slavery in all its forms. The Slavery Convention defined slavery as the status or condition of a person over whom any or all of the powers attaching to the right of ownership are exercised (Slavery Convention, art. 1). The prohibition of slavery was the first human rights issue to arouse international concern, yet slavery and slavery like practices remain a grave and persistent problem today.[48] Slavery and slavery like practices have underpinned the major global forms of political oppression, including apartheid, colonization, and imperialism. Like all crimes against humanity, gender shapes and influences enslavement.

Here, I continue to press the argument made in earlier sections that a narrow interpretation of gender leads scholars and legal practitioners to insert the rape of women into a legal narrative with no further attempts at investigating the social and political nature and nuances of rape as well as other harms women experience. In the case of enslavement in the context of Sierra Leone's armed conflict, TRC commissioners, the prosecutor, legal practitioners, and many human rights advocates have reduced women's experience of enslavement to a coital and conjugal experience. Appending sex (and more recently marriage) to slavery has become the defining distinction between men and women's experience of enslavement. According to this simplistic gender analysis, female slaves are sex slaves while their male counterparts are "just" slaves.

Contrary to the increasingly popular representation by legal practitioners and scholars of the international crime of "sexual slavery," with its emphasis on multiple or mass rapes of women and girls, Pamela Bridgewater (2005) provides an extensive review of the women's experience of enslavement in the United States. She describes a wide range of gender-based forms of violence, ranging from denying new mothers the opportunity to recover from labor, to nurse and otherwise care for their children, and to have legal protection from rape (ibid.: 115–17). She makes the important point that rape was not only a condition inherent to the female slave experience, but unfettered sexual access to women was central to the right of ownership that slave owners exercised over slaves (ibid.: 117–18).[49] Bridgewater shows that this sexual access to women extended to control and ownership of the reproductive potential and product of women. Thus, the slave owner owned children born from the rape of his female slaves.[50]

With the closing of the international slave trade in 1808, the enslavement of women still included physical labor, but it increasingly centered on bearing, nourishing, and rearing children needed for the continual replenishment of the slave labor force (ibid.: 119–20, quoting White 1999: 69). Slave breeding consisted of a concerted effort to increase the number of slave holdings by forcing female slaves to reproduce (ibid.: 120). Breeding methods varied and could include the rape by slave owners of their slaves or more systematic methods where "good breeders" were paired or sold to the market (ibid.: 121). In many ways, the sexual vulnerability and reproductive potential of women shaped the female experience of slavery to the extent that it was an important rallying point in abolitionist campaigns and even characterized congressional debates over the Thirteenth Amendment (ibid.: 125).[51]

Brenda V. Smith's (2006) work on women in prisons has been useful and enlightening in expanding the narrow approach to gendering enslavement.[52] Her approach to gender analysis requires that women's as well as men's experiences be seen as gendered. Smith points out that sexual violence is a reality for both women and men in prison, and she shows that sexual violence against male slaves and male prisoners takes different shapes than violence against women slaves or women prisoners. She writes, "It would be tempting to say that sexual abuse in institutional settings primarily affects women, and therefore—like slavery—an identifiable group is targeted for discriminatory treatment. That, however, is not true. Both male and female prisoners frequently face sexual abuse by both staff and other inmates as a means of domination" (ibid.: 279).

Applying the analyses of Smith and Bridgewater to the outcomes of the prosecution of enslavement by the Special Court exposes an entirely insufficient interpretation of the gendered nature of slavery, which refers to abducted women and girls as sex slaves and abducted men and boys as slaves. Extending this justice narrative to transnational slavery would cloud and not clarify the gendered realities of the slave experience. Jeffrey J. Pokorak adds a helpful social dimension to the definition of slavery when he writes that "slavery is commonly understood as the control of all aspects of a slave's social interactions" (2006–2007). Bearing this in mind, we can see that describing male slaves as "just" slaves also precludes the development of a narrative describing the ways male slaves experienced gender-specific forms of slavery, including but certainly not limited to sexual and reproductive exploitation. The breeding of male and female slaves, the rape of women, the separation of children from their parents, the destruction of the African and African-American family—these abuses against slaves are clearly gendered and resonate in the slave experience from different epochs and locales. The gendered analysis should be understood to reflect that enslaved men also suffered gender-specific harms. Sexual and reproductive ownership of male slaves was seen in various ways, including the denial of their fundamental right to be fathers and husbands (Bridgewater 2005: 126), and reduced them to a reproductive role with women not of their own choosing that is analogous to bulls in the practice of animal husbandry. Further, castration was regarded as a legitimate punishment and form of oppression of male slaves (Smith 2006: 579). Such exercises of ownership over male slaves were gender-specific harms degrading the masculinity of male slaves and denying their humanity.

Another notable study on gender and enslavement is provided by historian Casper Erichsen (2005). Erichsen describes the enslavement of the Nama peoples held summarily as prisoners of war on Shark Island in what was then German South West Africa (now Namibia). His gender-specific analysis of women's experience describes how women prisoners of war (POWs) were stripped of all sexual autonomy and human dignity as German soldiers voyeuristically photographed their naked forms and raped them. Erichsen's gender analysis of slavery like practices and conditions on Shark Island also examines the reasons why women made up the largest population in POW camps and that their exploitation as forced labor was massive. He is able with this gender analysis of sexual and other forms of exploitation to draw a link to the disproportionate number of women's deaths from hunger, malnutrition, exposure to the elements, and other subhuman conditions maintained in the camps. This important narrative transcends the focus on sex in order to distinguish male enslavement from that of women. Had Erichsen simply described Nama women as sex slaves of the Germans, we would still be missing a full, nuanced narrative on ways in which gender shaped women's experience of armed conflict and enslavement in German South West Africa.[53]

The historical examples of transatlantic and colonial slavery illustrate that ownership of slaves inherently includes sexual and reproductive ownership. The sexual and reproductive exploitation of a slave is comparable to the exploitation of his/her labor as he/she harvests the slave owner's field or repairs his home. It is the right of ownership that allows a slave to toil under the most egregious conditions and to submit to sexual exploitation. This right of ownership, with all it entails and its gender manifestations, should be examined in order that women's and men's gendered experiences be fully revealed, distinguished, condemned, and remedied.

Armed conflict has also depended on slavery and slavery like practices.

The enslavement of Chinese men by Japanese corporations during World War II, the enslavement of up to two hundred thousand women by the Japanese Imperial Army before and during World War II, the enslavement of Europeans in labor camps by the Nazi government during World War II, the enslavement of Tutsi women during the 1994 genocide, and the enslavement of men and women detainees in the Former Republic of Yugoslavia are but a few examples of enslavement in contemporary conflicts.

The Nuremberg and Tokyo charters recognized the crime of enslavement as a crime against humanity, but they provided no elaboration of the specific acts and motives that compose the elements of this crime. This omission was not remedied until the 1990s, when the International Criminal Tribunal for the Former Yugoslavia (ICTY) prosecuted enslavement. Two defendants, Kunarac and Kovac (the "Kunarac case") were charged with rape and enslavement as crimes against humanity. Kovac was charged singly with outrages upon personal dignity as violations of the laws of war. These charges arose from the mistreatment of women and children and allegations of forced labor in 1992 after the town of Foca was placed under the control of Serb forces. The Muslim and Croat inhabitants of the occupied town were rounded up and then assigned to detention facilities (Kunarac et al. Judgment, 22-02-2001).[54] The gender-specific nature of the enslavement of women in the former Yugoslavia was evident:

> The women were kept in various detention centers where they had to live in intolerably unhygienic conditions, where they were mistreated in many ways including, for many of them, being raped repeatedly. Serb soldiers or policemen would come to these detention centers; select one or more women, take them out and rape them. Many women and girls, including 16 of the Prosecution witnesses, were raped in that way. Some of these women were taken out of these detention centers to privately owned apartments and houses where they had to cook, clean and serve the residents, who were Serb soldiers. They were also subject to sexual assault. (Kunarac et al. Judgment para. 573–74)

According to the trial chamber, Kovac enslaved two women he kept in his apartment for a period of more than four months and two other girls for a week, after which he handed them over to other men (ibid., para. 749–52, 754, 756, 761, and 780).[55] Kovac was found guilty of enslavement, rape, and outrages upon personal dignity. The last count (outrages) related to Kovac's forcing the women to dance naked on a table while he sat on a sofa pointing weapons at them (ibid., para. 766–74).

The charges against Kunarac alleged that he kept two women in an abandoned house in Trnovace for six months. During this period, they were repeatedly raped by Kunarac and DP6, another man, treated as their personal property, and ordered to clean the apartment. The trial chamber accepted that even though the women were given keys to the front door, they had no realistic opportunity of escape. They were subject to other abuse, such as Kunarac inviting a soldier into the house so that he could rape "his" captive in exchange for money. The two women were treated as the personal property of Kunarac and DP6. The trial chamber determined that Kunarac established these living conditions in concert with DP6 and that both men personally committed the act of enslavement (ibid., para. 742). The trial chamber found Kunarac guilty of rape and enslavement. The appeals chamber confirmed that contemporary forms of slavery (as opposed to the traditional concept of slavery defined in the 1926 Slavery Convention [referred to as chattel slavery]) form part of enslavement as a crime against humanity under customary international law.[56]

The decision in the Kunarac case has been criticized for not fully conveying the fact that enslavement was particularly of a sexual nature and, therefore, sexual enslavement. Kelly Askin argues that the tribunal missed an opportunity to recognize the sexual nature of the enslavement but instead treated the enslavement as merely one of a large number of factors that indicated that enslavement had occurred (2003: 340). I argue in response that a gender analysis of crimes against humanity, such as torture, slavery, and imprisonment, does not call for a "sex tag." Sexual slavery, sexual detention, sexual imprisonment, and sexual torture will not shed light on men's and women's experiences of human rights abuses. Does the high incidence of sexual violence against male detainees make their experience sexual imprisonment? Does a torturer's targeting of male and female detainees' genitals warrant a description of sexual torture?[57] If an enslaved woman alleges that 5 percent of her experience was sexual violence and the other 95 percent was related to labor, such as farming her captor's fields, is she "just a slave" or "just a sex slave"? These questions are looking for "sex" and not gender and the ways in which gender shapes the commission and experience of crimes against humanity. Looking for sex in crimes against humanity reduces women's narrative to a sexualized version of what happened to men and obstructs the gender analysis.

The approach taken by the prosecutor and the trial chamber in the

Kunarac case avoided "sexing" women's experience but still made a clear point that sex and the control of sexuality were core elements of enslavement. However, it was not necessary for the statute, prosecutor, or trial chamber in this case to categorize the experience of women as sexual enslavement because the "sexual" range of crimes enslaved women experienced are consistent with "the exercise of power" necessary to create an absolute slave-master relationship. The Kunarac decision provides a landmark recognition of the ways in which gender can significantly affect gross violations of human rights. Both men and women were enslaved in the context of the Yugoslav war; however, the trial chamber did not allow this fact to obscure the gender-specific manifestations of this international crime. The trial chamber did not describe slavery in a "neutral way." Rather, it produced a gender analysis that revealed the different shapes war crimes and crimes against humanity took when committed by combatants against men and against women civilians. In this case, women, unlike men prisoners, were detained in apartments or other suburban addresses and ordered to perform servile acts, such as cleaning, cooking, and being sexually available to their captors.

The Kunarac case clearly constructs the elements of gender-based violence occurring in the act of enslavement of women. Hegemonic gender relations shaped the nature of enslavement. It should be noted that performing servile acts and being confined to a bedroom may not and almost certainly did not reflect the lived gender reality of Serbian or Muslim women in the former Yugoslavia before the armed conflict. However, the fact that these forms of abuse were reserved for female detainees is the first step to their becoming gendered acts of violence. The second is that the space where the violations were committed affirmed an archaic (real or imagined) patriarchy that confined women to gendered spaces deemed private (the bedroom and the kitchen).[58] The attacks were a part of the wider persecution of Muslims; however, they clearly attacked women as a gender group.

In contrast to the approach taken by the ICTY and the work of such academics as Bridgewater, Smith, and Erichsen, the human rights discourse surrounding the enslavement of Asian peoples by the Japanese Imperial Army essentialized women's experience to multiple rapes (sexual enslavement) in contradistinction to men's experience of enslavement. The Women's International War Crimes Tribunal for the Trial of Japanese Military Sexual Slavery (the Women's Tribunal) sat in Tokyo from 8 to 12 December 2000. It was a people's tribunal, organized by international human rights advocates and Asian grassroots movements and its judgment lacked any legal force.[59] However, its moral force lay in examining the evidence and in developing a lasting historical record of the crimes committed in the past (De Brouwer 2005: 139). The Women's Tribunal was intended to pave the way for the government of Japan to recognize its full responsibility and to provide redress to enslaved women (ibid.). In its findings, sexual slavery was held to have been a crime against humanity in 1945 in the context of World War II. According to the tribunal, "Sexual slavery is not a new crime but rather a particularly outrageous, invasive and devastating form of enslavement defined as the 'exercise of any or all the powers of ownership over a person.' The conscription of the 'comfort women' as part of the 'material' of war represents the institutionalization of sexual slavery on an unprecedented scale, rooted in profoundly misogynistic and racist attitudes all too common in the world today."[60]

The finding of the Women's Tribunal was at odds with the Special Rapporteur on Violence Against Women's study of "military sexual slavery," released almost five years before the Women's Tribunal. The rapporteur emphasized that she did not intend to invent new crimes committed against women in armed conflict. She used the term *sexual* as an adjective to describe a form of slavery but not to denote a separate offense. She explained that the term *sexual* was used to highlight the historical and contemporary reality that slavery amounts to the treatment of a person as a chattel, which often includes sexual access and forced sexual activity. In all respects, sexual slavery is slavery and its prohibition is a *jus cogens* norm.[61]

In contrast to the rapporteur's report, the narrative from the Women's Tribunal on gender-based violence privileges multiple rapes and gang rapes as the sole and defining harm enslaved women suffered. It indicates correctly that the primary reason for their abduction was to provide labor in the form of sex to the Japanese military. However, there are few references to other egregious aspects of enslavement, such as beatings or torture; entertainment tasks, such as singing at recreation centers; forced labor, such as laundering military uniforms, digging, or farming; or carrying out covert military activities, such as spying on local communities or acting as translators or interpreters. The dominant narrative focuses exclusively on multiple rapes, gynecological examinations, treatment for sexually transmitted infections, forced abortion, forced use of contraception, miscarriages, and infertility. The Women's Tribunal presented this historiography of comfort women to the international community, and it characterizes the major academic works on the comfort women.[62]

Karen Parker and Jennifer F. Chew make a valuable contribution to broadening the range of abuses women suffered. They detail other forms of torture and abuse, including beatings, mutilations, murder, and being forced to watch the torture of fellow slaves. They also describe poor living conditions, such as inadequate nourishment, forced moves, and long distances to travel in wartime conditions. Many women died from lack of appropriate medical care for malaria, malnutrition, and broken bones and internal bleeding resulting from beatings (1993–94: 509).

Sel Wahng (Spade and Wahng 2004) is another voice of disruption. He criticizes the superficial scholarly analysis of the Korean sex slaves that renders them solely as victims of wartime rapes. His work reveals not only mass and multiple rapes but also the ways in which the act of enslavement assaulted and constructed gender. He speaks of the gendered and sexual erasure of Korean women, and its contribution to a Japanese nationalist agenda (ibid.: 244). One form of erasure was through the Japanese military's masculinization of Korean women's bodies. Wahng uses testimonies to show that Korean women were referred to during rapes as "bastards," "men," and "guys" and that they were subject to medical interventions that made them barren so that the rape of Korean female bodies was constructed as a sexually nonreproductive act (ibid.: 244 and 251). These women actually inhabited gendered territory beyond the culturally specific definitions of women, and the different gender constructions of Korean women, Asian women, Dutch women, and Japanese women created a hierarchy of sex slaves and aggravated or mitigated levels of abuse (ibid. 244).[63] These are important analyses and distinctions, contextualizing the rape of Korean women in the context of a colonial history with Japan, which had developed a mythology of Korean peoples' superhuman strength and suitability for forced labor (ibid.: 250). For my purposes, the special rapporteur's, Parker and Chew's, and Wahng's gender analyses of enslavement in the context of World War II inspire a greater attempt at investigating gender as it related to and shaped the enslavement of men and women in the context of the Sierra Leone conflict.

It is a worrying development for the advancement of gender analyses of international crimes that the Rome Statute of the ICC makes separate listings for enslavement and sexual slavery as distinct international crimes. The Rome Statute reaffirmed the well established definition of "enslavement" as the "exercise of any or all of the powers attaching to the right of ownership over a person . . . including the exercise of such power in the course of trafficking in persons, in particular, women and children" (Rome Statute, Art. 7 [1] [c]).

The prohibition against enslavement provided by the Rome Statute is clearly applicable in the context of the decision on the enslavement of women in the Kunarac case. The trial chamber stated that under its definition of enslavement, indications of enslavement often include, though not necessarily, sex and control of sexuality (Kunarac Judgment, para. 540 and 543). "Any or all of the powers attaching to ownership" would include the acts of sexual abuse and exploitation, and the reference in footnote 11 to "forced labor and servile status" adequately covers the gendered exploitation of women for domestic work.

However, the drafters of the Rome Statute felt that "all of the powers attaching to ownership" did not adequately encompass sexual violence perpetrated against women slaves. Thus, the Rome Statute introduced the crime of sexual slavery in Article 8 (2)[e](vi). In 2000, the Preparatory Commission to the ICC provided the specific elements or Elements of Crimes of sexual enslavement that distinguish it from the definition of enslavement in the following manner: "The perpetrator caused such person or persons to engage in one or more acts of a sexual nature."[64] A good number of international legal scholars and jurists welcomed the Rome Statute's construction of sexual violence as a crime separate from slavery as an overdue recognition of the sexual aspect inherent in slavery (De Brouwer 2005: 137). They regarded the move as a more correct way to describe certain harms that might otherwise have been narrowly referred to as "enforced prostitution" (Oosterveld 2004: 608; De Brouwer 2005: 137). The Women's Caucus for gender justice in the International Criminal Court supported the separate listing, arguing that women may be forced into maternity or temporary marriage complete with domestic duties, both of which might have sexual and nonsexual aspects. In this case, a prosecutor could charge both enslavement and sexual slavery (Oosterveld 2004: 624, quoting Women's Caucus Recommendations 1997). Others opined that sexual slavery recognizes the specific nature of the form of enslavement and ensures that it will be given the distinct attention it deserves. Moreover, victims of the crime of sexual slavery may need somewhat different forms of protective measures or redress than victims of other forms of slavery (Oosterveld 2004: 624, quoting Argibay 2001: 386).

These responses reinforced the application of the most limited insertion of gender into the crime of enslavement, namely, the inclusion of rape and other forms of sexual violence as the defining feature of the harm women suffered. They permit the institutions mandated to bring justice to conflict societies to maintain and indeed reinforce a patriarchal construction of African women as rape victims or potential rape victims. Women in conflict societies are cast in a perpetual state of sexual vulnerability and passivity. This portrayal allows that institutional protection of women becomes another form of oppression—silencing, essentializing, and undervaluing women's experiences. And in the longer process of postwar reconstruction and rehabilitation, programmatic efforts promoting gender equality will restrict their gaze and tailor their response to the monolithic rape-survivor identity of their women clients.

Conclusion

The monumental legal development in the Rome Statute and case law of the Sierra Leone Special Court that saw enslavement fragment into a separate "gendered" crime of sexual enslavement is a part of a wider movement by international justice mechanisms to limit the process of gender mainstreaming. The Special Court statute's inclusion of the crime of sexual enslavement and the prosecutor's decision to charge forced marriage under outrages upon personal dignity mirrors the approach taken by the Women's Tribunal. However, the construction of military sexual enslavement in the context of the "comfort women" in World War II is far from analogous with the contemporary context of child soldiering in Sierra Leone's civil war.

Susan Shepler's leading anthropological study of child soldiering provides an obvious yet often ignored truth. Shepler writes that the group that shoulders the heaviest burden of productive labor in African societies is not women but rather the young. She points out, for example, that indeed both men and women look forward to an old age in which the young support them (2005, quoting Bledsoe 1980: 186). Child labor almost defines childhood in Sierra Leone, and a child who does not work is a bad child (2005: 12). Conversely, a parent who does not make his or her child work is a useless parent who abdicates his or her responsibility to train the child in preparation for an independent adult life.

Shepler's work reveals many factors that begin to elucidate child soldiering in Sierra Leone. She disrupts the dominant narratives of "gendered domestic chores." This is an important feature since domestic work (presumably "girl's work") characterizes sexual slavery and forced marriage, according the Sierra Leone Special Court and the TRC. In fact, the labor boys and girls perform overlap in unexpected ways. A child (Shepler refers only to boys in her study) might have to sweep the house and compound, get water for the household's morning baths, find wood in the forest and bring it home, and then either go to school or work on the farm or in the garden.[65] If gender does not clearly define the nature of work entrusted to children, legal narratives placing evidence of "domestic" work as an element of sexual enslavement or forced marriage in Sierra Leone need to be challenged. Sexual violence in armed conflict occurs in specific historical, social, political, and economic contexts (Turshen 2001: 56). Such terms as "bush brides," camp followers, and "comfort women" are shaped not only by systematic rape but also by the unique combination of contexts in any given region of conflict. These contexts permit combatants to use rape as a socially constructed event. Turshen provides the powerful statement that because it is socially constructed, rape is neither inevitable nor unchangeable (ibid.). This statement should provide the impetus to investigate the social, historical, political, and economic context in order to challenge the use of rape as a weapon of war. An analysis focusing on "sex" alone will not sufficiently empower us to do this.

A focus on the sexual abuse of boys in state-run institutions also provides an important disruption. A 2009 report released by the Irish government made disclosures of brutality against children in industrial and reformatory schools, churches, and Christian schools. A striking feature of this report is the ready comparative gender analysis made possible by the fact that since the nineteenth century the bulk of state institutions in Ireland were gender segregated. So patterns emerge as one reads the report of how girls and boys experienced abuse and neglect in similar but also different ways. One striking conclusion drawn by the report is that, in general, girls' schools were not as physically harsh as boys' schools and that there was no persistent problem of sexual abuse in girls' schools. Abuse of girls was opportunistic and predatory by male employees or occurring in outside placements (Irish Child Abuse Commission 2009: 21). In contrast, sexual abuse in boys' schools was described as "systemic," "endemic," "chronic," and occurring at "disturbing levels." Much of the abuse described was attributed to Catholic Brothers; however, the report describes sexual abuse by peers. In one situation, vulnerable boys had to submit to sex in exchange for protection from older boys (ibid.).

The disruption raised is not the contest I distanced myself from in the introductory chapter, which would ask "did Irish boys or Irish girls suffer the most?" Challenging the legal necessity for a separate crime of sexual enslavement will not be done with claims that "boys were raped too and more frequently than girls."[66] My objective with this rather cursory reference to sexual violence against adolescents in state institutions is to raise the questions that a thorough gender analysis of incarceration, captivity, conscription, and enslavement would require.[67] What made the sexual abuse of Irish boys in industrial and reform schools a form of gender-based violence: the fact that it happened disproportionately to boys? My response is that what confirms the violence against boys as gender-based violence is the ways in which their sex and gender shaped the nature, extent, and impact of the abuse they suffered. For example, sexual violence against boys may have been so prevalent because boys' schools were located in especially remote areas because it might be considered that boys did not need family contact as much as girls or because boys were more likely to be under the care of the Catholic Brothers who were more likely to be sexual predators than nuns.[68] Further, boys may have been regarded as being more recidivist and corrupt than girls, and therefore their reporting of abuse would be treated as less credible by the authorities: hence, the culture of silence facilitated the endemic abuse committed against them.

These are just some gendered assumptions I have formed around dominant ideas of juvenile delinquency and masculinity and are more compelling than a mere head count of Irish victims of sexual violence disaggregated into sex. Elaborated gender considerations can change policy relating to current cases of juvenile custody, whether in foster care or government institution. However, the approach I described at the level of the Special Court reduces a gender analysis of enslavement to the rape of women and excludes any analysis of the ways in which slavery attacks male and female gender identities. This focus on women and sex presents a risk of "eroticizing" intercourse between women and male owners rather than exploring and challenging hegemonic gender relations that make such violence inherent in and even necessary to sustain military factions and hierarchies in state-run institutions for convicted prisoners or even developmentally disabled residents. If we approach enslavement not from a sex/lust perspective but from the hegemonic power perspective, we would leave room for a study of boys' and men's experiences of captivity. Further, we would gain a deeper understanding of the social and political underpinnings of sexual violence, as it disproportionately affects women but also as it affects men and their communities.

Katherine Franke illustrates the possibilities of such an approach with an example of punishment in ancient Rome. When a husband caught another man in bed with his wife, it was acceptable punishment for the husband or his male slaves, or both, to orally or anally rape the male offender (1997–98: 1149, quoting Richlin 1992: 215 and 256). She points out that while it is possible that the person administering the punishment in these circumstances derived erotic satisfaction from these practices, to fundamentally characterize them as erotic in nature is to radically distort their meaning (Franke 1997–98: 1149). Some interpretations better reflect the ways in which the participants understood the practices, the significance they held in the cultures in which they took place, and the unique ways in which sex can be a powerful tool to inflict myriad forms of harm (ibid.: 1149). When poorly considered and analyzed, the mere classification of practices as "sexual" holds out the danger of eclipsing other relations of power and symbolic acts, punishments, and practices that men and women experience collectively and also as individuals in gender-specific ways.

There Are No Raped Women Here

As a visiting scholar at the Center for Human Rights and Humanitarian Law at American University's Washington College of Law, I was invited to speak at a conference on international criminal prosecutions of gender-based violence. It was a dynamic conference, bringing together NGO representatives, academics from various disciplines, victims' rights advocates, and tribunal staff: judges, prosecutors, victim support officers, and defense counsel with firsthand experience of the Sierra Leone Special Court, the Rwanda and Yugoslav tribunals, and the International Criminal Court. In the final moments of the conference, Hannah, a participant, voiced her displeasure at the fact that the conference organizers did not invite victims of rape to the conference. She felt this omission reflected a wider omission by international criminal courts of meaningful victim representation and robbed the conference of victims' voices. Hannah's contribution took my mind back to two conferences I attended in The Hague where former child soldiers were indeed invited to participate. Both cases had angered me because I felt their participation was restricted to their being gawked at by us, the Western academics.

At the reception following the conference, I expressed my reservations about inviting African rape survivors to Maria, a fellow participant. She sympathized with my reservations but also added her own very striking response: "Why did Hannah assume that there were no rape victims in the conference room?"

My initial reaction to Maria's astute inquiry was disappointment in myself because despite my own personal experiences of gender-based discrimination (see the Introduction for an example), I had casually accepted Hannah's statement that there were no rape victims in our midst. And yet the global statistics on the prevalence of sexual violence against women make a fiction of the idea that in a room full of at least two hundred women that none harbored personal narratives of sexual violence or other forms of gender-based discrimination from our experiences of peace, conflict, armed conflict, the Third World, and the First World. I understood, rightly or wrongly, that Hannah's contribution was part of a human rights narrative that refers only to Third World victims and makes (sexual) victimhood synonymous with these women. Maria's question forced me out of the complacency that can arise in human rights law scholars when we embrace the comforting narrative that rape and other abuses of human rights are happening to "those women." Too often, those women are "brown women," and they are made brown not necessarily by their race and complexion but by their illiteracy, poverty, and generally subordinate position in the global hierarchies of power. Those women are more likely to experience armed conflict and the mass of humanitarian interventions that accompany it. These features combine to allow academics (us) to impose "otherness" and muteness on brown women (them) even as we rush in to rescue women.[1] The war victims I encountered who were exhibited at "international" conferences in Europe looked disturbingly but also reassuringly like victims; they did not look like "us." They were exotics in ill-fitting clothes, unsuited for the cool European climate, and escorted by a humanitarian spokesperson. Maria reminded me to examine my own assumptions and essentializing construction of women victims.

Starting with a young Zambian woman in a floral summer dress in a Lusaka market, I have told stories about the veneration, ownership, and censorship of the bodies of African women that create an overpowering sense of vulnerability as well as an overpowering desire by our international and local communities to protect and shield us. And now a riddle: human rights laws, courts of law, customary courts, fathers and mothers, early marriage, vigilante street youths, and secret societies—what do these institutions that I have featured in this book all have in common? The answer is that their actions ostensibly have our (vulnerable African women's) protection as motivators. And indeed the quickly expanding body of human rights law and enforcement mechanisms are a testament to the desire to protect women from violence. However, the pain that law and justice can inflict, the omissions they make, the control they keep, the freedoms they confiscate, and the oppression they legitimate are part and parcel of their protection mechanisms in a patriarchal society. Looking back at the three tiers of human rights and humanitarian law, we see that their language of protection is a historically conditioned response that needs to be investigated and resisted as significant parts of it preclude the crafting of legal and social responses that empower survivors of gender-based violence and other forms of discrimination to overturn patriarchy (Otto 2002: 35). As it stands, the dominant narrative of gender and violence requires that the survivor must be disempowered not only by rape or other rights violation but also by the cloak of abject vulnerability imposed by the legal discourse, society, and other protectors.

There is, however, a fundamental difference between the universal human rights law framework and the larger group of protectors that includes parents arranging early marriages, older women policing the virginity of young women, and street youth conducting citizens' arrests of immodest girls. The family and community protectors understand gender inequality and discrimination because they live and navigate it every day as individuals and members of a community. They are local, and at different moments they experience the privileges as well as the oppression of gender hegemonies. They survive and prosper because they understand power and its distribution in their own household, clan, homestead, commune, village, sector, district, town, city, and metropolis. Thus, the teenaged boys who rescued me from rape in the market (see the Introduction) were able to intervene in a timely fashion because they clearly understood the gendered manifestations of power in the market. I was not able to protect myself because I (the student of law) did not understand that I was powerless. I would not (could not at the time) see my own vulnerability.

The evolution of international human rights law reminds me of that first-year law student. The birth of a universal framework was so deeply rooted in the discourse of equality and sameness that it could not readily insert patriarchy and other structural inequalities into its narrative of man and his fundamental freedoms. Patriarchy imposes, often violently, one authentic model of masculinity and a complementary but subordinate model of femininity. Patriarchy, heterocentrism, nationalism, and other essentializing sociopolitical systems sabotaged early human rights efforts to establish formal equality between "authentic" men, "deviant" men, and women. Likewise, efforts to insert gender and not only biological-sexual differences into the interpretation and enforcement of human rights laws were hampered when these hegemonic social structures were not exposed and transformed by mainstream social movements.

Thus, gender-based violence as a broad range of acts targeting femininity and masculinity remains underrepresented before transitional justice processes. The fact of sexual violence against women in conflict is recognized by us (legal observers, investigators, and prosecutors) as a serious but inherent phenomenon in the hegemonic relationship between man and his subordinates (women and weak men). Sexual violence attaches easily and even naturally to the bodies of women to such an extent that it becomes a natural leap to frame it as the defining or only significant harm that women experience in conflict. However, without a serious gender analysis, investigators and prosecutors cannot contribute to jurisprudence that captures the reality of gender-based violence as a crime against humanity and war crime. This is a conceptual failure that leaves a wide range of victims of gender-based war crimes and crimes against humanity outside of the justice process.

This omission leaves room for the appropriation of participating victims' voices by the justice process. TRC and tribunal transcripts are all too often composed of a small and apparently representative sample of the most sensational and heinous acts (breasts hacked off, forced acts of incest, necrophilia, pregnant women eviscerated, and so on and so forth). Old crimes, such as enslavement, receive new labels, such as "forced marriage" and "sex slavery." And the remaining backlog of cases is dropped for want of sustained interest from the international community, even though official explanations refer to a lack of sufficient evidence and the recalcitrance of victims and witnesses. At this point, the prosecutor's perspective can be likened to Aunt Hermien (see Chapter 2): the prosecutor accepts the inevitability and hypervisibility of rape and takes it for granted that "they were all raped." But by doing so, the prosecutor does not need to make any further analysis of gender and violence beyond the landmark conviction.

At times governments and tribunals are at loggerheads over certain aspects of justice. Disagreement can surround decisions over the seat of a tribunal or the perceived harshness or leniency of sentences. However, there are aspects of the justice process on which governments and tribunals concur, which brings me to the observation made by Fiounnuala Ní Aoláin that the international community plays a complex role in compounding gender inequality and unaccountability once entangled with a transitional society. There is a "transitional moment" that represents only one point on the continuum of a protracted legal and political engagement between the transitional state and the international community (2008: 38). There may be complicity in the dropping of charges against key actors in the peace process, there may be a mutual decision to focus on crimes against humanity and to ignore war crimes, and there may be a common interest in prosecuting child soldiering but not mass rape. There is indeed "an ideology to judging" (Rajagopal 2006: 26), particularly in transitional states engaged in massive democratization projects under the watchful eye of the international community. The processes, institutions, and values that drive change in transitional societies are deeply gendered (Ní Aoláin 2008: 2), which has yet to translate into gender competence or a sustained review of prosecutorial priorities with respect to gender, the interests tribunals represent and the constituents they serve, and their long-term political objectives in the postconflict state.

According to Martha Chamallas (2005: 38), a great virtue of narrative over theory is its ability to transcend false "either/and" dichotomies and present a nuanced "both/and" picture of social phenomena. My narratives throughout the book served to complicate gender and violence and to suggest that survivors of conflict cannot be reduced to a universal war story. Further, essentializing the victim only marginally benefits the iconic victim selected over others who cannot conform to this role. The iconic victim is aware that he/she must compromise and erase parts of his/her narrative in order to provide a match with the image of victimhood erected within the legal framework well before the examination in court. Thus, when appearing before the tribunal, a Hutu victim of a beating must emphasize her Tutsi sympathies, a Hutu rape victim should resemble a Tutsi woman, a Sierra Leonean girl who voluntarily joined the civil defense forces with her siblings must present herself as having been forcibly recruited for marriage, and a conscripted man must not refer to his rape as anything but torture.

This self-censorship can guarantee access to justice, but it also creates the apparent untruths in the narratives. The tragic outcome for the iconic victim is apparent in the case of "comfort women" discredited by revisionists who refer to these women as prostitutes because of serious inconsistencies in their narratives. Depending on the audience (for example, a feminist workshop, a formal court hearing, or an interview with the media), the individual testimony surrounding the recruitment of comfort women has been seen to vary dramatically. In one narrative, a woman will report that she was abducted by the Japanese; in a second narrative, she says she was given by her parents to the Japanese military; and in a third narrative, she relates that she applied for work with a dishonest local businessman and was then duped and trafficked. Maki Kimura argues that these are not inconsistencies or fabrications but that they reveal the survivors' awareness that they are straddling a virgin-whore dichotomy of women (2003: 11–13). It is my conclusion in this study that the tribunals and the human rights narratives create the benchmarks for "true victimhood" and victims learn with each testimony they give that justice, acknowledgment, and social and political absolution is forthcoming only when the prescribed form of victimhood is claimed.

The collapse of social and political institutions, including the institution of marriage, often results in accelerated social and political transformation. Postconflict societies as seen in countries such as Sierra Leone, Liberia, Rwanda, South Africa, and Uganda reveal that as institutions are reconfigured, gender equality can take root in previously unimagined spaces and at unprecedented rates. The rapid transformation in specific sectors of gender hegemonies is linked in part to the realization of the burden women bore under systems of oppression, be it apartheid or ethnic cleansing, and to the acknowledgment of the agency women exercised in subverting oppressors and protecting themselves and their communities from human rights violations.

However, by operating necessarily within a scope of temporal jurisdiction and focusing on gross violations of human rights during a specified period, the case law of ad hoc criminal trials obscures these transformations. The past and future are referenced only in order to evidence intent to commit a crime (where the government began arming civilians a year before the massacre, for example) or to evidence the impact of violations (for example, by showing that the ethnic composition of a town changed drastically after killings). What is lost are references to, for example, antiwar protests, and the support roles played by local and transnational family networks. An interdisciplinary and even ethnographic approach to analyzing legal narratives is needed in order to reveal gender transformations that occurred before, during, and in the aftermath of armed conflict. Once they are revealed and supported, these transformations can disrupt the human rights law and the justice narrative, which tend to project an overwhelmingly oppressive image of culture as the catalyst for atrocity and women's victimhood.

I join Omolara Ogundipe-Leslie and others who call for more narratives of African women's identities and lives, roles, and status beyond the conjugal and coital milieus (Ogundipe-Leslie 1994: 251). The conjugal and coital roles of African women have emerged as a preoccupation of transitional justice processes, to the extent that gender-based violence has been reduced to sexual violence against women and girls. This reductionist trend adds women to the ambit of war crimes and crimes against humanity but excludes gender and feminism from the analysis.

The repercussions of this exclusion are far reaching and are illustrated, for example, by the easy co-option by the prosecutor of forced marriage as a crime against humanity. The term "forced marriage" reveals the discursive power of rebels and local communities who accepted it and reminds us that the local justice process has discursive power to effectively influence law making and (transitional) justice process (Peetz 2008: 17). Where does this leave women and girls abducted by rebels and described by rebels, their communities, and the legal system as "bush brides"? There is no single answer to the long-term social and political implications for women and girls who experience rape and other forms of gender-based violence in armed conflict. Judith Zur (1993: 28, 30) writes of Guatemalan widows who rejected the military's branding of them as "wives of the guerrillas" because of its symbolic devaluation and its implicit threat to their sense of self. Conversely, Jelke Boesten (2008) describes how young Andean women and their families called upon military superiors to force soldiers to "domesticate" rape by marrying the girls and women they had raped. There is among women, perpetrators, and their communities the knowledge that names create reality. Jurists have yet to acknowledge that their legal narrative helped create and calcify the experience of bush marriage in Sierra Leone and left women few choices but to remain in the relationship or deny their entire experience of abduction in order to escape the pejorative title of "bush bride." Both choices required shunning their exercise of the right to access to justice.

The dominant judicial narrative of gender and violence asserts the simple dichotomies such that the major power struggle is between the Hutu and the Tutsi, the rebels and the army, the freedom fighter and the colonizer, the state and the terrorist, the men and the women, and so on. Binaries such as these conceal that the major power struggle is a gender struggle too and that armed conflict is in itself gendered. So the conclusion that some African women in South African detention centers delivered babies in prison without the aid of a midwife because apartheid was a racist system misses what a gender analysis would begin to capture: such maltreatment of women prisoners could reveal the threat that women political activists posed to white as well as black masculinities in a militarized state. A gender analysis would require that the victimization of South African women politicians was discussed in the context of men's socialization under apartheid and in the postapartheid era (May and Strikwerda 1994: 135). Masculinities belong in the gender analysis not to reveal analogous "male rapes" but to understand the communication of harm between perpetrators and victims around hegemonic power.

Transitional justice has become a standard feature of peace building and conflict resolution in Africa, and transitional justice narratives are constructing an African culture and history. Truth commissions are fairly overt in this objective, yet criminal justice processes are doing the same, though with less fanfare. Together they are creating a historiography of African women. An iconic image of the brown woman rape victim is emerging from this legal narrative. It is a representation that has the power to diminish women's participation in the process of peace building and the establishment of the rule of law and good governance.

Transitional justice has drawn the gaze of powerful international actors, such as the United Nations and the European Union, onto the bodies of African women. The lens they (we) look through is a legal and juristic one, and it has produced names such as "sex slave" that depoliticize women irreparably.[2] The lens shows us a perpetual victim whose abuse is made possible through the "rape culture" that characterizes African women's lives in peace and war.[3] The lens must be adjusted, and the view must move from quick studies of "sex in war" to serious analyses of the operation of "gender and violence" in humanitarian crises as well as in humanitarian intervention.

Notes

Introduction

1. Annemiek Richters (1988: 115) refers to my description of morality tales as the "omnipresence of rape fear," which can work "factually and symbolically to maintain or restore the gender biased, hierarchical order of society." Similarly, Susan J. Brison (1998: 11–27) writes that sexual violence victimizes not only those women who are directly attacked but all women. "The fear of rape has long functioned to keep women in their place." Latoya Peterson (2008: 209–20) would describe my experience in the Lusaka market as part of the "not rape" phenomenon. She explains the invisibility of the sexual harassment, intimidation, and coercion that young women experience but never speak of because it was "not actually rape." This "not rape epidemic" has a controlling and stifling effect on women's sexual autonomy and right to physical integrity. It also permits sexual aggressors who are "not rapists" to escape detection or punishment.

2. The attribution of culpability to rape victims is an international phenomenon. Speaking against the low conviction rate for rape cases in the United Kingdom, it has been said: "Alcohol seems to have become the new short skirt. The majority of cases resulting in an acquittal now involve a complainant who had been drinking" (Julie Bindel, 1 February 2007).

3. See Peyi Soyinka-Airewele (2004: 7) for an elaboration on the transformative impact of state violence on personal and political identity.

4. This and subsequent introductory narratives in this book are taken from private and informal conversations I had while on field visits to Sierra Leone (2007) and Rwanda (2004). In this and other introductory narratives, I intentionally obscure some prominent identifying factors, such as the names of chiefdoms or towns. Further, I apply pseudonyms where it seems appropriate to protect identities in the interest of privacy.

5. The words of Alessandro Portelli (1991: 53) on silences are pertinent to the silences on sexual violence in men's narratives: "The most important information may lie in what informants hide and in the fact that they do hide it, rather than in what they tell."

6. See Adam Jones for a detailed study on the gendercide of battle-aged men and how genocide disproportionately targets men. This gender-specific targeting of men has "attracted virtually no attention at the level of scholarship and public policy" (2004: 2).

7. The UN report on the fall of Srebrenica is widely quoted in the gendered narratives depicting men as the iconic victims. "Several thousand more men are still missing, and there is every reason to believe that additional burial sites, many of which have been probed but not exhumed, will reveal the bodies of thousands more men and boys" (UN Secretary-General 1999).

8. See Laura Suski (2009) for a detailed analysis of the motivation and outcome of humanitarianism that privileges the suffering of children.

9. See Stefan Kirchner's (2008: 2) description of the conflict in eastern Congo as hell in paradise, "a hell for women, that is." The claim inadvertently implies that Congolese men can still equate their daily lives to paradise despite the armed conflict and widespread rape of their womenfolk. Many academics and activists pressing for the privileging of women's experience tend to reduce women's gender experience of conflict to rape. This focus draws attention to widespread sexual violence but eclipses other dislocating and grave experiences, such as internal displacement, loss of property, loss of status arising from widowhood or loss of children, and food insecurity. See the Council of Europe's report on rape in armed conflict (2000), which replicates this reductionist tendency. Women are described as "the foremost victims of violations of international humanitarian law such as gang rape, forced prostitution, sexual slavery, forced insemination, torture and sexual abuse" (para. 3).

10. In describing her experience of the legal system, Sebold contrasts herself with rape survivors who are effectively barred from the justice process by disinterested or skeptical police investigators, prosecutors, and social workers because of their (the survivors') history of substance abuse, belonging to a minority race, or having had a domestic relationship with the perpetrator (Sebold 1999: 168, quoted by Martha Chamallas (2005: 14)). Susan J. Brison (1998: 15–16) also notes that she was spared suspicion from the police and medical personnel because she was a married woman, she was attacked by a stranger in a safe public place, and she bore the visible marks of strangulation and a severe beating to her face and body.

11. See Donald Piragoff (2001a, 2001b) for an excellent analysis of the negotiation and drafting of the Rules of Evidence and Procedure by States. He provides a rare insight into the many challenges posed by states in creating specific provisions for sexual violence, particularly relating to such issues as consent, corroboration, and in-camera testimony. See also André Klip's and Goran Sluiter's *Annotated Leading Cases of International Criminal Tribunals* (2007) which provide a legal commentary on the decisions of the ad hoc criminal tribunals for Rwanda and the former Yugoslavia, the Sierra Leone Special Court, the Timor Leste Special Panels for Serious Crimes, and more recently the International Criminal Court.

12. This body of literature has benefited from contributions from staff members or former staff members of the tribunals. See, for example, Saleem Vahidy et al. (2009), Sha-

nee Stepakoff and Michelle Staggs Kelsall (2007), Alison Cole (2008), Payam Akhavan (2005), and Patricia Viseur-Sellers (2001 and 2002). Nongovernmental organizations supporting women survivors of armed conflict have also produced evaluative studies of the victim and witness experience of transitional justice: see, for example, Kvinna till Kvinna (2004) and Dubravka Zarkov (2005). Activist-scholars Anne-Marie De Brouwer (2005) and Binaifer Nowrojee (2005) address the needs of victims and witnesses before the ad hoc criminal tribunals. And Heidy Rombouts (2006) and De Brouwer (2005) provide insightful studies on gender and reparations for the survivors of genocide in Rwanda.

13. See reports on the pressures women face from peers, family members, and colleagues to quit the formal workforce in order to raise children (Katrin Bennhold, 17 January 2010a and 2010b).

14. See Security Council Resolution 1325 (2000). This was the first resolution ever passed by the Security Council that specifically addresses the impact of war on women and the need to increase women's contributions to peace and conflict-resolution processes. See also Security Council Resolution 1820 (2008), which specifically states that rape is a weapon of war and can be a crime against humanity, and is a constitutive element of genocide. See also Security Council Resolution 1888 (2010).

15. The trial chamber in the case of Jean-Paul Akayesu (02-09-1998, para. 598 and 688) determined that coercive circumstances need not be evidenced by a show of physical force. Threats, intimidation, extortion, and other forms of duress that prey on fear or desperation may constitute coercion, and coercion may be inherent in certain circumstances, including armed conflict. This case also provides broad definitions of rape and sexual violence. A coercive circumstance arising from conflict could include stark conditions of internal displacement and occupation or permanent or temporary control by a military presence, such as a rebel group or colonial administration.

16. See Marta Cullberg Weston and the Kvinna till Kvinna Foundation (2002) describing the practical ways in which women's centers help women survivors overcome obstacles in the healing and recovery process in Bosnia-Herzegovina. The focus is far-reaching and addresses such issues as wartime traumatization, economic losses, the effects of war on families, the return process for refugees and internally displaced persons, and its traumas and fractured relationships with neighbors and communities, for example, dealing with wartime betrayals and collaboration.

17. Council of Europe, paras. 7, 8, and 11 (2000).

18. Scott Straus (2007) and Allan Thompson (2007) provide useful analyses on the role of the media as a propaganda tool in the buildup to the Rwandan genocide. See also Dubravka Zarkov (2001 and 2007) for specific references to the ways in which the media also uses gender stereotypes of masculinity or maleness to fuel armed conflict.

19. Marion Haroff-Tavel (2003: 185) describes variables of the aftermath, for example, when a natural disaster such as drought compounds the effects of protracted armed conflict, or months or even years after the end of the conflict, when donor fatigue sets in and a humanitarian crisis is renewed. See also Cynthia Cockburn (2001) for a gendered analysis of armed conflict and the insecurity that prevails in its aftermath.

20. Benjamin Ndabila Mibenge (2004: 32) describes how incidents of domestic violence increased dramatically when traumatized soldiers returned from the battlefield to their homes. "Upon their return from the (fighting, as part of the British land forces in the First and Second World War) wars, demobilized soldiers exhibited a propensity for violence, especially when they discovered that their wives had betrayed them in their absence." Fionnuala Ní Aoláin (2008: 19) refers to the "returning warrior," who has through conflict normalized the use of violence and views the home as another site in which to exercise power and control through physical force. She also writes of South Africa that "the perceived escalation of domestic violence rates post-Apartheid have raised deep concerns about the relationship between pre-existing apartheid violence and its spill over to a transitional society."

21. See Kristin B. Sandvik (2009) describing how the unprecedented focus on the extent and gravity of gender-based violence in situations of unrest and displacement has led to the recognition of refugee women as a particularly vulnerable group. See also Beth Vann (2002) on programmatic responses to gender-based violence against displaced populations. Amy G. Lewis (2006) provides an insight into the levels of violence that women experience in refugee camps and communities and provides case studies of multisectoral approaches taken by the UNHCR (UN Refugee Agency), including psychosocial, health, and security (including legal justice) responses in the African context.

22. See Judith Zur (1998) on the civil war in Guatemala and the domestic ways in which it was waged against communities and its impact on widows. See also Carolyn Nordstrom (1997) on the civil war in Mozambique and its impact on villagers.

23. See Karen Parker (2001) for an overview of humanitarian law, its historical development, and its present day treaty based and customary standards relating to the situation of women in contemporary wars, as well as to the rights and duties of women combatants and prisoners of war. See also Noëlle Quénivet (2005) for an in-depth critique of the feminist critique of international humanitarian law.

24. Some recent international headlines are illustrative: Craig Whitlock, "Vatican Turnaround: Holocaust Denier Must Recant," 4 February 2009; Mark Landler, "Austrian Court Frees British Author Jailed as Holocaust Denier," 21 December 2006; and *New York Times*, "Swiss Court Convicts Turkish Politician of Genocide Denial: Court Hands Down First Such Conviction," 9 March 2007. This last article reports that the politician was convicted under a 1995 Swiss law prescribing a three-year maximum penalty for those denying, belittling, or justifying any genocide.

25. Agreement for the Prosecution and Punishment of the Major War Criminals of the European Axis, and the Charter of the International Military Tribunal, London, 8 August 1945. I have intentionally left out the International Military Tribunal for the Far East (Tokyo Trials) because many legal commentators have argued persuasively that the impact of the Tokyo Trial has been minimal compared to that of Nuremberg as "its voluminous transcripts were placed in public archives but not published unlike the Nuremberg Trial which alone became the representative judicial act ending the war" (Brook 2007: 150). Madoka Futamura (2008: 9–10) also notes the absence of primary

source material from the Tokyo Trial and discusses its position as a "forgotten trial." The marginal space occupied by the Tokyo Trials in the annals of history has perhaps contributed to the international community's greater tolerance for denialism from the Japanese government about war crimes, whereas similar denialism is not tolerated from the German government or the general public.

26. In contrast, the denial of early nineteenth-century campaigns of genocide against the Armenian and Herero and Nama peoples are not widely criminalized in Europe because they were never made subject to comparable international criminal prosecution. The right to an apology and other forms of remedy is still contested by the German and Turkish governments and the descendants of the victims. The following headlines reveal that the debates over moral and legal responsibility persist: *Der Spiegel*, "Herero Massacre: General's Descendants Apologize for 'Germany's First Genocide,'" 10 August 2007; and Brian Knowlton, "Bush Urges Congress to Reject Armenian Genocide Resolution," 10 October 2007.

27. See Fiona Ross (2005), Rosalind Shaw (2005), and Beth Goldblatt and Sheila Meintjes (1996). Notable legal commentators include the International Center for Transitional Justice (ICTJ), which has published various research studies on truth commissions. ICTJ researchers are exemplary in that they often integrate gender into their case study evaluations of truth commissions, see ICTJ (2004). See also Jocelyn Getgen (2009) for a gendered legal analysis of a truth commission.

28. Admittedly, I refer to "victims" more than "survivors," but this usage is a nod to my professional relationship with the courts of law and the lawyer's parlance that refers to victims and witnesses, victim testimony, victim's rights, victim cross-examination, and so on.

Chapter 1. The Women Were Not Raped

1. The referenced events attracted intense, sensationalized, and prolonged media coverage in the United States. Some of the events, particularly the Kennedy Smith, Tyson, and Central Park cases, permeated popular culture outside the United States, in part owing to reporting by the international media. Trisha Meilli was attacked and raped while jogging in New York's Central Park in 1989. She was referred to as the "Central Park jogger" by the media. Four teens were convicted of the crime, but their convictions were vacated when another man, Matias Reyes, confessed in 1991. DNA evidence confirmed his confession. Bret Easton Ellis's book *American Psycho* (1991) is a psychological thriller about a young, attractive, and wealthy investment banker who is also a psychopath. The book contains scenes of graphic and (arguably) gratuitous violence against women, including mutilation, cannibalism, torture, and rape. William Kennedy Smith, a physician and member of a prominent American political family, was accused and charged with rape in 1991. Smith was acquitted. Mike Tyson, a heavyweight boxing champion, was accused and charged with rape in 1991. Tyson was convicted of rape and served three years of his six-year prison sentence. Defense counsel for both Tyson and Kennedy Smith claimed that sex had been consensual.

2. I deliberately use the fatalistic and stigmatizing terms "dying of AIDS" or "infected with HIV" as opposed to the more acceptable "living with HIV" or "living positive" because they match the tone of the discourse I found around women genocide survivors in 2004.

3. See Mibenge (2007b) for a discussion of the absence of the so-called "culture of silence" surrounding gender-based violence in Rwanda and how this stifles survivors' narratives while privileging the media and politicians in the broadcasting of a "rape of the nation" experience. See also Buss (2007) for a discussion of the hypervisibility of rape in postwar societies and its negative impact on prosecution and conviction in cases alleging sexual violence.

4. I borrow the term "single axis analysis" from Kimberlé Crenshaw (1989: 139–40).

5. The International Bill of Rights did not provide a definition of discrimination until the Human Rights Committee provided one in 1989: while these conventions (CERD and CEDAW) deal only with cases of discrimination on specific grounds, the HRC believes that the term "discrimination" as used in the Covenant (ICCPR) should be understood to imply any distinction, exclusion, restriction, or preference based on any grounds, such as race, color, sex, language, religion, political or other opinion, national or social origin, property, and birth or other status, and which has the purpose or effect of nullifying or impairing the recognition, enjoyment, or exercise by all persons, on an equal footing, of all rights and freedoms (General Comment 18 [1989], art. 7).

6. Margot L. Lovett (1996) provides a similar analysis of urban migration from western Tanzania and male strategies (colonial and indigenous) to control and mold female mobility and labor.

7. See also General Comment 18, art. 10, to the effect that the principle of equality sometimes requires state parties to take affirmative action in order to diminish or eliminate conditions that cause or help perpetuate discrimination prohibited by the ICCPR.

8. Mari J. Matsuda (1990–91: 1188–89) points out that all forms of oppression are not the same, but lists several emerging predictable patterns, which include the following: all forms of oppression involve taking a trait, X, which often carries with it a cultural meaning, and using X to make some group the "other" and to reduce their entitlements and power; all forms of oppression benefit someone, and sometimes both sides of a relationship of domination will have some stake in its maintenance; all forms of oppression implicate a psychology of subordination that involves elements of sexual fear, the need to control, hatred of self, and hatred of others .

9. See also Diane Otto's (2002) arguments that general comments and recommendations of all treaty bodies should more extensively mainstream gender into their authoritative interpretation of treaties.

10. Art. 17 of the ICCPR provides for the right of every person to be protected against arbitrary or unlawful interference with his privacy, family, home, or correspondence as well as against unlawful attacks on his honor and reputation.

11. The statement was apparently made by the CERD Committee chairperson when reporting to the chairpersons of the treaty committees' annual meeting.

12. Report of the sixth meeting of persons chairing the human rights treaty bodies (4 October 1995, para. 34). The recommendations were proposed by an expert group on the integration of gender perspectives into UN human rights activities and programs, which met in Geneva from 3–7 July 1995 to follow up recommendations from the 1993 World Conference on Human Rights (Otto 2002: 28).

13. The preamble to the General Comment provides that the comment arose from a thematic discussion with members of the CERD Committee, some governments, experts from the Sub-Commission for the Promotion and Protection of Human Rights, and NGOs that produced compelling evidence of the extent and persistence of descent based discrimination in different regions of the world.

14. CERD, General Comment 31, refers to protective measures for women and mothers who are non-nationals and subject to deportation while facing judicial proceedings (art. 25, 26, and 41).

15. The Maputo Protocol is a supplementary protocol to the Banjul Charter. The protocol was adopted by the African Union on 11 July 2003 in Maputo, the capital city of Mozambique.

16. Special rapporteurs, representatives, independent experts, or working-group members are appointed by the chairperson of the Commission on Human Rights after consultation with the five regional groups, which consist of member states of the commission. The appointees are independent, are not paid, and serve in a personal capacity for a maximum of six years. Currently, there are over thirty special-procedure mechanisms. See the website of the UN Office of the High Commissioner for Human Rights for a greater elaboration on the special procedures established by the UN Human Rights Council to address either specific country situations or thematic issues in all parts of the world http://www.ohchr.org/EN/HRBodies/SP/Pages/Welcomepage.aspx.

17. See also CEDAW General Recommendation 24 (1999), which interprets article 14 of CEDAW (on women and health) and gives special attention to older women and how their age may negatively affect their access to health care. "The Committee is concerned about the conditions of health care services for older women, not only because women often live longer than men and are more likely than men to suffer from disabling and degenerative chronic diseases, such as osteoporosis and dementia, but because they often have the responsibility for their aging spouses. Therefore, States parties should take appropriate measures to ensure the access of older women to health services that address the handicaps and disabilities associated with aging." This elaboration is more significant to women's full lives in that it goes beyond CEDAW's exclusive focus on women's sexual reproductive health, a major concern for women but also for men and governments. Articles 12 (1) and (2) refer specifically to pregnancy, confinement and the postnatal period, adequate nutrition during pregnancy and lactation, and family planning.

18. See also CEDAW's General Recommendation 21 (1994), articles 11–13, which address equality in the family and marriage. It acknowledges the different shapes marriage can take (while continuing to censor early, forced, and polygamous marriages)

and points out that in the public and private sphere, socially constructed gender roles for women are regarded as less valuable than men's. This devaluation of women's roles is identified as a factor in inequality and injustice within the family.

19. CEDAW's General Recommendation 19 (1992) on gender-based violence is also mindful of the different ways in which socioeconomic status can increase vulnerability to violence and other forms of gender-based discrimination. Speaking of rural women, it describes their increased vulnerability to gender-based violence because of traditional attitudes regarding the subordinate role of women that persist in many rural communities. Girls from rural communities are at special risk for violence and sexual exploitation when they leave the rural community to seek employment in towns.

20. Patricia Viseur-Sellers (2001: 281–90) clarifies that evidence of sexual abuse as well as male sexual abuse by the Gestapo, the Nazi S.S. forces, and ordinary German soldiers against Russian and French civilians was tendered by the Russian and French prosecutors, relying on witness testimony, police reports, medical certificates, and affidavits. Abuses included sexualized forms of torture of men, forced recruitment of girls and women into brothels, gang rapes, and sterility experiments on Jewish women. The defense neither objected nor raised a defense to counter the evidence of sexual violence. Despite this well-documented narrative of sexual violence, the Nuremberg judgment dealt with evidence of war crimes and crimes against humanity in an unspecific manner. Sexual violence was subsumed under the terms *atrocities* and *ill treatment*. Only killings, slave labor, and the persecution of Jews were addressed with any specificity. In contrast to the Nuremberg indictments, the Tokyo indictment explicitly alleged acts of sexual violence. Testimonies of sexual violence committed by invading Japanese troops or during the occupation of Borneo, the Philippines, Burma, Java, French Indochina, and China were submitted. The Tokyo judgment is unambiguous in that war crimes encompassed murder, rape, and other cruelties. Viseur-Sellers dispels the belief held by many international lawyers that evidence of sexual violence was not admitted at Nuremberg or Tokyo or, if it was admitted, that it was immaterial to the judgment.

21. First Geneva Convention for the Amelioration of the Condition of the Wounded and Sick in Armed Forces in the Field; Second Geneva Convention for the Amelioration of the Condition of Wounded, Sick and Shipwrecked Members of Armed Forces at Sea ; Third Geneva Convention Relative to the Treatment of Prisoners of War; and Fourth Geneva Convention Relative to the Protection of Civilian Persons in Time of War.

22. Nancy Lindisfarne (1994: 82–96) presents a compelling analysis of the ways in which gender norms creating powerful men and weak, chaste women contribute to a rape culture because penetrative sex, even forced, becomes integral to "becoming a man" and fulfilling the requirements of proper masculinity.

23. Rosalind Dixon (2002: 704) describes the dishonor that befalls a rape survivor as leaving female victims socially infertile by virtue of their unmarriageability or untouchability.

24. See for example, Geneva IV, articles (89) "Expectant and nursing mothers and children under fifteen years of age, shall be given additional food, in proportion to their

physiological needs;" and (132) "Each interned person shall be released by the Detaining Power as soon as the reasons which necessitated his internment no longer exist. . . . The Parties to the conflict shall, moreover, endeavor during the course of hostilities, to conclude agreements for the release, the repatriation, the return to places of residence or the accommodation in a neutral country of certain classes of internees, in particular children, pregnant women and mothers with infants and young children, wounded and sick, and internees who have been detained for a long time."

25. Noya Rimalt (2008) examines sexual harassment legislation in Israel, the United States, and Europe and the manner in which Israeli courts, in particular, talk about sexual harassment and conceptualize its harm. She concludes in part that the narrative of the courts is patriarchal and contrary to human rights discourse, because of its conceptualization of sexual harassment as an honor crime rather than a prima facie human rights violation. Thus, while woman complainants may gain access to justice, the narrative is not a true representation of the harm that sexual violence has caused. See also Monica Diggs Mange (2007) for a critique of U.S. antidiscrimination law and its failure to redress discrimination on the grounds of gender.

26. Common Article 3 to the Geneva Conventions of 12 August 1949: "In the case of armed conflict not of an international character occurring in the territory of one of the High Contracting Parties, each Party to the conflict shall be bound to apply, as a minimum, the following provisions: (1) Persons taking no active part in the hostilities, including members of armed forces who have laid down their arms and those placed "hors de combat" by sickness, wounds, detention, or any other cause, shall in all circumstances be treated humanely, without any adverse distinction founded on race, colour, religion or faith, sex, birth or wealth, or any other similar criteria. . . . To this end, the following acts are and shall remain prohibited at any time and in any place whatsoever with respect to the above-mentioned persons: (a) violence to life and person, in particular murder of all kinds, mutilation, cruel treatment and torture; (b) taking of hostages; (c) outrages upon personal dignity, in particular humiliating and degrading treatment; (d) the passing of sentences and the carrying out of executions without previous judgment pronounced by a regularly constituted court, affording all the judicial guarantees which are recognised as indispensable by civilised peoples. (2) The wounded and sick shall be collected and cared for."

27. ICRC on international humanitarian law at http://www.icrc.org/ihl.nsf/INTRO/475?OpenDocument and http://www.icrc.org/ihl.nsf/full/470?opendocument.

28. The prime ministers of India and Pakistan met and passed a declaration and treaty agreeing that women and girls abducted at partition be rescued from their respective territories and restored to their families (Butalia 2000: 109–11).

29. Arguably, article 2 (e) of the Genocide Convention (1948) identifies that forcibly transferring children of a national, ethnic, racial, or religious group to another group with the intent to destroy a group is an act of genocide. This action is of course a form of separation of children. However, in keeping with Ní Aoláin's analysis, the gender dimensions of forcibly transferring children are ignored in this legal categorization.

The legal categorization focuses on the transfer of children from the group. Thus, it ignores women's role as primary caregivers to children, as well as their sexuality and reproductivity.

30. Madeline Morris produces several historical U.S. military records indicating that the Criminal Investigation Branch of the Provost Marshal's office investigated an indeterminable number of rape reports committed by American troops during the breakout and liberation of France: "The invading soldiers came fully armed. . . . Many soldiers had the notion that French women generally were both attractive and free with their love. . . . Generally speaking, the rape cases of the French Phase fell into one broad pattern characterised by violence, though of different degrees. The use of firearms was common in perpetrating the offence" (Morris 1995–96: 667, quoting the Office of the Judge Advocate General, 1945: 241).

31. The objectives of the UN Decade for Women, running from 1976 to 1986, included the promotion of equality between men and women. And the 1985 Nairobi Forward Looking Strategies for the Advancement of Women grew out of the World Conference to Review and Appraise the Achievements of the UN Decade for Women. See Report of the World Conference to Review and Appraise the Achievements of the United Nations Decade for Women: Equality, Development and Peace (1986).

32. Ratna Kapur (2002: 20–21) challenges the positive contribution of these tribunals, which often invite women who have experienced the most heinous human rights abuses. Kapur argues that these testimonies produce a sensationalized and essentializing (negative) culture and gender narrative in the process of rousing a strong reaction from the international community.

33. Preparations for the World Conference on Women: Action for Equality, Development and Peace (1992), held in Beijing in November 1995. The purpose of this conference was to review and appraise the advancement of women since 1985 in terms of the Nairobi Forward Looking Strategies for the Advancement of Women and to mobilize men and women at both the policy-making and grassroots levels to achieve their objectives.

34. Para. 137 also notes that women and children constitute some 80 percent of the world's millions of refugees and other displaced persons, including internally displaced persons. They are threatened by deprivation of property, goods, and services and deprivation of their right to return to their homes of origin, as well as by violence and insecurity.

35. The UN Secretary-General reiterated this sentiment: with respect to women's experience of conflict, women are increasingly seen not exclusively as victims of rape, but rather as exercising agency and adopting multiple roles that may include or exclude the victim role. For example, women and adolescent girls may also support fighting forces and prolong the conflict in numerous ways; they may infiltrate opposition groups for the purposes of passing information, hide or smuggle weapons under their clothing and via their children, and support or care for fighters. Individual women combine various roles at once, such as a displaced person, a community activist, a small business

owner, a soldier, and a homeless person (Secretary-General Report on Women, Peace and Security (2002), para. 47).

36. Security Council Resolution 872 (1993) established an international tribunal for the purpose of prosecuting persons responsible for serious violations of international humanitarian law committed in the territory of the former Yugoslavia.

37. The UN Commission on Human Rights was established in 1946 and replaced by the UN Human Rights Commission in 2006.

38. Website of the Office of the High Commissioner for Human Rights, http://www.ohchr.org/EN/HRBodies/SP/Pages/Introduction.aspx.

Chapter 2. All the Women Were Raped

1. For the mandates of the prosecutor, the president of the trial chamber, and the trial chambers, see ICTR Statute, art. 10-15 and 17–19.

2. Akayesu Amended Indictment 06-06-1997: Akayesu was the mayor of Taba Commune and was responsible for maintaining law and public order in his commune. At least two thousand Tutsis were killed in Taba between 7 April and the end of June 1994, while he was still in power. The prosecutor charged that the killings in Taba were committed openly and were so widespread that, as mayor, Akayesu must have known about them. Although he had the authority and responsibility to do so, Akayesu never attempted in any way to prevent the killing of Tutsis in the commune. He was found guilty of genocide; direct and public incitement to commit genocide; and the crimes against humanity of extermination, murder, torture, rape, and other inhuman acts. See also Akayesu Judgment 02-09-1998.

3. Muhimana et al. Amended Indictment 20-10-2000: Muhimana was the counselor of Gishyita commune in the Kibuye prefecture. He was charged with acting individually and in concert with others to mobilize civilians and gendarmes in the persecution of Tutsi civilians in the Kibuye prefecture and Bisesero area. He was convicted of genocide and rape and murder as crimes against humanity. See also Muhimana Judgment and Sentence 28-04-2005.

4. Gacumbitsi Indictment 01-06-2001: Gacumbitsi was the mayor of Rusumo commune in the Kibungo prefecture. He was charged with ordering, instigating, participating in, and aiding and abetting in genocidal massacres and rapes. He failed to take reasonable measures to prevent soldiers, gendarmes, militias, and civilian militias under his authority from the persecution of Tutsi civilians. Sexual violence was widespread and systematic in Rusumo commune. He was convicted of genocide, and extermination, rape, and murder as crimes against humanity. See also Gacumbitsi Judgment 17-06-2004.

5. Niyitegeka Indictment 11-07-1997: Niyitegeka was a journalist and the minister of information of the interim government on 9 April. He was a member of the ruling party, the Mouvement Démocratique Républicain (MDR), and its chairman in the Kibuye Prefecture (1991–1994). He was also a member of the national political bureau. He was charged with individually committing acts of genocide and crimes against

humanity and using his authority to incite the persecution of Tutsis. He was convicted of genocide, conspiracy to commit genocide, direct and public incitement to commit genocide, and the crimes against humanity of extermination, murder, and other inhumane acts. See also Niyitegeka Judgment 16-05-2003.

6. Ntuyahaga Indictment 26-09-1998: Ntuyahaga was a major in the Rwandan Army at the outset of the genocide. As an officer of the armed forces, he was charged with responsibility for the genocide and widespread atrocities committed by the army against the Tutsi civilian population. He was also charged with failing to protect Prime Minister Agathe Uwingiliyimana from assassination and for facilitating the killing of Belgian peacekeepers. The prosecutor withdrew the indictment in order to allow the Belgian government to prosecute Ntuyahaga. The ICTR indictment was withdrawn and Ntuyahaga was released. He voluntarily surrendered to the Belgian government and was convicted of the murder of the Belgian peacekeepers in July 2007. He is now serving a twenty-year sentence in Belgium.

7. Bagosora Amended Indictment 31-07-1998: Bagosora held the office of *directeur de cabinet* in Rwanda's Ministry of Defense. In this capacity he managed the day-to-day affairs of the ministry in the absence of the defense minister. In the buildup to the genocide, he presided over a military commission mandated to design a "Final Solution" that would exterminate Tutsi civilians in Rwanda. He was the highest authority in the Ministry of Defense during the genocide. He was convicted of genocide; the crimes against humanity of murder, the murder of peacekeepers, extermination, rape, persecution, other inhumane acts; and three counts of serious violations of Article 3 of the Geneva Conventions and Additional Protocol II as follows: violence to life, violence to the lives of the peacekeepers, and outrages upon personal dignity. See also Bagosora et al. Oral Summary 18-12-2008 and Bagosora et al. Judgment 18-12-2008.

8. Ndindiliyimana et al. Amended Indictment 25-10-2002: Ndindiliyimana was the chief of staff of the Gendarmerie Nationale. At the outset of the genocide, he formed the senior ranks of the interim government that led and conducted the genocide. He was found guilty of genocide, crimes against humanity (murder), crimes against humanity (extermination), and violations of Article 3 Common to Geneva Convention and Additional Protocol II (murder). The trial chamber considered mitigating factors, including Ndindiliyimana's character, his reputation as a political moderate who attempted to oppose extremist forces, his support for the Arusha Accords, his cooperation with UNAMIR, his attempts to stop the killings and to save the lives of Tutsi, and the insignificant degree of control that Ndindiliyimana actually exercised over the gendarmes in Rwanda during the events of 1994, in particular, his material ability to prevent and punish crimes. See also Ndindiliyimana et al. Judgment and Sentence 17-05-2011, para. 78, 79, 2188-2242.

9. See Zdravko Mucić et al. Judgment 16-11-1998, para. 159, and De Brouwer (2005: 27). See also article 38 of the Statute of the International Court of Justice, which names the sources of international law as international conventions, whether general or particular, establishing rules expressly recognized by the contesting states; international

custom, as evidence of a general practice accepted as law; the general principles of law recognized by civilized nations; judicial decisions; and the teachings of the most highly qualified publicists of the various nations, as subsidiary.

10. Chapter VII (art. 39–42) of the UN Charter addresses action to be taken by member states with respect to threats to the peace, breaches of the peace, and acts of aggression.

11. See Mibenge (2002) for a detailed description of early conflicts between the transitional government of Rwanda and the UN Security Council relating to temporal jurisdiction, sentencing practices, and the seat of the tribunal in Arusha.

12. This fundamental flaw in location is also tied to the association of Arusha with the failed Arusha Accords (1993) that many felt precipitated President Habyarimana's assassination and the genocide. Alice Karekezi, an observer of the ICTR, stated in an interview that "Arusha where the international tribunal has its seat . . . is in the memory of Rwandese a sign of failure. . . . I spoke of the Arusha Agreement on August '93. . . . It was a failure . . . a failure which [sic] name is Genocide" (Karekezi 2008).

13. This brief and general history draws extensively from the timeline of the conflict advanced by the case law of the International Criminal Tribunal for Rwanda.

14. The nature of the ethnic or racial distinction and division in Rwanda is debated by scholars. My own position is that at different precolonial, colonial, and postcolonial periods, ethnicity was a semifluid political, social, cultural, and even economic construct.

15. From 1990 onward, the political assassinations of Hutu opposition leaders by rival parties was a prominent feature of politics in Rwanda. See Taylor (1999b: 158–59) for accounts of assassinations and reprisal assassinations between Hutu factions from the North and South. However, the political assassinations following the assassination of President Habyarimana are widely described as representing a shift from political rivalry to genocidal massacres. The assassination of Juvenal Habyarimana, Agathe Uwilingiyimana, and other senior Hutu politicians was necessary to create a power vacuum leading to the formation of a ruling party that could effect the genocidal campaign.

16. For the role of media discourse and propaganda inciting genocide, see Cassandra Cotton (2007), Nikki Slocum-Bradley (2008), and Daniel Rothbart and Thomas Bartlett (2008).

17. Participation in killings differed throughout Rwanda. In some places, the authorities as well as civilians killed readily and vigorously; in other areas, such as central and southern Rwanda, where the Tutsi were numerous and well integrated and where the ruling party had few supporters, many Hutu refused initial orders to kill and even joined Tutsi in fighting off assailants. Only under punitive actions, ranging from fines to threats of death, did the Hutu give up their opposition to genocide. See Human Rights Watch (1999b: 11).

18. See Paul Magnarella (1997) for an overview of Security Council Resolutions, General Assembly Resolutions, the ICTR statute, and other legal and judicial responses to the genocide.

19. Binaifer Nowrojee (2007: 109) points out that no rape charges were even brought by the Office of the Prosecutor in 70 percent of the adjudicated cases. In the 30 percent that included rape charges, only 10 percent were found guilty for their role in the widespread sexual violence. Double that number, 20 percent, were acquitted because the court found that the prosecutor had not proved this charge beyond a reasonable doubt. See also Breton-Le Goff (2002) for an analysis of trends in sexual violence prosecutions in indictments by the ICTR from 1995 to 2002.

20. Honoré Rakotomanana, the first deputy prosecutor of the ICTR (1995–1997), stated in an interview that "the reason they have not collected rape testimonies is because African women don't want to talk about rape. . . . We haven't received any real complaints. It's rare in investigations that women refer to rape." See Human Rights Watch (1996).

21. Fiona De Londras (2009: 12) describes the reorientation of prosecutorial priorities following the arrival of Carla del Ponte as prosecutor in 1999. On taking office, Del Ponte announced her intention to prosecute 153 suspects by 2005. This ambitious plan required the "streamlining" or "rationalization" of the Office of the Prosecutor (OTP), which included dismantling the investigation unit dedicated to examining and investigating crimes relating to sexual violence (President of the ICTR 2001). Apparently, a clear prosecutorial decision was taken to deprioritize sexual violence, possibly because investigating and prosecuting such crimes is especially labor and resource intensive, and instead to focus on other crimes. The incongruence between the marginalization of sexual violence by the OTP and its centrality to the Rwandan genocide is clear and holds clear implications for the position of sexual violence before the tribunals: it is important as long as it does not get in the way of other, more easily prosecuted crimes. Strong protests were posted by feminist groups such as the NGO Coalition for Women's Human Rights (2002) against the prosecutor's decision not to pursue sexual violence charges in the Cyangugu and Muvunyi cases despite the prosecutor's possession of comprehensive evidence of sexual violence. See Muvunyi Decision on the Prosecutor's Motion for Leave to File an Amended Indictment 23-02-2005. See also Ntagerura, Bagambiki and Imanishimwe Decision on the Application to File an Amicus Curiae Brief 24-05-2001.

22. Nowrojee (2007: 113) speaks further of the prosecutor's "squandered opportunities," "periods of neglect," and "repeated mistakes" in the investigation and prosecution of sexual violence. Interviews conducted by Buss (2009:152) with tribunal staff from the OTP and Registry reveal some concurrence with the major criticisms from observers: a shifting political commitment by the OTP, the poor investigation of sexual crimes and the poor drafting of rape charges in indictments.

23. Nowrojee (2005: 4 and 24) describes one notorious incident in the Nyiramasuhuko et al. (Amended Indictment 01-03-2001), when trial chamber judges apparently burst out laughing while witness TA, a victim of multiple rapes during the genocide, was being cross-examined in inappropriate detail about the events leading up to her rape.

24. See the Special Rapporteur (1998), para. 11 and 12, for victims' concerns about the ability of the Victim and Witness Unit (VWU) to protect them from repercussions

after testifying. She raises, from the victim's perspective, issues of relocation and claims of violent reprisals, among other concerns. The report also includes a response from the VWU describing the logistical and financial challenges it faces in providing protection to victims and witnesses.

25. This protracted civil war has been the subject of various studies and even international court action. See the International Court of Justice's Press Release 2002/15, referring to the Democratic Republic of the Congo's proceedings for provisional measures against Rwanda citing massive human rights violations by Rwanda on Congolese territory. The application of the DRC was ultimately dismissed when the International Court of Justice found that it had no jurisdiction to entertain the application. See also Press Release 2006/4 of 3 February 2006, referring to armed activities on the territory of the Congo.

26. See Lydia Polgreen (2008) for a detailed account of the regional conflict involving the Congo-based Hutu militia force known as the FDLR (Forces Démocratiques de Libération du Rwanda), numerous Congolese rebel groups, and Congolese civilians. For accounts of the nature of the sexual violence against women in the DRC and impediments to justice, see Human Rights Watch (2005), Amnesty International (2008), and De Vries (2007).

27. Security Council Resolution 955 (1994) establishes an international tribunal "for the sole purpose of prosecuting persons responsible for genocide and other serious violations of international humanitarian law committed in the territory of Rwanda and Rwandan citizens responsible for genocide and other such violations committed in the territory of neighboring States, between 1 January 1994 and 31 December 1994 and to this end to adopt the Statute of the International Criminal Tribunal for Rwanda."

28. This emphasis is made more pronounced when one considers that the International Criminal Tribunal for the Former Yugoslavia (ICTY) was created to prosecute persons responsible for serious violations of international humanitarian law committed in the territory of the former Yugoslavia since 1991. There was no reference to "genocide" in the enacting statute despite the strong allegations of genocide and ethnic cleansing made against the Serb government by the media and United Nations human rights investigators before the establishment of the tribunal.

29. Genocide Convention (1948), art. 2(2)(d) (Imposing measures intended to prevent births within the group) and art. 2(2)(e) (Forcibly transferring children of the group to another group). I note that the attendant gender role of rearing children is also widely understood to be a biological function as women's so-called maternal instinct is often linked to hormonal and other physical attributes, such as producing milk or having higher levels of estrogen.

30. Ní Aoláin (2000b: 57) concluded (and I find it applicable to the case at hand) with respect to the laws of war that it is a construction that "lacks breadth, encompassing only a fraction of what women actually experienced as sexual harm and which was intended as such by their captors."

31. Taken from the testimony of witness JJ as heard by the Special Rapporteur on 24

October 1997 when observing the trial against Jean-Paul Akayesu at the International Criminal Tribunal for Rwanda, Arusha. *Interahamwe* refers to Hutu militia groups during the 1994 genocide. See Special Rapporteur (1998): para. 10.

32. This analysis would apply also in cases where the victim of rape is visibly pregnant or carrying a nursing child. In the major cultures of the world, these factors raise greater public outrage in cases of rape and other forms of gender-based violence. Victim testimony from the major conflicts of the 1990s all include variations on the rape and mutilation of pregnant women.

33. UN General Assembly Resolutions A/Res/59/137 and A/Res/64/226 recognized the extremely high number of traumatized children and women victims of rape and sexual violence, and urged the international community to provide adequate assistance to them—specifically in the shape of justice programs. See also the Report of the Secretary General on Assistance to Survivors of the 1994 Genocide in Rwanda. It provides a status report of the challenges to the delivery of relief and rehabilitation assistance by the United Nations and its partners to survivors of the 1994 genocide in Rwanda (2009).

34. ICTR Statute Article 3, Crimes Against Humanity: "The International Tribunal for Rwanda shall have the power to prosecute persons responsible for the following crimes when committed as part of a widespread or systematic attack against any civilian population on national, political, ethnic, racial or religious grounds: a) Murder; b) Extermination; c) Enslavement; d) Deportation; e) Imprisonment; f) Torture; g) Rape; h) Persecutions on political, racial and religious grounds; i) Other inhumane acts."

35. See also Meredeth Turshen's (2001: 65) theory that there is economic value in women's reproductive and productive potential as well as their right to property. It was not until 2000 that a law on inheritance and marriage settlements granted women individual property rights in Rwanda.

36. "Although Beatrice was not wealthy, she had hired a local man to do work for her. In the violence following April 6, 1994, that man demanded sex from Beatrice. She perceived his demands as coming from a desire to exert his authority over a woman who occupied a different class than him" (2008a).

37. A second companion, described as a Hutu woman, is able to take two of the murdered woman's Tutsi children and pass them off as her own, thus saving their lives (Buss 2008a).

38. Jayashri Srikantiah (2007: 199) provides an excellent analysis of the limits of agency in the context of trafficking. It provides a useful analogy with women's agency and its limits in the context of armed conflict.

39. This account of being tracked down and sexually assaulted was repeated ad verbatim in the Amended Indictment against Ndindiliyimana et al. (25-10-2002, para. 5.7). The Bagosora judgment (oral summary) repeats that "the Prime Minister fled her home and hid at a neighboring compound. She was found, killed and then sexually assaulted" (18-12-2008, para. 23).

40. The trial chamber in the Niyitegeka judgment was confronted with a similar violation of a dead (as opposed to dying) woman. It decided that vaginally penetrating

a corpse with a stick could not be rape but still amounted to a crime against humanity under the category of "other inhumane act" (16-05-2003, para. 463–667).

41. The term "Hutu Power" has come to define a political movement that was spelled out by the Hutu Ten Commandments, a manifesto for ethnic segregation and exclusion. The primary goal of Hutu Power was to preserve Hutu dominance and supremacy in all areas of life and reject any form of power sharing between the extremist political parties and Tutsi or Hutu opposition parties. It demanded absolute loyalty to the ruling party and at its most extreme manifestation called for the extermination of the Tutsi as well as Hutu opponents to the government of Juvenal Habyarimana.

42. This claim should not be taken to suggest that rape and other forms of sexual violence were widespread in Rwanda before the conflict. Christopher Taylor (1999b: 157–58) observes that in more peaceful times, Rwanda was not characterized by a high incidence of rape. However, after the 1990 invasion of Rwanda by the RPF, the nation became increasingly militarized and violent. Sexual violence became widespread, but this was not a "normal" state of affairs.

43. Others have noted that all Tutsi women were targeted for rape and that educated, elite women were attacked regardless of their ethnicity (Mzvondiwa Ntombizodwa 2007: 101, quoting Newbury 1988).

44. The Bagosora Amended Indictment describes the early years of Rwanda's First Republic as under the domination of the Hutu of central and southern Rwanda—led by Gregoire Kayibanda. However, in 1973, ethnic and political tension between the North and South resulted in a military coup by General Juvenal Habyarimana on 5 July, shifting power from civilian to military hands and from the Hutu of central Rwanda to the Hutu of the northern prefectures of Gisenyi and Ruhengeri (Habyarimana's native region) (31-07-1998, para. 1.2 and 1.3). See also Mamdani (2000) for a detailed account and analysis of the North-South political and economic divide in Rwanda. See Peter Uvin (1998) for a detailed study of the *Akazu* northern power base. And Erin K. Baines (2003: 485) argues persuasively that the *Akazu* spurred on anti-Tutsi discourse as a means of diverting attention from class and regional tensions in Rwanda.

45. See the reference in the Kambanda Judgment and Sentence (04-09-1998, para. 39 (iv)). "Jean Kambanda acknowledges his participation in a high level security meeting at Gitarama in April 1994 between the President, Theodore Sindikubwabo, himself and the Chief of Staff of the Rwandan Armed Forces (FAR) and others, which discussed FAR's support in the fight against the Rwanda Patriotic Front (RPF) and its 'accomplices', understood to be the Tutsi and Moderate Hutu."

46. Sexual mutilation is listed alongside such genocidal measures as forced sterilization in the Rutaganda (06-12-1999), Akayesu (02-09-1998), and Musema (27-01-2000), Judgements under Article 2(2)(d) of the statute (genocide as a measure to prevent births). See also the Akayesu Judgment, para. 507.

47. Bagosora Trial Chamber Decision on motions for judgement of acquittal (02-02-2005 [at note 63]).

48. In the context of the armed conflict in the former Yugoslavia and elsewhere,

Dubravka Zarkov (1997) explains the low reporting of sexual violence against men as linked to the fact that masculinity is inseparable from power and thus unimaginable as victimized. Victimized man is not a man. Within the definition of masculinity in our societies, men are always and only rapists and thus unrapable.

49. Dallaire testified as follows regarding sexual violence: "Some of the sites . . . and you could see by the layout of the women and so on that rape and then mutilation had happened . . . that is I am speaking about my observers and myself that young girls, young women, would be laid out with their dresses over their heads, the legs spread and bent. You could see what seemed to be semen drying or dried. And it all indicated to me that these women were raped. And then a variety of materials were crushed or implanted into their vaginas; their breasts were cut off. . . . A number of the women had their breasts cut off or their stomach open. . . . I would say generally at the sites you could find younger girls and young women who had been raped or, you know, deducting that they were raped. . . . I would say that not many sites that were reported did not have such scenes of rape" (Bagosora Trial Chamber Decision on motions for judgment of acquittal, 02-02-2005 [at note 63]).

50. Sivakumaran (2007: 257–58) notes that in some conflicts, the sexual violence seems sporadic and ad hoc, while in others, it is clearly more systematic. He provides an illustrative list of conflicts where sexual violence against men has been chronicled in the more distant past as well as in contemporary conflicts—in Ancient Persia and the Crusades, as well as by the Ancient Greek, Chinese, Amalekite, Egyptian, and Norse armies. It has occurred in the conflicts in El Salvador, Chile, Guatemala, and Argentina. It has been perpetrated in the conflicts in Greece, Northern Ireland, Chechnya, Turkey, and the former Yugoslavia. It has been a feature of the conflicts in Sri Lanka, Iraq-Kuwait, Coalition-Iraq, and the Sino-Japanese war. It has been present in the conflicts in Liberia, Sierra Leone, Kenya, Sudan, the Central African Republic, Burundi, Uganda, Rwanda, the Democratic Republic of the Congo, Zimbabwe, and South Africa.

51. There has been some discussion of the symbolic meanings of castration in Rwanda. See Alison Des Forges's explanation that in precolonial times some Tutsi kings would decorate a ceremonial drum with the genitalia of defeated enemy rulers (2007: 45). Hutu propaganda used this historical image to circulate a false claim that Burundi's president was castrated, when in fact he was killed by a bayonet blow to his chest in 1993. J. L. Ranck (1998: 45) produces a lurid cartoon depicting the first elected president of Burundi, Ndadaye, hanging on a cross while the leaders of the RPF castrate him. The cartoon caption reads: "Finish off this stupid Hutu, let us hang his genitals on a drum." It could also be argued that the castration of Kabanda was understood at the local level as toppling or emasculating Tutsi kings.

52. Katherine M. Franke (1997–98: 1158 and 1160) examines sexual acts being used as an instrument of gender- and race-based terror in a case of policy brutality in the form of sodomy and argues that any body part could be considered a sexual or intimate body part depending on the context.

53. Franke (1997–98: 1168–69) makes a similar observation of the ICTY proceed-

ings in the Meakic (also known as Mejakic) case. Zeljko Mejakic was the Commander of a detention camp established by Serbian forces in a former mining complex in the village of Omarska, in northwestern Bosnia and Herzegovina during the conflict. This camp was notorious for its subhuman living conditions, harsh interrogations, severe beatings, killings and sexual assault of non-Serb detainees. Franke argues that the case acknowledges the sexual element of torture that women suffered while concealing the sexual element suffered by men in comparable contexts and conditions. The torture and humiliation of female prisoners was prosecuted as wilfully causing great suffering or serious injury to body or health and rape, but the torture and humiliation of male prisoners, even when it specifically targeted the genitals, was prosecuted as willfully causing great suffering or serious injury to body or health and other inhumane acts. The Tadic case provides another example. Dusan Tadic was the President of the Local Board of the Serb Democratic party in Kozarac and the charges against him also centered on grave abuses committed against prisoners at Omarska Camp, including torture, rape and killing. In the Tadic case, the defendant was charged with committing a crime against humanity under Article 5(g) (rape) against a woman prisoner. However, in another case, the defendants beat a male prisoner, after which they forced two other male prisoners to lick the beaten prisoner's buttocks and penis, and then to bite off one of his testicles. The prosecutor charged Tadic with a grave breach under Article 2(b) (torture or other inhumane treatment), a violation of the laws or customs of war under Article 3 (cruel treatment), and a crime against humanity under Article 5(i) (other inhumane acts) of the statute. Dusko Tadic was not charged with violating Article 5(g) of the Statute (rape), even though the conduct included forced fellation and other sex- and gender-based violence.

54. Kirsten Campbell (2007: 422–24) complicates my analysis somewhat with her analysis of the legal proceedings before the ICTY. Campbell points out the disproportionately high number of cases and counts involving sexual violence against male victims. First, prosecutions against these cases are in clear contrast to the general lack of visibility of male sexual assault in the Yugoslavian conflict, both in terms of media coverage and in comparison to the institutional and legal focus on sexual violence against women. Second, the high proportion of counts of male sexual assault is surprising given the generally agreed on predominance of sexual violence against female victims in the conflict. The high number of male sexual violence prosecutions by the ICTY does not reflect the presumed gender differential patterns and scales of sexual assaults. While the highest estimated number of women raped is fifty thousand, there are no claims that the number of men sexually assaulted is comparable to the widespread and systematic rape of women. She accounts for this discrepancy by the fact that the high number of counts of male sexual assault may be explained by the disproportionate number of male witnesses appearing before the tribunal. Eighty percent of tribunal witnesses were male and 20 percent were female.

55. Gerard Prunier (1995: 292) writes that as the French humanitarian intervention in Rwanda began, the Hutu extremist radio invited Hutu women to welcome the

Europeans: "You Hutu girls wash yourselves and put on a good dress to welcome our French allies. The Tutsi girls are all dead, so now you have your chance." I regard this as a disingenuous call from the radio and its allusion that witness BJ and other Hutu girls enjoyed uninterrupted lives secure from violence during the genocide. The radio invitation was also framed in the context of the colonial ideology of Hamitism, which depicted Tutsi women as more desirable to European men than Hutu women. See Taylor (1999a: 156).

56. Opportunistic killings of Hutus by Hutu militias were also widespread. "Young men who hung around the [road] barriers, often drunk or under the influence of marijuana, plundered, raped and even killed Hutu bystanders and passers-by. Sometimes they confiscated identity cards from victims so that they could claim that they were Tutsi. They paraded through the sectors with the firearms meant for use at the barriers, extorting what they wanted from unarmed neighbors" (Des Forges 1999: 572).

57. Nils Christie (1977: 4) describes lawyers as particularly good at stealing conflicts from victims.

Chapter 3. All Men Rape

1. In my early interaction with the chief, I regarded him as a "big" man and comported myself as a "small" woman (his daughter). I later realized that the chief regarded and spoke to me as a "big" woman because of such features as my apparent worldliness and advanced education. I adjusted my interaction with him accordingly.

2. Bintu was a "big" woman. When I walked down the street with her, women applauded or cheered her on as we passed. She was one of the few elected women government representatives in the region. I also observed that she participated in and even dominated my conversations with the mayor and the chief. Richard Fanthorpe's (2007: 10) observations on the role of the chief shed some light on my deferential attitude toward Chief Sesay. He writes that chiefs remain leading political figures in rural areas. It remains their prerogative to authorize all initiation rites in their chiefdoms. Paramount and other high-ranking chiefs are expected to serve as patrons of these rites, attending them in person if possible and making contributions to their cost and the public celebrations that accompany them.

3. It is this final point that probably made me burst out laughing. Fortunately, the chief and his nephew, our chaperone, joined in my laughter, although it was obviously at their (men's) expense.

4. My understanding of the family and marriage positions them as institutions comparable to the Truth Commission or Special Court in their capacity to identify, legitimate, and censor gender roles and gender-based violence.

5. Both the African Charter on the Rights and Welfare of the Child (1990) (art. 1) and the Convention on the Rights of the Child (1989) (art. 1) provide that a child is any human being below the age of eighteen years. The TRC report specifically indicates its adherence to the Convention on the Rights of the Child, the Women's Convention, the Universal Declaration of Human Rights, ICCPR, ICESCR, and other major human

rights instruments (Truth and Reconciliation Report, vol. 1, cap.1, para. 54–55 [hereafter TRC 1:1: 54–55]).

6. One assumes that if two fifteen-year-olds were married, both the bride and the groom would be regarded by human rights advocates as children and as victims of early marriage.

7. In 2009, Sierra Leone's Parliament passed the Registration of Customary Marriage and Divorce Act (Chapter 140 of the Laws of Sierra Leone, Act No. 1 of 2007). This law does not prohibit child marriage per se, but it requires parental consent if either spouse is below the age of eighteen (art. 5). Moreover, customary courts are given the power to dissolve a marriage if either spouse is under the age of eighteen at the time of marriage and when requesting the dissolution. It is still too early to predict how successfully children will be able to avail themselves of this law. The TRC concluded its report several years before the enactment of this new legislation, and so I do not refer to the 2009 act further.

8. The report describes the enslavement of boys and girls during the armed conflict. In order to make a gender distinction on enslavement, the TRC commissioners refer to girls' experience of slavery as "forced marriage," "bush marriage," and "sexual slavery." And while I argue that any conjoining of bush and forced with marriage wrongly suggests a conjugal arrangement and conceals the egregiousness of enslavement, I do use these terms as they are applied by the TRC. However, I use the term early marriage in place of forced marriage, bush marriage, and sexual slavery.

9. The nature and extent of gender-based violence is rarely fully revealed in transitional justice processes. Gender-based violence is often depoliticized so as to remove it from the political domain. See Jocelyn Getgen (2009) for a critique of the Peruvian Truth Commission's exclusion of enforced sterilization of low-income indigenous Quechua-speaking women from its purview. The narrative of more than two hundred thousand affected women was denied a political acknowledgment.

10. The SLPP was defeated in a democratic election in the 2007 general elections by the All People's Congress (APC) led by President Bai Koroma. The peaceful handover of power was favorably reported by the international press. See Will Ross, "Democracy Wins in Sierra Leone Polls," 18 September 2007.

11. I found it especially helpful that Ferme and Coulter studied communities in very different geographical regions and at different points in the armed conflict. This variation created some sharp differences in their representation of practices and traditions and served as a reminder that gender is experienced differently in different locations, times, and spaces. See also Caroline Bledsoe (1980) and Bledsoe and Anastasia Gage (1994) for ethnographic research on women, marriage, and gender in Sierra Leone. See also Janneke van Gog (2008) for an excellent study of the experience of girls and women returning to their hometowns after abduction and forced marriage by armed groups.

12. Carolyn Nordstrom explains that "people have learned that, politically and militarily, knowledge is a dangerous thing. How did one come by such knowledge? Who was one fraternizing with to gain such knowledge? And worse, how are people using

or misusing, this knowledge? These questions can result in death. When I first asked people who did not know me what was going on in the war, who the President was, or just about any other question, I often got the reply, I really don't know. As I sat and talked with people, shared food, explained my work and the people whose friendships I valued, made return trips, listened to their stories and shared my own, people's 'answers' changed. They did know what Mozambique was, who represented the power brokers" (1997: 81–82).

13. I thank Susan Shepler for pointing out to me that polygamous unions make it easier for Sierra Leonean women to maintain rights to the matrimonial home in the case of divorce.

14. This brief and general history draws extensively from the timeline of the conflict advanced by Keen (2005) and the TRC report.

15. The settlement of Freetown—the "province of freedom"—was established in 1787 as a British settlement and a settlement for former slaves. The Krios who constitute 2 percent to 3 percent of the population are descended from former slaves from the United States, Britain, and Jamaica who settled in Freetown between 1787 and 1850. Krios are also made up of recaptives, or slaves rescued from slave ships stopped by the British Navy on the high seas after the enactment of the Anti-Slavery Act of 1807 (Hirsch 2005: 23).

16. The Panel of Experts for Sierra Leone (2000) was appointed pursuant to Security Council Resolution 1306 to investigate the link between the trade in diamonds and the trade in weapons. The experts described "conflict diamonds" as "diamonds that originate in areas controlled by forces fighting the legitimate and internationally recognized government of the relevant country" (para. 144).

17. David Keen (2005: 1, 147, 155, and 158) describes how at different stages in the conflict, such states as Guinea, Liberia, and Libya were implicated as having directly acted as belligerents in the conflict or as supporting actors. Regional and international forces have also played active roles in the conflict, such as the Economic Community of West Africa (ECOWAS) and the UN Mission in Sierra Leone. And at a crucial moment, the Sierra Leone government called on the South African mercenary corporation Executive Outcomes to challenge ex–Sierra Leone Army and rebel fighters. ECOWAS and Executive Outcomes also enjoyed close cooperation not only with government forces but also with the Civil Defense Force whose leaders were charged by the prosecutor with war crimes and crimes against humanity. To varying degrees some members of these groups have also been implicated in organized crime and human rights violations, such as trafficking in arms, diamonds, drugs, and women and children.

18. I describe the Peace Accord in greater detail in Chapter 4.

19. Ferme's (2001: 101) description of how relationships between sons-in-law and mothers-in-law are marked by avoidances and strictly proscribed contact and behavior make the specific cultural sensitivities of this incident clearer.

20. See also the testimony of witnesses about brothers forced to identify and then rape their sisters (TRC 3b:3: 295 and 332).

21. Four members of the commission were Sierra Leonean: the commission chairman, Bishop Joseph Humper; the commission deputy chair, Laura Marcus-Jones, a former judge of the Sierra Leone High Court; Professor John Kamara, a college principal and veterinary surgeon; and Sylvanus Torto, a professor of public administration. The remaining three foreign commissioners were proposed by the UN high commissioner for human rights: Satang Jow, a former minister of education in the Gambia; William Schabas, a Canadian and a former director of the Irish Center for Human Rights; and Yasmin Sooka, a South African lawyer and former commissioner on the TRC in South Africa.

22. See Rashida Manjoo (2007), Beth Goldblatt and Sheila Meintjes (1996), and Ross (2005) for gender critiques of the conditions for the inclusion and exclusion of women's experience of political violence in South Africa's truth-telling process.

23. See Fiona Ross (2005: 230) who criticizes the omission of the torture of women political activists from the South African Truth and Reconciliation process. She describes that the Trauma Center for Victims of Violence conducted research on detainees in Zwelethemba in 1995. None of the five women in the focus group who had been detained were interviewed in the process. Ross attributes this omission to the fact that the center recorded only those who were detained for periods exceeding forty-eight hours. The center made the mistaken assumption that those detained for shorter periods were not tortured or otherwise mistreated.

24. The Campaign for Good Governance, Council of Churches, and Forum for African Women Educationalists are NGOs based in Sierra Leone that at different stages of the war attempted to provide such services as health care and counseling to survivors of sexual violence. They collated evidence of the widespread rape of women and girls. Physicians for Human Rights (2002: 10) acknowledges their support in their own research process.

25. During the tenure of the Sierra Leone TRC, UNIFEM was the women's fund at the United Nations. It focused its activities on supporting the implementation at the national level of existing international commitments to advance gender equality. Advancing gender justice, transforming harmful traditional practices, and ending violence against women were some of its principle thematic areas. The Beijing Platform for Action and the Convention on the Elimination of All Forms of Discrimination Against Women provided the framework for the work of UNIFEM. Security Council Resolutions 1325 (2000) on women, peace, and security, and 1820 (2008) on sexual violence in conflict became crucial references for UNIFEM's work in support of women in conflict and postconflict situations. In July 2010, UNIFEM and three other UN entities that focused exclusively on gender equality and women's empowerment were merged in order to create UN Women, the UN entity for gender equality and empowerment of women. The creation of UN Women came about as part of the UN reform agenda, bringing together resources and mandates for greater impact.

26. Funding for the commission primarily came from international sources, including $500,000 to more than $1 million from the United States, the United Kingdom, and

the European Union, as well as significant support from Denmark, Norway, and Sweden. The Sierra Leone government also provided some initial support, which covered the costs of the commission's first office space (International Center for Transitional Justice 2004: 3).

27. According to the report, the TRC Legal and Reconciliation Unit worked intensively with witnesses and a number of counseling agencies in Sierra Leone. The unit provided witnesses with referrals to counseling agencies where appropriate. The reconciliation unit also ensured that follow-up sessions were provided by trained counselors after the hearings. Counselors visited the witnesses later in their homes and completed questionnaires that dealt with the impact and consequences of appearing before the commission (TRC 3b:3: 28).

28. There were also many women who opted to make written statements only to the commission and who chose not to appear before any hearings. As far as girls under eighteen years of age were concerned, the commission employed a policy that all testimony would be given in-camera and that mechanisms would be found to have this testimony heard without making identities public (TRC 3b:3: 26; TRC 4:4: 19). Statement takers also received training on how to take testimonies sensitively from children who had been sexually violated (TRC 4:4: 18).

29. I thank Professor Noya Rimalt's students in the course on Women, Gender and War at Georgetown University Law School (20 April 2009) for questioning the conclusion in an early draft of this work that a chapter on women indicated gender mainstreaming into the narrative of the TRC report. Mainstreaming gender and women's concerns into the report would have required that women's experience was also inserted into the different volumes of the report. Gender mainstreaming has been described as the strategy established by member states of the United Nations to achieve gender equality. Gender mainstreaming is defined in the Economic and Social Council's agreed conclusions 1997/2 as "the process of assessing the implications for women and men of any planned action, including legislation, policies or programs in all areas and at all levels. It is a strategy for making the concerns and experiences of women and men an integral dimension of design, implementation, monitoring, and evaluation of policies and programs in all political, economic, and societal spheres so that women and men benefit equally and inequality is not perpetuated. The ultimate goal is to achieve gender equality. Gender mainstreaming entails bringing the perceptions, experience, knowledge, and interests of women and men to bear on policy making, planning, and decision making." See Secretary-General (2002), para. 13: 4.

30. On education, politics, economic status, and sexuality, see TRC 3b:3: 35–42, 43–60, 67–70, and 81–83, respectively.

31. The link between early marriage and other violations of the rights of the girl child are supported by notable child experts. "She's (the child bride) likely to experience early and forced sexual intercourse without protection, exposing her to potential injury and infection. In childbearing, she is more likely than a woman who marries late to experience complications, give birth to an underweight or stillborn baby or die. She

must drop out of school, stunting her intellectual growth and often isolating her from her peers" (World Vision 2008: 3).

32. See Barbara Arneil's (2001: 43–44) critique of second-wave feminists who used wives as a unit of analysis for a universal woman.

33. *The Queen v. Tang* (2008), 16. The High Court of Australia cautioned against inappropriate applications of the term *slavery*. It underscored that it was important to recognize that harsh and exploitative labor conditions do not themselves amount to slavery. The court used the example that prostitution is exploitative; however, it is not a form of slavery.

34. Judge Kirby, *The Queen v. Tang* (2008), 49 quoting Simpson's (2007: 159) use of the phrase "enemy of mankind."

35. Section 27 provides that no law shall make any provision that is a discriminator either of itself or in its effect. And section 27 (4) makes exceptions for adoption, marriage, divorce, burial, the sharing and distribution of property on death, or other interests of personal law.

36. The Mohammedan Act, Chapter 96 of the Laws of Sierra Leone (1960); the Civil Marriage Act, Chapter 97 of the Laws of Sierra Leone (1960); the Matrimonial Causes Act, Chapter 102 of the Laws of Sierra Leone (1960).

37. See Coulter's (2005) account of the initiation of over a hundred girls in a town that had been destroyed by war. She notes how the initiation was the first since the war displaced villagers and that its new postconflict utility was to reconfigure disrupted family and kinship ties. The initiation ceremony also illustrated that war had altered gender relations, for example, the visible presence of men in the celebratory stage of the ceremony was a postwar innovation. Coulter shows that initiation became more than a women's journey or event; in this case, it was a central event in the reconciliation and rehabilitation of a war-devastated community.

38. I began to suspect that if he failed to meet his financial obligations toward the child, the mother of the child could alienate the child from him and transfer paternity to another financial provider.

39. While visiting the chief, I observed a flurry of movement throughout the day in a large square outside his residence. The court was in session. Sessions were presided over by the chief's representatives, and they resolved all manner of conflicts. One case involved a member of a men's society who was fined for not informing the chief before launching a male initiation ceremony. My interview with the chief was interrupted as his representative asked the chief to suggest the fine that should be paid by the wrongdoer.

40. There is no single centralized women's society, and each society is shaped by many influences, including Islamic culture, political history, tribal composition, coastal or interior geography, and border influences.

41. Richard Fanthorpe makes the interesting point that rape, along with other serious crimes, violates Sande as well as the laws of male societies. Violations of these laws might be adjudicated by the society in the bush, and those found guilty of the most

serious violations might even be sacrificed to assuage this spirit (Fanthorpe 2007: 4, quoting Bellman 1975: 125).

42. It is unclear what effect the civil war had on the activities and cohesion of women's secret societies. In contrast, it has been noted by researchers that leaders of the male societies were often targeted for humiliating beatings and attacks by rebels (Henry 2006: 386). Fanthorpe (2007: 13–14) writes that the end of the armed conflict has seen the secret societies reestablished and mass initiations of boys and girls hosted throughout the country. He also describes that the societies have increased in stature as a result of their ability to mobilize their youth in national and local government elections.

43. Human rights studies are wont to reduce the Bundu to a society that mutilates girls' genitalia.

44. Ratna Kapur (2002: 10) also points out that a gratuitous connection is invoked between culture and violence in the Third World, although it is not invoked in a similar way when discussing violence against women in various Western contexts.

45. Heather Baldwin (2006: 20–21) cautions that portraying women as agentless victims helps raise sympathy for their plight, but the harm is that they come to believe they are victims unable to have any control over their own lives. This belief may lead to serious consequences for their mental and physical health. In addition, researchers and aid workers respond with interventions and programs focusing only on the victim status.

46. Stripping women of agency when they take on roles that contravene the roles of their gender socialization is similar to the stripping away of children's agency by the language of human rights. Susan Shepler (2005) describes how former child combatants strategically resist or assist in their depoliticization by human rights workers.

47. Human Rights Watch suggested a link between bush marriages and marriages by capture which were common at the turn of the nineteenth to twentieth centuries in Sierra Leone according to a study by Sierra Leonean legal scholar Joko Smart (HRW 2002: 42, quoting Smart 1983: 29). "In tribal wars, the conquerors would kill the male inhabitants of the vanquished village and capture the women who subsequently became the wives of the conquerors. The 'marriage' was validated by the captor's public declaration of his intention to cohabit with his captive wife. Such a wife was regarded as a slave and her children could not inherit from their father" (ibid.). I consider the juxtaposition of these two forms of abduction by Human Rights Watch too facile and tenuous to maintain. I have not encountered other suggestions that combatants justified sexual slavery or forced marriage by claiming to be reviving a practice that fell into disuse a century or more ago.

48. In peacetime, Coulter (2006: 188) explained that in the Kuranko community, women were politically and economically subordinate. However, the most prestigious position for a woman was that of Mammy Queen. The responsibilities of the Mammy Queen were often to mediate between parties and to settle disputes within households, between men and women, and also between women. Indeed, certain grievances would be brought to the Mammy Queen even before being passed on to the chief or traditional courts.

49. *Bush* has taken on negative connotations with respect to original or indigenous peoples in central and southern Africa who have retained their traditional livelihoods and lifestyles and are regarded by urbanites as immune to modernization and therefore backward. I encountered this attitude as a teenager living in Kenya and Namibia, where being called "bush" or a "bush man" was a taunt about one's village manners (village being regarded by urbanites as uncivilized) and later saw this in Rwanda where the Twa forest gatherers were regarded as inferior and uneducatable "bush people" who could not advance themselves. See Liisa Malkki (1995) for a detailed analysis of the depiction of the Twa as "bush" by Hutu refugees in Tanzania.

50. However, as an interesting aside, I refer to Coulter's account of an interview where a girl explained that the rebels did not live in the bush as one would think but that they occupied village homes and turned villagers out to sleep in the bush: "The villagers lived in the bush, we lived in their houses" (2006: 181). And Ferme points out that in times of conflict "farms and work spaces hidden in the forest are the first temporary shelters for refugees from villages, and hence they are the potential beginnings of new permanent settlement" (2001: 14).

51. Traditionally, initiation was a protracted period, up to two years in the bush with girls of the same age, and girls who underwent initiation through the secret women's societies were treated with deference and feted by their communities (Human Rights Watch 2003: 27).

52. Just as girls endured a prolonged initiation process in the bush, so did boys under the auspices of the men's Poro Society.

53. Myriam Denov and Christine Gervais (2007: 604–5) also point out that these survival strategies ultimately reflect poorly on women who survive captivity and enslavement because women slaves are seen as untrustworthy, promiscuous, and seductive. They are considered to have chosen to align themselves with their captors and are responsible for their own victimization.

54. Dyan Mazurana and Susan McKay (2004: 3) write that in Sierra Leone, the higher the status of a male commander, the more abducted girls he was given as a wife.

55. This form of attachment is also addressed as a form of psychobiological consequence of severe trauma. One of the most pernicious effects of torture is that in their attempt to maintain attachment bonds, victims turn to the nearest source of hope to regain a state of psychological and physiological calm. Under situations of emotional deprivation, they may develop strong emotional ties to their tormentors. This traumatic bonding is thought to occur among hostages, abused children, and abused spouses. The need to stay attached contributes to the denial and dissociation of the traumatic experience, and in order to preserve an image of safety and to avoid losing the hope of the existence of a protector, victims may begin to organize their lives around maintaining a bond with and placating their captors (Saporta and van der Kolk 1992: 154–55).

56. Arneil (2001: 46) demonstrates that attempts by feminist scholars to universalize women are dismissive of such issues as race and class. She exemplifies this within the American context where the African American women's historical experience of slavery

and the native Americans' experience of colonization must be included before feminists can claim to include all groups of women in their analysis.

57. Special Rapporteur (2007): para. 52.

58. Ferme describes a young woman with a "big woman" status. She was from outside Kpuawala and married to a younger man whom she supported financially. Unlike him, she had attended school and could write and speak English. She was cosmopolitan in her grooming and attire and stated that she was not a "bush person" like her neighbors. During her business trips (she was a dancer and a businesswoman and often traveled to perform), her mother-in-law lamented her absence because her daughter-in-law took care of her and fed her unlike her own son who had not supported her in years (Ferme 2001: 174).

59. Ferme explains that the links between marriage and slavery help place in context the degrees of dependence that underpin the Mende notion that everybody is under someone's patronage. She used this patronage notion to consider marriage and other relations as incorporated within a family universe.

60. See also Kiran Cunningham's (1996: 336) study on gender, marriage, and power in Mende society in Sierra Leone. She writes that "in addition a woman may marry a man from the outside, live in his village, divorce him, marry another man, and move back to Kpetema to be with him."

61. Cunningham (1996: 346) also suggests that extended visits to one's natal village were a ruse for women to divorce and seek remarriage.

62. What might pass as marriage under a Western construction of the union may not be a marriage in Sierra Leone or other African cultures. A man and woman may cohabit and bear children, but they may not be married until the man makes his final installment of gifts to the woman's parents. Or a man and woman may not undergo a marriage ceremony until the woman courted falls pregnant, thereby affirming that the union is fertile. See Kenneth Omeje's (2001) excellent critique of community activists, women's rights campaigners, missionaries, and the state's failure to "liberate" women known as cult women from sexual exploitation among the "Bangu" peoples of sub-Saharan Africa. He illustrates that confronting this harmful traditional practice from a doctrinalist paradigm, particularly human rights theory, has only reinforced the practice and further disempowered women victims of the practice.

63. "Sometimes they (police, school principals, chiefs, Poro members) would be forcibly sodomized, branded with RUF slogans, or executed. All were deliberate attempts to attack or overturn shared values, ideological norms and traditional institutions" (Henry 2006: 386).

Chapter 4. All Women Are Slaves

1. The brief nature of my stay in Sierra Leone meant that I conducted interviews solely with the Victims and Witness Unit at the Sierra Leone Special Court. I was unsuccessful in securing an invitation as a guest researcher from the Registry before my arrival or in establishing confidential relationships with Special Court staff. The lack of

institutional accreditation made even a physical entrance into the Special Court burdensome (due to security checks), which shaped my decision to focus on more accessible local institutions, such as the police, the Ministry of Gender, NGOs, and international NGOs. Jayashri Srikantiah's (2007: 158) experience and observation that despite an inability to access empirical evidence from institutions, hypotheses can be drawn by researchers in order to identify flaws in the institutional implementation of gendered processes was instructive to me at this point.

2. A suspended death sentence hung over Sankoh's head at the signing of the Lomé accord. This arose from his arrest (detention under house arrest) in 1997 by Nigeria, which subsequently handed him over to Sierra Leone in July 1999. The United Nations, the Organization of African Unity, and the Commonwealth were moral guarantors of the Lomé accord. Representatives of Benin, Burkina Faso, Ghana, Guinea, Liberia, Libya, Mali, Nigeria, Britain, and the United States were also present (Adebayo 2002: 97–99). The special representative of the secretary-general appended to his signature of the Lomé agreement a statement that the United Nations did not consider that the amnesty provisions of the agreement would apply to international crimes of genocide, crimes against humanity, war crimes, and other serious violations of international humanitarian law.

3. Other important factors for the failure of the Lomé accord include the destabilizing influence of Liberia, which continued to provide arms and purchase diamonds from the RUF; obstructionism by the RUF leadership; the exclusion of the AFRC-SLA from the agreement; the weakness of support from the international community in the demobilization process; and the weak international peacekeeping effort (Keen 2005: 253).

4. Special provisions were provided for the potential prosecution of juvenile offenders, or those children over fifteen but under eighteen years of age at the time of the crime (Special Court Statute, art. 8 [2]).

5. Foday Sankoh died of ill health on 29 July 2003 in the hospital in UN custody. Samuel Hinga Norman, a leader of the CDF, died on 22 February 2007 following surgery while in UN custody. Sam Bockarie, an RUF general, was reportedly shot dead in the Ivory Coast on 6 May 2005 when Liberian government forces attempted to arrest him. Johnny Paul Koroma, the former coup leader and head of state of Sierra Leone (May 1997–February 1998), was indicted as the chairman of the AFRC. He fled Sierra Leone before he could be tried. His whereabouts are still unknown.

6. The Special Court Agreement Act was enacted by Sierra Leone's Parliament in 2002. The act gives legal effect to the powers and competences of the Special Court within the legal system of Sierra Leone.

7. An Amnesty International press release also broached concern that the work of the Special Court made little impact on Sierra Leoneans (Amnesty International 2009). I was in Sierra Leone when Charles Taylor was extradited to Sierra Leone by the Nigerian government on 29 March 2007, and Samuel Hinga Norman was airlifted to Dakar, Senegal, on 17 February 2007 for surgery and died from medical complications on 22 February 2007. Norman was described in the CDF indictment as the national

coordinator of the CDF and the leader and commander of the Kamajors with *de jure* and *de facto* command and control over operations of that group. On both occasions, I called one of my Sierra Leonean host families for a security briefing before leaving my lodgings to head into downtown Freetown. My informants in this case were a couple, Mr. and Mrs. Koroma (pseudonyms), both of whom worked at a ministry in downtown Freetown. Mr. Koroma was a proud card-carrying Kamajor. In both cases, my family members were amused that I imagined news from the Special Court would affect their routines. They told me in no uncertain terms that I should continue with my regular business and report to work exactly as they intended to. Their message to me was that life went on for Sierra Leoneans, and the work and dramas of the Special Court held no special significance for them.

8. The Statute for the Sierra Leone Special Court provides as follows: "Article 5 (a)— Crimes under Sierra Leonean Law: The Special Court shall have the power to prosecute persons who have committed the following crimes under Sierra Leonean law: (a) Offences relating to the abuse of girls under the Prevention of Cruelty to Children Act, 1926 (Cap. 31): (i) Abusing a girl under 13 years of age, contrary to section 6; (ii) Abusing a girl between 13 and 14 years of age, contrary to section 7; (iii) Abduction of a girl for immoral purposes, contrary to section 12."

9. According to Chapter 31 of the Laws of Sierra Leone, article 15 of the PCCA provides that "when a person is accused of defiling a minor it shall be a sufficient defence if the person so charged had reasonable cause to believe that the girl was of or above the specified age." And article 10 provides that "defiling a minor is a misdemeanor—unless the child was a common prostitute or of known immoral character."

10. Three of the Special Court judges are Sierra Leonean, namely, Justice Rosolu John Bankole Thompson (trial chamber), Justice Jon Kamanda (appeals chamber), and Justice George Gelaga King (presiding judge of the appeals chamber). Other judges have originated from Senegal, Uganda, Cameroon, Nigeria, Samoa, Austria, Canada, and Northern Ireland.

11. Similarly, a high representation of women in Parliament should not lead to the presumption that women-friendly laws will follow. If the institutional culture of Parliament remains patriarchal, colonial, and elitist, its laws will continue to reflect these characteristics irrespective of the gender of parliamentarians. I thank Karen Colvard of the H. F. Guggenheim Foundation for raising this point at the Emory University conference on Gender Violence and Gender Justice in May 2009 in her presentation "Western Feminism and Gender Issues in the Developing World."

12. Article 8 (1) of the statute provides that the Special Court and domestic courts shall have concurrent jurisdiction and article 8 (2) provides that the Special Court shall have primacy over national courts, and further, that at any stage of the procedure, the Special Court may formally request a national court to defer its competence.

13. Article 6 (c) of the charter of the International Military Tribunal (Nuremberg) does not refer to rape as a crime against humanity and only includes "murder, extermination, enslavement, deportation and other inhumane acts committed against any

civilian population, before or during the war; or persecutions on political, racial or religious grounds."

14. Article 2 of the Sierra Leone Special Court Statute provides that "the Special Court shall have the power to prosecute persons who committed the following crimes as part of a widespread or systematic attack against any civilian population: (a) Murder, (b) extermination, (c) enslavement, (d) deportation, (e) imprisonment, (f) torture, (g) rape, sexual slavery, enforced prostitution, forced pregnancy and any other form of sexual violence; (h) persecution on political, racial, ethnic or religious grounds; and (i) other inhumane acts." Article 7 of the statute of the ICC (Rome Statute) extends the crime of rape in a similar fashion: "Rape, sexual slavery, enforced prostitution, forced pregnancy, enforced sterilisation, or any other form of sexual violence of comparable gravity are listed."

15. Article 3 addresses violations of article 3 common to the Geneva Conventions including, "(a) violence to life, health and physical or mental well-being of persons, in particular murder as well as cruel treatment such as torture, mutilation or . . . and (e) outrages upon personal dignity, in particular humiliating and degrading treatment, rape, enforced prostitution and any form of indecent assault."

16. I compare the Special Court prosecutor's "gender mandate" to the ICTR prosecutor's "genocide mandate." As I described in Chapter 2, the "genocide mandate" was contained in the Security Council Resolution stating the international community's conviction that genocide occurred in Rwanda. Based on this mandate, it would have been unthinkable for the prosecutor for Rwanda not to include a genocide charge in every indictment it issued. I elaborated on this genocide mandate and its impact on the prosecutor's investigations of gender-based violence in Chapter 2.

17. Article 16 (4) of the Special Court statute divides the WVU into two units: a protection, security, and movement unit with nearly thirty staff members and a psychosocial support unit with around ten staff members. The former manages all logistical and security arrangements for witnesses, including the identification and maintenance of safe houses.

18. Dyan Mazurana and Khristopher Carlson (2004: 12) provide an interesting perspective of a former girl fighter who argued that combining "marriage" with fighting was a strategy for security. At the age of fifteen, she was an RUF frontline fighter, and felt it was better to be a fighter as well as a wife to a common soldier because you could better protect yourself with your own weapon, you had greater access to food and loot, and your chances of escape were greater, unlike captive "wives" of commanders who were closely guarded with little chance of escape. This testimony shows how girls donned different roles strategically and that classifying this fifteen-year-old rebel frontline fighter as a wife and ending the analysis at that point is to produce an incomplete and even demeaning narrative.

19. Sesay, Kallon and Gbao Judgment Summary 25-02-2009. The trial chamber confirmed the prosecutor's limited interpretation of active hostilities: the chamber has found that after their military training, the children were assigned specific functions

within the RUF. Certain children were retained by commanders for domestic labor or to go on food-finding missions, and the chamber has found that this use does not constitute active participation in hostilities (para. 49).

20. See Susan Shepler (2005) on the cultural context of child recruitment into fighting forces in Sierra Leone. Other groundbreaking studies on the central role that girl soldiers play in Africa's armed conflicts include Mazurana and Carlson (2004), Save the Children (2004–2005) and Mazurana and McKay (2006).

21. Sierra Leone ended its national demobilization, demilitarization, and repatriation program in December 2003. Since the program began in 1998, 72,500 former combatants have been demobilized (Mazurana and Carlson 2004: 2, quoting Bradley and Fusato and Maughan 2002). This figure includes 4,751 women (6.5 percent) and 6,787 children (9.4 percent), of whom 506 are girls (Mazurana and Carlson 2004: 2).

22. The Sierra Leone Special Court's WVU demonstrated a commitment and an ability to provide follow-up supervision and support to witnesses. See Saleem Vahidy et al. (2009) for an internal WVU review of the services it provided to victims and witnesses.

23. The point is that boys also suffer serious social and psychological repercussions after returning from the bush. This experience may not be linked to bearing children or the loss of virginity as is the case with girls returning from the bush. However, this should not *per se* make their experience less harmful. It should be viewed instead through a gender lens, which would reveal the very specific ways boys experienced harm and how it affected their reintegration after demobilization.

24. The Berkeley Report does not elucidate on whether the prosecutor regarded Aisha's relationship as "marriage" or "sexual slavery" and whether the witnesses and victims services supported her in seeking alternatives to this relationship. The report notes that Aisha is a pseudonym.

25. According to officials organizing the demobilization, demilitarization, and repatriation process, "wives," including those who had been abducted, were to be explicitly excluded from formal entrance into the program. The focus of the program was on the main fighting forces, and "minority" groups would not be taken into consideration. However, since women and girls frequently played multiple roles, a narrow classification of them as "wives" resulted in programmatic errors. Mazurana and Carlson (2004) found that while 60 percent of women and girls indicated having served as a "wife," only 8 percent claimed that it was their primary responsibility or role.

26. I adopt these terms in this specific instance in the context of the North as representing (in the most broad and simplistic way) the wealthy developed nations and the South as representing developing nations. In this paradigm, the South is dependent on the North for development assistance, agency, and policy. The North is positioned as economically superior and leverages this status to assert moral and cultural superiority.

27. The UN rule of law tools for postconflict states refer to the fact that children are often excluded from justice processes by "widespread traditional views of childhood across all regions of the world" (OHCHR 2009: 20).

28. See Balakrishnan Rajagopal (2006) for a discussion on the West as the source of the international human rights law framework.

29. See Mats Utas (2005) for a detailed analysis and case study of civilian girls and women in the context of the Liberian civil war who employed their sexuality as a survival tool to compete for and win senior military men and the relative security these relationships provided.

30. I borrow the phrase "deviants of childhood" from Laura Suski (2009: 207).

31. The report concludes that women and girls were deliberately targeted by all armed groups. It also condemns the sexual exploitation of women and girls by humanitarian workers who were known to have demanded sex in exchange for assistance.

32. Mazurana and Carlson (2004: 11) point out that the government supplied the CDF with weapons and financial and logistical support.

33. The decision not to exempt some groups from accountability is in sharp contrast to the South Africa Truth Commission, which failed to comprehensively facilitate truth-telling processes with respect to violence committed in extraterritorial liberation camps of the (now ruling) African National Congress.

34. Another myth that was left untouched by the Sierra Leone Truth Commission was that women did not play a military role in the CDF. Mazurana and Carlson's (2004: 12–13) field-based data on the demobilization, demilitarization, and repatriation process revealed the presence of fully initiated female members in the CDF beginning in the early 1990s. Women were included in all ceremonies, amulets, and scarification; they served as frontline fighters, commanders, initiators, spiritual leaders, medics, herbalists, spies, and cooks.

35. See Macartan Humphreys and Jeremy M. Weinstein (2004: 10) whose interviews with CDF combatants revealed many instances of sexual violence. "One Kamajor farmer noted that whether or not you were raped depended on whether the woman was pregnant, nursing a child, or younger than 12 years old."

36. Norman et al. Prosecution Request to Amend Indictment, 02-08-2004.

37. Ibid., para. 10 (c).

38. Sesay, Kallon and Gbao Decision on Prosecution Application for Leave to File an Interlocutory Appeal against Decision 01-06-2004, para. 42.

39. Norman, Fofana and Kondewa Majority Decision on the Prosecution's Application 02-08-2004, paras. 4 and 6.

40. Norman, Fofana and Kondewa Decision on Prosecution Appeal Against the Trial Chamber's Decision of 2 August 2004, 19-01-2005, para. 44.

41. Shanee Stepakoff and Michelle Staggs Kelsall (2007) present various accounts of the chamber calling for the redaction of any hint of sexual violence in the testimony of victims and witnesses.

42. For a legal commentary on the appeals chamber decision, see Chiseche Mibenge (2007b).

43. In contrast, the ICTR was very amenable to extending time limits with respect to the amendment of indictments. In the Barayagwiza case, the trial chambers

acknowledged that an extension of time could prejudice the rights of the accused and ordered that the accused receive damages for such harm (Mibenge 2007a).

44. Rosalind Shaw (2007: 194–95) details a teenager's testimony describing the brutal attack and murder of his mother by an RUF rebel. The rebel was known to the family and had in the past made unwelcome sexual advances toward the boy's mother. On the same day of the murder, the CDF took over their village. The boy and his siblings reported the murder to the CDF who summarily killed the man they identified. The testimony brings to light that in some cases civilians were involved in reprisal killings, either directly or through informing on others. Colin Knox and Rachel Monaghan (2002: 51–60) in the context of political violence in South Africa and Ireland present the ambiguities and contestation in responding to the question, who are the victims?

45. Norman, Fofana and Kondewa Dissenting Opinion of Judge Pierre Boutet on the Decision on Prosecution Request for Leave to Amend the Indictment 05-08-2004, paras. 23-33 (hereafter Dissenting Opinion of Boutet).

46. See Valerie Oosterveld (2009) for the most comprehensive account of the appeal chamber's review of the trial chamber decision. It should be noted that in this appeal the prosecutor did not seek the remittal of the case to the trial chamber for the consideration of additional counts on gender crimes even if the appeal chamber upheld his request. See Fofana and Kondewa Appeals Judgment 28-05-2008, para. 415.

47. Fofana and Kondewa, Partially Dissenting Opinion of Judge Winter 28-05-2008, para. 73.

48. Special Rapporteur (2008).

49. See also Yvonne Corcoran Nantes (1998: 160–61), who describes sexual violence as inherent to slavery in Brazilian society where female slaves were also expected to engage in sexual labor. From an early age, pubescent females were given to young males in the household and were subject to all manner of abuse. The master of the household would expect to have the female slave of his choosing wherever, however, and whenever it pleased him. It was also customary to offer slave women to male house guests. Marriage and family life were generally denied to the slave population.

50. Pamela Bridgewater (2005: 118) describes legislation enacted in part of the United States regulating this reality. These laws focused on prohibiting children born from such rapes from inheriting property from their owner-father.

51. The Thirteenth Amendment to the U.S. Constitution officially abolished slavery and involuntary servitude, except as punishment for a crime. It was adopted on 6 December 1865.

52. Smith's analysis is particularly relevant as she describes the sexual exploitation of incarcerated women as a modern corollary to slavery.

53. See Rachel Anderson (2005) for a descriptive account of harsh detention and labor conditions, including medical experimentation against the Herero people. See also Krista O'Donnell's (1999: 36) research on domestic work in German South West Africa in 1904–1915 and the white patriarchal control over the bodies of black women workers. She describes the exercise of the so-called paternal right of correction over work-

ers through sexual violence against African women. Women were viewed primarily as reproductive or sexual agents, and the punishments reflected this attitude, for example, treading on pregnant women until they miscarried.

54. Kunarac et al. Judgment 22-02-2001.

55. The factors confirming the enslavement included that 1) the women were not allowed to leave the apartment unaccompanied by Kovac and were also psychologically detained because even if they had managed to escape from the apartment, they would have had nowhere to go (they were also aware of the risks if they were recaptured); 2) Kovac sold three of the witnesses; 3) twice he handed two of the witnesses over to a group of soldiers for almost a fortnight, and they were continuously raped by them; 4) he engaged in mistreatment, such as beating; 5) he laid claim to exclusivity over one of his victims whom he raped almost every night he spent in the apartment; 6) the women lived in poor conditions and suffered from lack of food; and 7) the women had to do household chores, including cooking and cleaning the apartment.

56. Kunarac et al. Appeals Chamber Judgment 12-06-2002, para. 117.

57. In the 1980s, literature began to emerge that focused on the psychological as well as sexological aspects of torture. Political exiles in Europe, who were from the Middle East, North Africa, and Latin America, began to provide insight into the sexual traumatization arising from torture focusing on the sex and gender of prisoners. This form of torture can consist of forcing the prisoners to take part in humiliating or deviant sexual relations (this characterized the torture of male Muslim prisoners in the Yugoslav war context). Torture can be carried out by inflicting physical pain to the genitals, which brings the prisoner to associate pain or panic with sexuality. I believe that greater attention to this literature from the psychological or medical fields would enhance the competence of legal researchers and practitioners dealing with gender and gross violations of human rights. See Inger Agger (1989: 309).

58. There is very often a disconnection between real and imagined gender realities. For example, a community may agree that men are the breadwinners and have primary responsibility for financially maintaining the home. However, men and women may be expressing an idealized image of men's gender role while denying the reality that women in their community have historically and traditionally created and maintained the bulk of household wealth through their commercial transactions in the informal sector. I thank Brandon Hamber of INCOR University of Ulster for raising this point at the Emory University Conference on Gender Violence and Gender Justice in May 2009 in his presentation "Masculinity and Transition. Crisis or Confusion?" Christopher Taylor (1999b: 155) in his analysis of gender hegemonies in the context of the Rwanda genocide also notes that Hutu extremists sought to reassert a male dominance that had probably never existed in Rwanda's actual history.

59. See Phillip Piccigallo (1979: 179–80) for one of the few existing detailed studies of the entire Allied Eastern war crimes operations. The study reveals that Dutch military courts tried 448 cases involving more Japanese accused (1,038) than any other nation save the United States. A civilian hotel proprietor in Batavia, Washio Awochi, was

charged with the war crime of the enforced prostitution of twelve Dutch women and girls. He was found guilty and sentenced to ten years' imprisonment.

60. The Women's International War Crimes Tribunal for the Trial of Japanese Military Sexual Slavery, summary of findings (2000), para. 24.

61. Special Rapporteur (1995): paras. 11, 17, and 30.

62. See Yuki Tanaka (2002).

63. While the Women's Tribunal identifies sexual enslavement as misogynistic and racist, its analysis falls short of distinguishing between the different racial categories and hierarchies existing between and among Asian peoples.

64. See the Finalized Draft Text of the Elements of Crimes (2000).

65. I recall my own surprise at waking up at dawn to find Uncle Abduh, the "man of the house," cooking fish on a brazier on the back porch in preparation for a family outing to the beach. I asked a dependent in the home if Uncle Abduh always cooked, and she replied, "He cooks the fish." Uncle Abduh cooking the family meal while the women swept or in my case slept may not be representative of the distribution of labor in Sierra Leonean households. I use the story to show how my own impression of traditional male (i.e., fishing) and female tasks (i.e., cooking the fish) may not tally with the Sierra Leonean reality. Certainly, according to Shepler's study, the gendered division of labor is far from clear with respect to children.

66. This would not be disruptive; it would be counterproductive, as it could be used to normalize girls' experience and even sexual violence.

67. See also Just Detention International's reporting on the particular vulnerability of incarcerated gay and transgender men. These groups are disproportionately targeted for rape and other forms of sexual violence than self-identified heterosexual men in the same conditions of detention. My own analysis concludes that men who are not authentic men, in this case, violating the laws of heteronormality, are singled out by apparently heterosexual men for sexual violence as a form of discipline, humiliation, or punishment (Fact Sheet 2009a and 2009b).

68. I acknowledge the ease with which I accept the dominant image of a sexual predator as male. I therefore add the recently released (and very disruptive) statistics from the U.S. Bureau of Justice, which reveal high levels of sexual abuse of youth in juvenile facilities. Approximately 95 percent of all youth (male and female) reporting staff sexual misconduct said they had been victimized by female facility staff. In 2008, 42 percent of staff in juvenile facilities under state jurisdiction were female (U.S. Department of Justice 2010).

Conclusion

1. I thank Professor Pamela Scully (Emory University, Women's Studies) and Professor Sita Ranchod-Nilsson (Institute of Developing Nations at Emory University) for bringing a diverse group of scholars together at the May 2009 Emory University conference on Gender Violence and Gender Justice: Critical Perspectives on Post-Conflict Societies. We shared vivid and intimate discussions on "brown women" and "those

women" and on the ways our own theory and practice reproduce these harmful categories. The candid disclosure of many speakers at this conference strongly motivated the tone of this final chapter.

2. See Salah M. Hassan (2003: 115–27) for a critical essay of the "scientific" lens that objectified African women's bodies. Hassan describes the work of artist Hassan Musa as deconstructing or adjusting this and other lenses through his representations of iconic black women performers such as Sara Baartman and Josephine Baker.

3. The term *rape culture* makes rape appear to be a practice that is unchallenged and even accepted by all African men and women.

Works Cited

Adedeji, Adebayo. *Comprehending and Mastering African Conflicts*. London: Zed Books, 1999.

Adekeye, Adebajo. *Building Peace in West Africa: Liberia, Sierra Leone and Guinea Bissau*. Boulder, Colo.: Lynne Rienner, 2002.

Agger, Inger. "Sexual Torture of Political Prisoners: An Overview." *Journal of Traumatic Stress* 2:3 (1989): 305–18.

Akhavan, Payam. "The Crime of Genocide in the ICTR Jurisprudence." *Journal of International Criminal Justice* 3:4 (2005): 989–1006.

Amnesty International. *Sierra Leone: Childhood—A Casualty of Conflict*. Amnesty International, 30 August 2000.

———. *Marked for Death: Rape Survivors Living with HIV/AIDS in Rwanda*. Amnesty International, 5 April 2004.

———. *Democratic Republic of Congo North Kivu: No End to War on Women and Children*. Amnesty International, 29 September 2008.

———. Press release. "Sierra Leoneans Unaware of Charles Taylor Trial." 14 July 2009.

Anderson, Rachel J. "Redressing Colonial Genocide Under International Law: The Hereros' Case of Action Against Germany." *California Law Review* 93 (2005): 1155–89.

Anghie, Antony. "The Evolution of International Law: Colonial and Postcolonial Realities." In *International Law and the Third World: Reshaping Justice*, ed. Richard Falk, Balakrishnan Rajagapol, and Jacqueline Stevens, 35–50. New York: Routledge-Cavendish, 2008.

———. "Rethinking the Concept of Harm and Legal Categorizations of Sexual Violence During War." *Theoretical Inquiries in Law* 1:2 (2000a): 307–40.

———. "Sex-Based Violence and the Holocaust—A Reevaluation of Harms and Rights in International Law." *Yale Journal of Law and Feminism* 12:1 (2000b): 43–84.

Ní Aoláin, Fiounnuala D., and Rooney Eilish. "Underenforcement and Intersectionality: Gendered Aspects of Transition for Women." *International Journal of Transitional Justice* 1 (2007): 338–54.

———. "Women, Security and the Patriarchy of Internationalized Transitional Justice." University of Minnesota Law School, Minneapolis, Legal Studies Research Paper Series, No. 08-40, SSRN, 2008.

Argibay, Carmen M. "Sexual Slavery and the 'Comfort Women' of World War II." *Berkeley Journal of International Law* 22 (2001): 387–88.

Arneil, Barbara. "Women as Wives, Servants and Slaves: Rethinking the Public/Private Divide." *Canadian Journal of Political Science* 34:1 (2001): 29–54.

Askin, Kelly. D. "Sexual Violence in Decisions and Indictments of the Yugoslav and Rwandan Tribunals: Current Status." *American Journal of International Law* 93:1 (1999): 97–123.

———. "Prosecuting Wartime Rape and Other Gender-Related Crimes Under International Law: Extraordinary Advances, Enduring Obstacles." *Berkeley Journal of International Law* 21 (2003): 288–349.

Baines, Erin K. "Body Politics and the Rwanda Crisis." *Third World Quarterly* 24:3 (2003): 479–93.

Baldwin, Heather. "Fighting to Survive in Rwanda: War, Agency and Victimhood." Ph.D. diss., *Boston College Books and Theses,* paper AAI3238815, 2006.

Bellman, Beryl Larry. *Village of Curers and Assassins: On the Production of Fala Kpelle Cosmological Categories.* The Hague: Mouton, 1975.

Bennhold, Katrin. "The Female Factor: The Good Mother, and Modern Politician." *New York Times,* 17 January 2010a.

Bennhold, Katrin. "The Female Factor: In Germany, a Tradition Falls, and Women Rise." *New York Times,* 17 January 2010b.

Bledsoe, Caroline. *Women and Marriage in Kpelle Society.* Stanford, Calif.: Stanford University Press, 1980.

Bindel, Julie. "Why Is Rape So Easy to Get Away With?" *Guardian Unlimited,* 1 February 2007.

Bledsoe, Caroline, and Anastasia J. Gage. "The Effects of Education and the Social Stratification on Marriage and the Transition to Parenthood in Freetown, Sierra Leone." In *Nuptiality in Sub Saharan Africa: Contemporary Anthropological and Demographic Perspectives,* ed. Caroline H. Bledsoe and Gilles Pison, 148–67. Oxford: Clarendon, 1994.

Blommaert, Jan, Mary Bock, and Kay McCormick. "Narrative Inequality in the TRC Hearings: On the Hearability of Hidden Transcripts." In *Discourse and Human Rights Violations,* ed. Christine Anthonissen and Jan Blommaert, 33–64. Amsterdam: John Benjamins, 2007.

Boesten, Jelke. "Marrying Your Rapist: Domesticated War Crimes in Peru." In *Gendered Peace: Women's Struggles for Post-War Justice and Reconciliation,* ed. Donna Pankhurst, 205–27. New York: Routledge, 2008.

Bradley, Sean, Massimo Fusato, and Philippe Maughan. "Sierra Leone: Disarmament, Demobilization and Reintegration (DDR)." In *Findings Infobrief Africa Region,* ed. P. C. Mohan, no. 81. Washington, D.C.: World Bank, 2002.

Breton-Le Goff, Gaëlle. *Analysis of Trends in Sexual Violence Prosecutions in Indictments by the International Criminal Tribunal for Rwanda (ICTR) from November 1995 to November 2002.* Coalition of Women's Human Rights in Conflict Situations, 28 November 2002.

Bridgewater, Pamela D. "Ain't I a Slave: Slavery, Reproductive Abuse and Reparations." *University of California Women's Law Journal* 14 (2005): 89–161.

Brison, Susan J. "Surviving Sexual Violence: A Philosophical Perspective." In *Violence Against Women: Philosophical Perspectives,* ed. Stanley G. French , Wanda Teays, and Laura M. Purdy, 11–26. Ithaca, N.Y.: Cornell University Press, 1998.

———. "The Uses of Narrative in the Aftermath of Violence." In *On Feminist Ethics and Politics,* ed. Claudia Card, 200–26. Lawrence: University Press of Kansas, 1999.

Brook, Timothy., and Radhabinod Pal. "On the Rape of Nanking: The Tokyo Judgment and the Guilt of History." In *The Nanking Atrocity 1937–1938: Complicating the Picture,* ed. Bob Tadashi Wakabayashi, 149–80. New York: Berghahn, 2007.

Bunch, Charlotte, and Niam Reilly. *Demanding Accountability: The Global Campaign and Vienna Tribunal for Women's Human Rights.* New York: Center for Women's Global Leadership and UNIFEM, 1994.

Buss, Doris. The Curious Visibility of Wartime Rape: Gender and Ethnicity in International Criminal Law. *Windsor Journal of Access to Justice* 25 (2007), 3–22.

———. "Rethinking Rape as a Weapon of War." Unpublished manuscript, 2008a. Copy with author.

———. "Sexual Violence, Ethnicity and the Limits of Intersectionality in International Law." In *Intersectionality and Beyond: Law, Power and the Politics of Location,* ed. Emily Grabham, Davina Cooper, Jane Krishnadas, and Didi Herman, 105–23. London: Routledge-Cavendish, 2008b.

———. "Rethinking Rape as a Weapon of War." *Feminist Legal Studies* 17 (2009): 145–63.

Butalia, Urvashi. *The Other Side of Silence: Voices from the Partition of India.* Durham, N.C.: Duke University Press, 2000.

Byrnes, Andrew. "Women, Feminism and International Human Rights Law—Methodological Myopia, Fundamental Flaws or Meaningful Marginalisation? Some Current Issues." *Australian Year Book of International Law* 12 (1988): 205–40.

Campbell, Kirsten. "The Gender of Transitional Justice: Law, Sexual Violence and the International Criminal Tribunal for the Former Yugoslavia." *International Journal of Transitional Justice* 1 (2007): 411–32.

Card, Claudia. *The Atrocity Paradigm: A Theory of Evil.* New York: Oxford University Press, 2004.

Chamallas, Martha. "Lucky: The Sequel." *Ohio State University Moritz College of Law Working Paper Series,* Paper 15, 2005.

Charlesworth, Hilary. "Feminist Methods in International Law." *American Journal of International Law* 93 (1999): 379–94.

Christie, Nils. "Conflicts as Property." *British Journal of Criminology* 17:1 (1997): 1–14.

Cockburn, Cynthia. *Gender, Armed Conflict and Political Violence*. Washington D.C.: World Bank: 10 and 11 June 1999.

———. "The Gendered Dynamics of Armed Conflict and Political Violence." In *Gender, Armed, Conflict and Political Violence,* ed. Caroline O. N. Moser and Fiona C. Clark, 13–30. London: Zed, 2001.

Cole, Alison. "Prosecutor v. Gacumbitsi: The New Definition for Prosecuting Rape Under International Law." *International Criminal Law Review* 8:1–2 (2008): 55–86.

Colvard, Karen. "Western Feminism and Gender Issues in the Developing World." Conference on Gender Violence and Gender Justice. Emory University, Atlanta, Georgia, May 2009.

Cook, Nicolas. *Diamonds and Conflict: Policy Proposals and Background*. Washington, D.C.: Congressional Research Service/Library of Congress, 2000.

Corcoran Nantes, Yvonne. "Chattels and Concubines: Women and Slavery in Brazil." In *Gender and Catastrophe,* ed. Ronit Lentin, 155–70. London: Zed, 1998.

Cotton, Cassandra. 2007. "Where Radio Is King: Rwanda's Hate Radio and the Lessons Learned." *Atlantic International Studies Journal* 4 (Spring 2007), 4–11.

Coulter, Chris. "Reflections from the Field: A Girl's Initiation Ceremony in Northern Sierra Leone." *Anthropological Quarterly* 78:2 (2005): 431–41.

———. *Being a Bush Wife: Women's Lives Through War and Peace in Northern Sierra Leone*. Uppsala, Sweden: Uppsala University, 2006.

Crenshaw, Kimberlé. "Demarginalising the Intersection of Race and Sex: A Black Feminist Critique of Anti-Discrimination Doctrine, Feminist Theory and Anti-Racist Politics." *Feminist Theory and Antiracist Politics, University of Chicago Legal Forum* 139 (1989): 138–67.

Cruise O'Brien, Donal B. "Lost Generation? Youth Identity and State Decay in West Africa." In *Postcolonial Identities in Africa,* ed. Richard Werbner and Terence Ranger, 55–74. London: Zed, 1996.

Cullberg Weston, Marta. *War Is Not Over with the Last Bullet: Overcoming Obstacles in the Healing Process for Women in Bosnia-Herzegovina*. Stockholm: Kvinna till Kvinna Foundation, 2002.

Cunningham, Kiran. "Let's Go to My Place: Residence, Gender and Power in a Mende Community." In *Gender Kinship Power: A Comparative and Interdisciplinary History,* ed. Mary Jo Maynes, Anne Waltner, Birgitte Soland, and Ulrike Strasser, 335–51. New York: Routledge, 1996.

Dauer, Sheila. "Indivisible or Invisible, Women's Human Rights in the Public and Private Sphere." In *Women, Gender and Human Rights: A Global Perspective,* ed. Marjorie Agosin, 65–83. Piscataway, N.J.: Rutgers University Press, 2001.

De Brouwer, Anne-Marie. *Supranational Criminal Prosecution of Sexual Violence: The ICC and the Practice of the ICTY and the ICTR*. Antwerp: Intersentia, 2005.

De Londras, Fiona. "Prosecuting Sexual Violence in the Ad Hoc International Criminal Tribunals for Rwanda and the Former Yugoslavia." *University College Dublin Working Papers in Law, Criminology and Socio-Legal Studies*, Research Paper 06/2009, 2009.

De Vries, Janine. *Sexual Violence Against Women in Congo: Obstacles and Remedies for Judicial Assistance.* Leiden, Germany: Stichting NJCM-Boekerij, 2007.

Denov, Myriam, and Christine Gervais. "Negotiating (In)Security, Resistance, and Resourcefulness Among Girls Formerly Associated with Sierra Leone's Revolutionary United Front." *Signs: Journal of Women in Culture and Society* 32:4 (2007): 885–910.

Des Forges, Alison. "Call to Genocide: Radio in Rwanda 1994." In *The Media and the Rwanda Genocide,* ed. Allan Thompson, 41–55. London: Pluto, 2007.

———. *Leave None to Tell the Story: Genocide in Rwanda.* New York: Human Rights Watch and la Fédération Internationale des Ligues des Droits de l'Homme, 1 March 1999.

Diggs Mange, Monica. "The Formal Equality Theory in Practice: The Inability of Current Anti-Discrimination Law to Protect Conventions and Unconventional Persons." *Columbia Journal of Gender and Law* 16:1 (2007): 1–42.

Dirlik, Arif, "Culturalism as Hegemonic Ideology and Liberating Practice." *Cultural Critique* 6 (1987): 13–50.

Dixon, Rosalind. "Rape as a Crime in International Humanitarian Law: Where to from Here?" *European Journal of International Law* 13:3 (2002): 697–719.

Dolgopol, Ustinia, and Snehal Paranjape. *Comfort Women: An Unfinished Ordeal—Report of a Mission.* Geneva: International Commission of Jurists, 1994.

Enloe, Cynthia. *Globalization and Militarism: Feminists Make the Link.* New York: Rowman & Littlefield, 2007.

Erichsen, Casper W. *The Angel of Death Has Descended Violently Among Them: Concentration Camps and Prisoners-of-War in Namibia, 1904–8.* Leiden, Germany: African Studies Center, 2005.

Fanthorpe, Richard. *Sierra Leone: The Influence of the Secret Societies, with Special Reference to Female Genital Mutilation.* Geneva: Writenet/UNHCR, 2007.

Feliciati, Clara Chapdelaine. "Restorative Justice for the Girl Child in Post Conflict Rwanda." *Journal of International Women's Studies* 7:4 (2006): 14–35.

Ferguson, Niall. *Empire: The Rise and Demise of the British World Order and the Lessons for Global Power.* New York: Basic, 2003.

Ferme, Mariane C. *The Underneath of Things: Violence, History, and the Everyday in Sierra Leone.* Berkeley: University of California Press, 2001.

Finnegan, William. *A Complicated War: The Harrowing of Mozambique.* Berkeley: Universty of California Press, 1992.

Franke, Katherine M. "Putting Sex to Work." *Denver University Law Review* 75 (1997–98): 1139–80.

Futamura, Madoka. *War Crimes Tribunals and Transitional Justice: The Tokyo Trial and the Nuremberg Legacy.* New York: Routledge, 2008.

Gallagher, Anne. "Ending the Marginalisation: Strategies for Incorporating Women into the United Nations Human Rights System." *Human Rights Quarterly* 19 (1997): 283–333.

Gasana, Emmanuel, Jean-Bosco Butera, Deo Byanafashe, and Alice Karakezi. "Rwanda."

In *Comprehending and Mastering African Conflicts,* ed. Adebayo Adedeji, 141–73. London: Zed, 1999.

"Herero Massacre: General's Descendants Apologize for 'Germany's First Genocide.'" *Der Spiegel,* 10 August 2007.

Getgen, Jocelyn E. "Untold Truths: The Exclusion of Enforced Sterilizations from the Peruvian Truth Commission's Final Report." *Boston College Third World Law Journal* 29:1 (2009): 1–34.

van Gog, Janneke. *Coming Back from the Bush: Gender, Youth and Reintegration in Northern Sierra Leone.* Leiden, Germany: African Studies Center, 2008.

Goldblatt, Beth, and Sheila Meintjes. *Gender and the Truth and Reconciliation Commission: A Submission to the Truth and Reconciliation Commission.* Johannesburg: Center for Applied Legal Studies/Gender Research Project, 1996.

Goldstone, Richard J. "Prosecuting Rape as a War Crime." *Case Western Reserve Journal of International Law* 34:3 (2002): 277–86.

Hamber, Brandon. "Masculinity and Transition. Crisis or Confusion?" Conference on Gender Violence and Gender Justice. Emory University, Atlanta, Georgia, May 2009.

Happold, Matthew. "Child Soldiers in International Law: The Legal Regulation of Children's Participation in Hostilities." *Netherlands International Law Review* 47:1 (2000): 27–52.

Haroff-Tavel, Marion. "Coping with the Aftermath of Armed Conflict: The Role of the Humanitarian Community." *Refugee Survey Quarterly* 22:4 (2003): 185–94.

Hassan, Salah M. "Hassan Musa's ArtAfricanism: The Artist as a Critic." In *Looking Both Ways: Art of the Contemporary African Diaspora,* ed. Laurie Ann Farrell, 115–28. New York/Ghent: Museum for African Art and Snoeck, 2003.

Henry, Doug. "Violence and the Body: Somatic Expressions of Trauma and Vulnerability During War." *Medical Anthropology Quarterly* 20:3 (2006): 379–98.

Hidalgo, Jose, Hussein Sadruddin, and Natalia Walter. "Human Trafficking in the United States: Expanding Victim Protection Beyond Prosecution Witnesses." *Stanford Law and Policy Review* 16:2 (2005): 384–90.

Hirsch, John L. *Sierra Leone, Diamonds and the Struggle for Democracy.* International Peace Academy Occasional Paper Series. Boulder, Colo.: Lynne Rienner, 2005.

Human Rights Watch. *Shattered Lives: Sexual Violence During the Rwandan Genocide and Its Aftermath.* New York: Human Rights Watch, 4 September 1996.

——. *Getting Away with Murder, Mutilation, and Rape: New Testimony from Sierra Leone.* New York: Human Rights Watch, 24 June 1999a.

——. *Leave None to Tell the Story: The Genocide in Rwanda.* New York: Human Rights Watch, 1 March 1999b.

——. *We'll Kill You If You Cry: Sexual Violence in the Sierra Leone Conflict.* New York: Human Rights Watch, 15 January 2002.

——. *Seeking Justice: The Prosecution of Sexual Violence in the Congo War.* New York: Human Rights Watch, 7 March 2005.

Humphreys, Macartan, and Jeremy M. Weinstein. *Handling and Manhandling Civilians in Civil War*. Presented at the conference, Techniques of Violence in Civil War, PRIO, Oslo, Norway, August 20-21, 2004.

Humphreys, Macartan, and Jeremy M. Weinstein. "Handling and Manhandling Civilians in Civil War." *American Political Science Review* 100:3 (2006): 429-47.

Hyden, Goran. *Institutions, Power and Policy Outcomes in Africa*. London: Overseas Development Institute, 2008.

Hyun, Chulho. *Childhood Lost: Assistance for Children Orphaned by AIDS in Uganda*. New York: UNICEF, 2007.

International Center for Transitional Justice. *The Sierra Leone Truth and Reconciliation Commission: Reviewing the First Year*. New York: International Center for Transitional Justice, 2004.

International Court of Justice. "The Democratic Republic of the Congo (DRC) Initiates Proceedings against Rwanda citing Massive Human Rights Violations by Rwanda on Congolese Territory." Press Release 2002/15, 28 May 2002.

International Court of Justice . "Armed Activities on the Territory of the Congo." Press Release 2006/4, 3 February 2006.

International Crisis Group. *Sierra Leone: The State of Security and Governance*. New York: International Crisis Group, Africa Report 67, 2003.

Irish Commission to Inquire into Child Abuse. The Final Report of the Commission to Inquire into Child Abuse, 20 May 2009.

Jackson, Michael. The Kuranko: Dimensions of Social Reality in a West African Society. London Hurst, 1977.

Jacobson, Ruth. "Complicating 'Complexity': Integrating Gender into the Analysis of the Mozambican Conflict." *Third World Quarterly* 20:1 (1999): 175-87.

Jones, Adam. "Gender and Genocide in Rwanda." In *Gendercide and Genocide*, ed. Adam Jones, 98-137. Nashville: Vanderbilt University Press, 2004.

Just Detention International. "Fact Sheet: LGBTQ Detainees Chief Targets for Sexual Abuse in Detention." Los Angeles: Just Detention International, 2009a.

———. "Fact Sheet: Incarcerated Youth and Extreme Risk of Sexual Abuse." Los Angeles: Just Detention International, 2009b.

Kalshoven, Frits. *Constraints on the Waging of War*. New York: Springer, 2008.

Kapur, Ratna. "Postcolonial Erotic Disruptions: Legal Narratives of Culture, Sex, and Nation in India." *Columbia Journal of Gender and Law* 10 (2000-2001): 333.

———. "The Tragedy of Victimisation Rhetoric: Resurrecting the 'Native' Subject in International/ Postcolonial Feminist Legal Politics." *Harvard Human Rights Journal* 15:1 (2002): 1-28.

Karekezi, Alice. Interview with Harry Kreisler. *Justice for Women in Rwanda*, Conversations with History series, Institute of International Studies, Office of Media Services, University of Berkeley, (2008), http://www.youtube.com/watch?v=Gd_PAqy9Pi8.

Keen, David. *Conflict and Collusion in Sierra Leone*. New York: Palgrave, 2005.

Kelsall, Tim. *Going with the Grain in African Development?* Discussion paper no. 1. London: Overseas Development Institute, 2005.

Kimura, Maki. *Listening to Voices: Testimonies of "Comfort Women" of the Second World War.* London: LSE Gender Institute, New Working Paper Series 8, 2003.

Kirchner, Stefan. *Hell in Paradise: War, Rape and Failure in the Congo.* Seminar on Women in War, University of Paris I. Pantheon Sorbonne, 2008.

Klip, André, and Goran Sluiter. "The Special Court for Sierra Leone 2003–2004." In *Annotated Leading Cases of International Criminal Tribunals IX.* Antwerp: Intersentia, 2007.

Knowlton, Brian, "Bush Urges Congress to Reject Armenian Genocide Resolution." *New York Times,* 10 October 2007.

Knox, Colin, and Rachel Monaghan. *Informal Justice in Divided Societies: Northern Ireland and South Africa.* New York: Palgrave Macmillan, 2002.

Kunowah-Tinu Kiellow, Mohamed. *The Legality of the Amnesty Enshrined in the Lomé Peace Agreement.* Freetown, Sierra Leone: Sierra Express Media, 2008.

Kvinna till Kvinna Foundation. *Voices from the Field: About Prosecution of Sexualized Violence in an International Context.* Stockholm: Kvinna till Kvinna Foundation, 2004.

Landler, Mark. "Austrian Court Frees British Author Jailed as Holocaust Denier." *International Herald Tribune,* 21 December 2006.

Lewis, Amy G. "Gender Based Violence Among Refugee and Internally Displaced Women in Africa." *Georgia Immigration Law Journal* 20 (2006): 269–91.

Lindisfarne, Nancy. Variant Masculinities, Variant Virginities: Rethinking "Honour and Shame." In *Dislocating Masculinities: Comparative Ethnographies,* ed. Andrea Cornwall and Nancy Lindisfarne, 82–96. London: Routledge, 1994.

Lovett, Margot L. "'She Thinks She's Like a Man': Marriage and (De)Constructing Gender Identity in Colonial Buha, Western Tanzania, 1943–1960." *Canadian Journal of African Studies* 30:1 (1996): 52–68.

MacCormack-Hoffer, Carol P. "Bundu: Political Implications of Female Solidarity in a Secret Society." In *Being Female: Reproduction, Power and Change,* ed. Dana Raphael, 155–63. The Hague: Mouton, 1975.

Magnarella, Paul J. "Judicial Responses to Genocide: The ICTR and the Rwanda Genocide Courts." *Africa Studies Quarterly* 1:1 (1997): 17–32.

Malkki, Liisa H. *Purity and Exile: Violence, Memory, and National Cosmology Among Hutu Refugees in Tanzania.* Chicago: University of Chicago Press, 1995.

Mamdani, Mahmood. "When Does Reconciliation Turn into a Denial of Justice? The Truth According to the Truth and Reconciliation Commission." Pretoria: HSRC Publishers, 1998.

Manjoo, Rashida. "Gender Injustice and the South African Truth and Reconciliation Commission." In *Gendered Peace: Women's Struggles for Post-War Justice and Reconciliation,* ed. Donna Pankhurst, 137–55. London: Routledge, 2007.

Matsuda, Mari J. "Beside My Sister, Facing the Enemy: Legal Theory Out of Coalition." *Stanford Law Review* 43 (1990–91): 1183–92.

May, Larry, and Robert Strikwerda. "Men in Groups: Collective Responsibility for Rape." *Hypatia* 9:2 (1994): 134–51.

Mazurana, Dyan, and Khristopher Carlson. *From Combat to Community: Women and Girls of Sierra Leone.* Washington, D.C.: Women Waging Peace, 2004.

Mazurana, Dyan, and Susan McKay. *Where Are the Girls? Girls in Fighting Forces in Northern Uganda, Sierra Leone and Mozambique: Their Lives During and After War.* Montreal: Rights and Democracy, 2004.

McClendon, Thomas V. *Gender and Generations Apart: Labor Tenants and Customary Law in Segregation-Era South Africa, 1920s to 1940s.* Portsmouth, N.H.: Heinemann, 2002.

McCormick, Richard W. "Rape and War, Gender and Nation, Victims and Victimizers: Helke Sander's *BeFreier und Befreite.*" *Camera Obscura* 46:1 (2001): 99–141.

Menon, Ritu, and Kamla Bhasin. "Abducted Women, the State and Questions of Honour: Three Perspectives on the Recovery Operation in Post-Partition India." In *Embodied Violence: Communalising Women's Sexuality in South Asia,* ed. Kumari Jayawardena and Malathi de Alwis, 1–32. London: Zed, 1996.

Mibenge, Benjamin Ndabila. *Civil Military Relations in Zambia: A View from the Military.* Pretoria, South Africa: Institute of Security Studies, 2004.

Mibenge, Chiseche. "Concurrent Application of International, National and African Laws in Rwanda." In *Treaty Enforcement and International Cooperation in Criminal Matters,* ed. Rodrigo Yepes-Enríquez and Lisa Tabassi, 95–105. The Hague: TMC Asser, 2002.

———. "Commentary: The Right to Appeal in the Case of Samuel Hinga Norman et al." In *The Special Court for Sierra Leone 2003–2004 in Annotated Leading Cases of International Criminal Tribunals IX,* ed. André Klip and Goran Sluiter, 844–48. Antwerp: Intersentia, 2007a.

———. "Gender, Ethnicity and Exclusion: The Right to a Remedy for Victims of Wartime Rape." In *Gender, Conflict and Development,* ed. Dubravka Zarkov, 145–79. Delhi: Zubaan, 2007b.

Mitchell, David S. "The Prohibition of Rape in International Humanitarian Law as a Norm of Jus Cogens: Clarifying the Doctrine." *Duke Journal of Comparative and International Law* 15:2 (2005): 219–58.

Morris, Madeline. "By Force of Arms: Rape, War, and Military Culture." *Duke Law Journal* 45:4 (1995–96): 651–781.

Muddell, Kelli. "Capturing Women's Experiences of Conflict: Transitional Justice in Sierra Leone." *Michigan State Journal of International law* 15 (2007): 85–100.

Mzvondiwa Ntombizodwa, Cecilia. "The Role of Women in the Reconstruction and Building of Peace in Rwanda. Peace Prospects for the Great Lakes Region." *African Security Review* 16:1 (2007): 99–107.

Newbury, Catherine. *The Cohesion of Oppression: Clientship and Ethnicity in Rwanda, 1860–1960.* New York: Columbia University Press, 1988.

Nordstrom, Carolyn. *What John Wayne Never Told Us: Sexual Violence in War and Peace.* Unpublished paper, 1991.

———. *A Different Kind of War Story.* Philadelphia: University of Pennsylvania Press, 1997.

Nowrojee, Binaifer. *Your Justice Is Too Slow: Will the ICTR Fail Rwanda's Rape Victims?* Geneva: UN Research Institute for Social Development, Occasional Paper 10, 2005.

———. "Your Justice Is Too Slow: Will the International Criminal Tribunal for Rwanda Fail Rwanda's Rape Victims?" In *Gendered Peace: Women's Struggles for Reconciliation and Justice,* ed. Donna Pankhurst, 107–36. New York: Routledge, 2007.

O'Donnell, Krista. "Poisonous Women: Sexual Danger, Illicit Violence and Domestic Work in German Southern Africa 1904–1905." *Journal of Women's History* 11:3 (1999): 31–54.

Office of the Judge Advocate General, Department of War, History of the Judge Advocate General's Office in the European Theatre, 18 July 1942 – 1 November 1945. Unpublished manuscript, on file with the Office of the Chief of Military History, Historical Manuscript File, no. 8-35 AA v.1, 1945.

Ogundipe-Leslie, Omolara. *Recreating Ourselves: African Women and Critical Transformations.* Trenton, N.J.: Africa World Press, 1994.

Omeje, Kenneth. "Sexual Exploitation of Cult Women: The Challenges of Problematising Harmful Traditional Practices in Africa from a Doctrinalist Approach." *Social and Legal Studies* 10 (2001: 45–60).

Oosterveld, Valerie. "Sexual Slavery and the International Criminal Court: Advancing International Law." *Michigan Journal of International Law* 25 (2004): 606–51.

———. "The Special Court for Sierra Leone's Consideration of Gender Based Violence: Contributing to Transitional Justice?" *Human Rights Review* 10:1 (2009): 73–98.

Otto, Dianne. "Gender Comment: Why Does the UN Committee on Economic Social and Cultural Rights Need a General Comment on Women?" *Canadian Journal of Women in Law* 14 (2002): 1–52.

Pankhurst, Donna. "The 'Sex War' and Other Wars: Towards a Feminist Approach to Peace Building." *Development in Practice* 13:2–3 (2003): 154–77.

———. *Gendered Peace: Women's Struggles for Reconciliation and Justice.* New York: Routledge, 2007.

Parker, Karen. "Human Rights of Women During Armed Conflict." In *Women and International Human Rights Law: Toward Empowerment,* Volume 3, ed. Kelly Askin and Dorean M. Koenig, 283–323. New York: Transnational, 2001.

Parker, Karen, and Jennifer F Chew. "Compensation for Japan's World War II War Rape Victims." *Hastings International Law and Comparative Law Review* 17:3 (1993–94): 497–549.

Patel, Ricken. *Sierra Leone's Uncivil War and the Unlimited Intervention That Ended It.* Case Study for the Carr Center for Human Rights Policy, mimeo. Cambridge, Mass.: Harvard University, 2002.

Pateman, Carole. "Feminist Critique of the Public Private Dichotomy." In *Public and Private in Social Life,* ed. Stanley I. Benn and Gerald F. Gaus, 281–303. New York: St. Martin's, 1983.

Peetz, Peter. *Discourses on Violence in Costa Rica, El Salvador, and Nicaragua: Laws and the Construction of Drug and Gender Related Violence.* Working Paper 80. Hamburg: German Institute of Global Area Studies, 2008.

Penn, Helen. "The World Bank's View of Early Childhood." *Childhood* 9:1 (2002): 118–32.

——. *Unequal Childhoods: Young Children's Lives in Poor Countries.* London: Routledge, 2005.

Peterson, Latoya. "The Not-Rape Epidemic." In *Yes Means Yes! Visions of Female Sexual Power and a World Without Rape,* ed. Jaclyn Friedman and Jessica Valenti, 209–20. Berkeley, Calif.: Seal, 2008.

Physicians for Human Rights. *War-Related Sexual Violence in Sierra Leone: A Population Based Assessment.* Boston: Physicians for Human Rights, 2002.

Piccigallo, Phillip R. *The Japanese on Trial: Allied War Crimes Operations in the East 1945–1951.* Austin: University of Texas Press, 1979.

Piragoff, Donald K. "Evidence." In *The International Criminal Court: Elements of Crimes and Rules of Procedure and Evidence,* ed. Roy S. Lee et al., 349–401. New York: Transnational, 2001a.

——. "Procedural Justice Related to Crimes of Sexual Violence." In *International and National Prosecution of Crimes Under International Law, Current Developments,* ed. Horst Fischer, Claus Kress, and Sascha Rolf Luder, 385–421. Berlin: Berlin Verlag, 2001b.

Pokorak, Jeffrey P. "Rape as a Badge of Slavery: The Legal History of, and Remedies for Prosecutorial Race-of-Victim Charging Disparities." *Nevada Law Journal* 7:1 (2006–2007): 1–54.

Polgreen, Lydia. "Militias in Congo Tied to Government and Rwanda." *New York Times,* 12 December 2008.

Portelli, Allesandro. *The Death of Luigi Trastulli and Other Stories: Form and Meaning in Oral History.* New York: State University of New York Press, 1991.

Pottier, Johan. "Escape from Genocide: The Politics of Identity in Rwanda's Massacres." In *Violence and Belonging: The Quest for Identity in Post-Colonial Africa,* ed. Vigdis Broch-Due, 195–205. London: Routledge, 2005.

Pouligny, Beatrice. *The Forgotten Dimensions of Transitional Justice Mechanism: Cultural Meanings and Imperatives for Survivors of Violent Conflicts.* Paris: Center for International Studies and Research, 2007.

President of the International Tribunal for Rwanda. Sixth Annual Report of the International Criminal Tribunal for the Prosecution of Persons Responsible for Genocide and Other Serious Violations of International Humanitarian Law Committed in the Territory of Rwanda and Rwandan Citizens Responsible for genocide and Other Such Violations Committed in the Territory of Neighboring States between 1 January and 31 December 1994 submitted to the Security Council and to the General Assembly. For the period from 1 July 2000 to 30 June 2001. A/56/150 – S/2001/863, 2001.

Prunier, Gerard. *The Rwanda Crisis 1959–1994: History of a Genocide.* London: Hurst, 1995.

Quénivet, Noëlle N. R. *Sexual Offenses in Armed Conflict and International Law.* Ardsley, N.Y.: Transnational, 2005.

Rajagopal, Balakrishnan. "Counter-Hegemonic International Law: Rethinking Human Rights and Development as a Third World Strategy." *Third World Journal* 27:5 (2006): 767–83.

Ranck, J. L. *The Politics of Memory and Justice in Post Genocide Rwanda.* Ph.D. diss., University of California, Berkeley, 1998.

Reno, William. "The Political Economy of Order Amidst Predation in Sierra Leone." In *States of Violence: Politics, Youth and Memory in Contemporary Africa,* ed. Edna G. Bay and Donald L. Donham, 37–57. Charlottesville: University of Virginia Press, 2006.

Richards, Paul. *Fighting for the Rainforest: War, Youth and Resources in Sierra Leone.* London: Heinemann, 1996.

Richlin, Amy. *The Garden of Priapus: Sexuality and Aggression in Roman Humor,* revised edition. Oxford: Oxford University Press, 1992.

Richters, Annemiek. "Sexual Violence in Wartime. Psycho-Sociocultural Wounds and Healing Processes: The Example of the Former Yugoslavia." In *Rethinking the Trauma of War,* ed. Patrick J. Bracken and Celia Petty, 112–28. London: Free Association, 1998.

Rimalt, Noya. "Stereotyping Women, Individualising Harassment: The Dignitary Paradigm of Sexual Harassment Law Between the Limits of Law and the Limits of Feminism." *Yale Journal of Law and Feminism* 19 (2008): 391–447.

Rombouts, Heidy. *Gender and Reparations in Rwanda.* New York: International Center for Transitional Justice, 2006.

Rose, Laurel L. "Orphans' Land Rights in Post-War Rwanda: The Problem of Guardianship." *Development and Change* 36:5 (2005): 911–36.

Ross, Fiona C. *Bearing Witness: Women and the Truth and Reconciliation Commission in South Africa.* London: Pluto, 2002.

———. "Women and the Politics of Identity: Voices in the South African Truth and Reconciliation Commission." In *Violence and Belonging: The Quest for Identity in Post-Colonial Africa,* ed. Vigdis Broch-Due, 214–36. London: Routledge, 2005.

Ross, Will. "Democracy Wins in Sierra Leone Polls." *BBC News,* 18 September 2007

Rothbart, Daniel, and Thomas Alexander Marks Bartlett. "Rwandan Radio Broadcasts and Hutu/Tutsi Positioning." In *Global Conflict Resolution Through Positioning Analysis,* ed. Fathali M. Moghaddam, Rom Harre, and Naomi Lee, 169–88. New York: Springer, 2008.

Sachs, Albie. "Experiences Under Repression in South Africa." In *Dealing with the Past: Truth and Reconciliation in South Africa,* ed. Alex Boraine, Janet Levy, and Ronel Scheffer, 20–25. Cape Town, South Africa: IDASA, 1997.

Sandvik, Kristin Bergotora. "The Physicality of Legal Consciousness." In *Humanitari-*

anism and Suffering: The Mobilization of Empathy, ed. Richard Ashby Wilson and Richard D. Brown, 223–44. New York: Cambridge University Press, 2009.

Sanin, Kyra, and Anna Stirnemann. *Child Witnesses at the Special Court.* Berkeley: War Crimes Studies Center/University of California, 2006.

Saporta, Jose A., and Bessel A. van der Kolk. "Psychobiological Consequences of Severe Trauma." In *Torture and Its Consequences: Current Treatment Approaches,* ed. Metin Basoglu, 151–81. Cambridge: Cambridge University Press, 1992.

Save the Children. *The Road to Reintegration: Save the Children and Coalition to Stop Use of Child Soldiers, Call for Action: Working with Child Soldiers in West Africa.* Westport, Conn.: Save the Children, 2004–2005.

Schatzberg, Michael G. *Political Legitimacy in Middle Africa: Father, Family, Food.* Bloomington: Indiana University Press, 2002.

Sebold, Alice. *Lucky: A Memoir.* California: Bay Back, 1999.

Shaw, Rosalind. *Rethinking Truth and Reconciliation Commissions: Lessons from Sierra Leone.* Washington, D.C.: United States Institute of Peace, 2005.

———. "Memory Frictions: Localizing the Truth and Reconciliation Commission in Sierra Leone." *International Journal of Transitional Justice* 1 (2007): 183–207.

Shepler, Susan. "The Rites of the Child: Global Discourses of Youth and Reintegrating Child Soldiers in Sierra Leone." *Journal of Human Rights* 4 (2005): 197–211.

Sideris, Tina. "Problems of Identity, Solidarity and Reconciliation." In *The Aftermath: Women in Post-Conflict Transformation,* ed. Sheila Meintjes, Anu Pillay, and Meredeth Turshen, 46–62. London: Zed, 2001a.

———. "Rape in War and Peace: Social Context, Gender, Power and Identity." In *The Aftermath: Women in Post-Conflict Transformation,* ed. Sheila Meintjes, Anu Pillay, and Meredeth Turshen, 142–58. London: Zed, 2001b.

Sierra Leone Lawyers Centre for Legal Assistance. *Unequal Rights: Discriminatory Laws against Women in Sierra Leone.* Freetown: LAWCLA, 2004.

Simpson, Gerry. *Law, War and Crime: War Crimes Trials and the Reinvention of International Law.* Cambridge: Polity, 2007.

Sivakumaran, Sandesh. "Sexual Violence Against Men in Armed Conflict." *European Journal of International Law* 18 (2007): 257–58.

Slocum-Bradley, Nikki R. "Discursive Production of Conflict in Rwanda." In *Global Conflict Resolution Through Positioning Analysis,* ed. Fathali M. Moghaddam, Rom Harre, and Naomi Lee, 207–26. New York: Springer, 2008.

Smart. Joko. *Sierra Leone Customary Family Law.* Freetown: Fourah Bay College Bookshop, 1983.

Smith, Brenda V. "Battering, Forgiveness and Redemption." *American University Journal of Gender, Social Policy and the Law* 11:2 (2003): 921–62.

——— "Rethinking Prison Sex: Self Expression and Safety." *Columbia Journal of Gender and Law* 15 (2006): 185–234.

Soyinka-Airewele, Peyi. "Subjectivities of Violence and the Dilemmas of Transitional Governance." *West Africa Review* 6 (2004): 1-42.

"Swiss Court Convicts Turkish Politician of Genocide Denial: Court Hands Down First Such Conviction." *New York Times*, 9 March 2007.

Spade, Dean, and Sel Wahng. "Transecting the Academy." *GLQ: A Journal of Lesbian and Gay Studies* 10:2 (2004): 240–53.

Srikantiah, Jayashri. "Perfect Victims and Real Survivors: The Iconic Victim in Domestic Human Trafficking Law." *Boston University Law Review* 87 (2007): 157–211.

Stepakoff, Shanee, and Michelle Staggs Kelsall. "When We Wanted to Talk About Rape: Silencing Sexual Violence at the Special Court for Sierra Leone." *International Journal of Transitional Justice* 1:3 (2007): 355–74.

Straus, Scott. "What Is the Relationship Between Radio and Violence? Rethinking Rwanda's 'Radio Machete.'" *Politics Society* 35 (2007): 609–37.

Suski, Laura. "Children, Suffering, and the Humanitarian Appeal." In *Humanitarianism and Suffering: The Mobilization of Empathy,* ed. Richard Ashby Wilson and Richard D. Brown, 202–22. New York: Cambridge University Press, 2009.

Tanaka, Yuki. *Japan's Comfort Women: Sexual Slavery and Prostitution During World War II and the US Occupation.* London: Routledge, 2002.

Taylor, Christopher. C. *Milk, Honey and Money: Changing Concepts in Rwandan Healing.* Washington, D.C.: Smithsonian Institution, 1992.

———. "A Gendered Genocide: Tutsi Women and Hutu Extremists in the 1994 Rwanda Genocide." *PoLAR* 22:1 (1999a): 42–54.

———. *Sacrifice as Terror: The Rwandan Genocide of 1994.* New York: Berg, 1999b.

Thompson, Allan, ed. *The Media and the Rwanda Genocide.* London: Pluto, 2007.

Turshen, Meredeth. "The Political Economy of Rape: An Analysis of Systematic Rape and Sexual Abuse of Women During Armed Conflict in Africa." In *Victims, Perpetrators or Actors? Gender, Armed Conflict and Political Violence,* ed. Caroline O. N. Moser and Fiona C. Clark, 55–68. London: Zed, 2001.

Uhler, Oscar and Coursier Henri. The ICRC Commentary on the Geneva Conventions of 12 August 1949 (IV). Geneva: International Committee of the Red Cross, 1958.

U.S. Department of Justice. *12 Percent of Adjudicated Youth Report Sexual Victimization in Juvenile Facilities During 2008–9.* NCJ 228416. Washington, D.C.: U.S. Bureau of Justice Statistics, 2010, http://bjs.ojp.usdoj.gov/content/pub/press/svjfry09pr.cfm.

Utas, Mats. "Victimcy, Girlfriending, Soldiering: Tactic Agency in a Young Woman's Social Navigation of the Liberian War Zone." *Anthropology Quarterly* 78 (2005): 403–43.

Uvin, Peter. *Aiding Violence: The Development Enterprise in Rwanda.* West Hartford, Conn.: Kumarian, 1998.

Vahidy, Saleem, Simon Charters, and Rebecca Horn. "Witnesses in the Special Court for Sierra Leone: The Importance of the Witness–Lawyer Relationship." *International Journal of Law, Crime and Justice* 37:1 (2009): 25–38.

Vann, Beth. *Gender Based Violence: Emerging Issues in Programs Serving Displaced Populations.* New York: Reproductive Health for Refugees Consortium, 2002.

Viseur-Sellers, Patricia. "The Context of Sexual Violence: Sexual Violence as Violations of Humanitarian Law." In *Substantive and Procedural Aspects of International Criminal Law: The Experience of International and National Courts*, ed. Gabrielle Kirk McDonald and Olivia Swaak-Goldman, 263–323. The Hague: Kluwer Law International, 2001.

———. "Sexual Violence and Peremptory Norms: The Legal Value of Rape." *Case Western Reserve Journal of International Law* 34:3 (2002): 287–303.

White, Deborah Gray. *Ar'n't I a Woman? Female Slaves in the Plantation South*. New York: W. W. Norton, 1999.

Whitlock, Craig. "Holocaust Denier is Ordered to Recant – Otherwise, Vatican Says, Cleric Can't Come Back." *Washington Post Foreign Service*, 5 February 2009.

Wilkerson, Abby L. "Her Body Her Own Worst Enemy: The Medicalization of Violence Against Women." In *Violence Against Women: Philosophical Perspectives*, ed. Stanley G. French, Wanda Teays, and Laura M. Purdy, 123–38. Ithaca, N.Y.: Cornell University Press, 1998.

World Vision. *Before She's Ready: 15 Places Girls Marry by 15*. World Vision, 2008.

Zarkov, Dubravka. "War Rapes in Bosnia: On Masculinity, Femininity and Power of the Rape Victim Identity." *Tijdschrift voor Criminologie* 39:2 (1997): 140–52.

———. "The Body of the Other Man: Sexual Violence and the Construction of Masculinity, Sexuality and Ethnicity in Croatian Media." In *Victims, Perpetrators or Actors? Gender, Armed Conflict and Political Violence*, ed. Caroline O. N. Moser and Fiona Clark, 69–82. London: Zed, 2001.

———. *Working Through the War: Trajectories of Non-Governmental and Governmental Organizations Engaged in Psycho-social Assistance to Victims of War and Family Violence in the ex-Yugoslavia States*. Utrecht: Admira Foundation and Pharos, 2005.

———. *Media, Ethnicity and Gender in the Break-up of Yugoslavia*. Durham, N.C.: Duke University Press, 2007.

Zur, Judith. "The Psychosocial Effects of 'La Violencia' on Widows of El Quiche, Guatemala. *Gender and Development* 1:2 (1993): 27–30.

Zwingel, Susanne. *Gendered Responsibilities for War and Peace: Strategies of Political, Socio-Economic and Psychological Reconstruction in Post-War Germany*. Presented at the 100th annual meeting of the American Political Science Association, Chicago, 2004.

UN and Regional Reporting

Council of Europe Committee on Equal Opportunities for Women and Men, *Report on Rape in Armed Conflicts*, Document 8668, 15 March 2000.

Organisation for African Unity. *Rwanda the Preventable Genocide: The Report of the International Panel of Eminent Personalities to Investigate the 1994 Genocide in Rwanda and the Surrounding Events*. Addis Ababa, Ethiopia: Organisation for African Unity, 2000.

Panel of Experts for Sierra Leone. Report of the Panel of Experts, established by

Resolution 1306 (2000), paragraph 19, in relation to Sierra Leone, S/2000/1195, 20 December 2000

Coomaraswamy, Radhika. Special Rapporteur on violence against women, its causes and consequences, *Addendum Report on the mission to the Democratic People's Republic of Korea, Republic of Korea and Japan on the issue of military sexual slavery in wartime,* E/CN.4/1996/53/Add.1, 4 January 1996.

———. Report of the Special Rapporteur on violence against women, its causes and consequences, "Addendum Report of the mission to Rwanda on the issues of violence against women in situations of armed conflict," E/CN.4/1998/54/Add.1, 4 February 1998.

———. Report of the Special Rapporteur on violence against women, its causes and consequences, "Addendum Report of the mission to Sierra Leone,"
E/CN.4/2002/83/Add.2, 11 February 2002.

Ertürk, Yakin. Report of the Special Rapporteur on violence against women, its causes and consequences, "Intersections Between Culture and Violence Against Women," A/HRC/4/34, 17 January 2007.

Shahinian Gulnara. Report of the Special Rapporteur on contemporary forms of slavery, including its causes and consequences, A/HRC/9/20, 28 July 2008.

UN Division for the Advancement of Women. Sexual Violence and Armed Conflict: United Nations Response. Geneva: UNDAW and Women2000, 1988, http://www.un.org/womenwatch/daw/public/W2000andBeyond.html.

UN Report of the World Conference to Review and Appraise the Achievements of the United Nations Decade for Women: Equality, Development and Peace, 15-26 July 1985 in Nairobi, 1986.

UN Secretary-General report on *Women, Peace and Security,* submitted pursuant to Security Council Resolution 1325 (2000). New York: UN Publications, 2002.

UN Office of the United Nations High Commissioner for Human Rights. Rule of Law Tools for Post-Conflict States: National Consultations of Transitional Justice. New York and Geneva: UN Publications, 2009.

UN Secretary General report of the sixth meeting of persons chairing the human rights treaty bodies, convened pursuant to General Assembly Resolution 49/178 of 23 December 1994, "Human Rights Questions: Implementation of Human Rights Instruments," Doc. A/50/505, 4 October 1995.

UN Secretary-General report pursuant to General Assembly Resolution 53/55, "The Fall of Srebrenica," 15 November 1999.

UN Secretary-General's report on *Assistance to Survivors of the 1994 Genocide in Rwanda, particularly Orphans, Widows, and Victims of Sexual Violence.* Submitted to the General Assembly in compliance with its request in Resolution 62/96. Secretary-General A/64/313, 20 August 2009.

Case Law—International Criminal Tribunal for Rwanda

The Prosecutor v. Jean-Paul Akayesu Amended Indictment ICTR-96-4-T, 06-06-1997.

The Prosecutor v. Jean-Paul Akayesu Judgment ICTR 96-4-T, 02-09-1998.

The Prosecutor v. Théoneste Bagosora Amended Indictment, ICTR-96-7-I, 31-07-1998.

The Prosecutor v. Théoneste Bagosora, Gratien Kabiligi, Aloys Ntabakuze, and Anatole Nsengiyumva Trial Chamber Decision on Motions for Judgment of Acquittal, ICTR-98- 41-T, 02-02-2005.

The Prosecutor v. Théoneste Bagosora, Gratien Kabiligi, Aloys Ntabakuze and Anatole Nsengiyumva Oral Summary, ICTR-98-41-T, 18-12-2008.

The Prosecutor v. Théoneste Bagosora, Gratien Kabiligi, Aloys Ntabakuze and Anatole Nsengiyumva Judgment, ICTR-98-41-T, 18-12-2008.

The Prosecutor v. Sylvestre Gacumbitsi Indictment, ICTR-2001-64-T, 01-06-2001.

The Prosecutor v. Sylvestre Gacumbitsi Judgment, ICTR-2001-64-T, 17-06-2004.

The Prosecutor v. Jean Kambanda Judgment and Sentence, ICTR-97-23-S, 04-09-1998.

The Prosecutor v. Mika Muhimana, Clement Kayishema, Ignace Bagilishema, Charles Sikubwabo, Aloys Ndimbati, Vincent Rutaganira, Obed Ruzindana, Ryandikayo First Indictment, ICTR-95-1-I, 20-10-2000.

The Prosecutor v. Mikaeli Muhimana Revised Amended Indictment, ICTR-95-B1-I, 03-02- 2004.

The Prosecutor v. Mikaeli Muhimana Judgment and Sentence, ICTR-95-1B-T, 28-04-2005.

The Prosecutor v. Alfred Musema Judgment and Sentence, ICTR-96-13-A, 27-01-2000.

The Prosecutor v. Tharcisse Muvunyi Decision on the Prosecutor's Motion for Leave to File an Amended Indictment, ICTR-2000-55A-TT, 23-02-2005.

The Prosecutor v. Georges Rutaganda Judgment, ICTR-96-3-T, 06-12-1999.

The Prosecutor v. Augustin Ndindiliyimana, Augustin Bizimungu, Protais Mpirianya, Francois-Xavier Nzuwonemeye and Innocent Sagahutu Amended Indictment (Joinder), ICTR-2000-56-I, 25-10-2002.

The Prosecutor v. Augustin Ndindiliyimana, Augustin Bizimungu, Francois-Xavier Nzuwonemeye and Innocent Sagahutu Judgment and Sentence, ICTR-00-56-T, 17-05- 2011.

The Prosecutor v. Elezier Niyitegeka, Indictment ICTR-97-27-I, 11-07-1997.

The Prosecutor v. Elezier Niyitegeka, Prosecutor's Submission of the Harmonised Amended Indictment ICTR-96-14-T, 125-11-2002.

The Prosecutor v. Elezier Niyitegeka, Judgment ICTR-96-14-T, 16-05-2003.

The Prosecutor v. André Ntagerura, Emmanuel Bagambiki and Samuel Imanishimwe Decision on the Application to File an Amicus Curiae Brief According to Rule 74 of the Rules of Procedure and Evidence Filed on Behalf of the NGO Coalition for Women's Human Rights in Conflict Situations, ICTR-99-46-T, 24-05-2001.

The Prosecutor v. Bernard Ntuyahaga Indictment, ICTR-98-40-I, 26-09-1998.

The Prosecutor v. Pauline Nyiramasuhuko and Shalom Ntahobali Amended Indictment, ICTR- 97-21-I, 01-03-2001.

Case Law—Sierra Leone Special Court

The Prosecutor v. Samuel Hinga Norman, Moinina Fofana and Allieu Kondewa Prosecution Request to Amend the Indictment Against Samuel Hinga Norman, Moinina Fofana and Allieu Kondewa, SCSL-04-14-PT, 09-02-2004.

The Prosecutor v. Samuel Hinga Norman, Moinina Fofana and Allieu Kondewa Decision on Prosecution Request for Leave to Amend the Indictment, SCSL-04-14-PT, 20-05-2004.

The Prosecutor v. Issa Hassan Sesay, Morris Kallon and Augustine Gbao Decision on Prosecution Application for Leave to File an Interlocutory Appeal Against Decision on Motion for Concurrent Hearing of Evidence Common to Cases, SCSL-2004-15-PT and SCSL-2004-16-PT, SCSL-04-16-PT, 11-06-2004.

The Prosecutor v. Samuel Hinga Norman, Moinina Fofana and Allieu Kondewa Majority Decision on the Prosecution's Application for Leave to File an Interlocutory Appeal Against the Decisions on the Prosecution's Request for Leave to Amend the Indictment Against Samuel Hinga Norman, Moinina Fofana and Allieu Kondewa, SCSL-04-14-T, 02-08-2004.

The Prosecutor v. Samuel Hinga Norman, Moinina Fofana and Allieu Kondewa Dissenting Opinion of Judge Pierre Boutet on the Proseuction's Application for Leave to File an Interlocutory Appeal against the Decision on the Prosecution's Request for Leave to Amend the Indictment Against Samuel Hinga Norman, Moinina Fofana and Allieu Kondewa, SCSL-04-14-T-172, 05-08-2004.

The Prosecutor v. Samuel Hinga Norman, Moinina Fofana and Allieu Kondewa Decision on Prosecution Appeal Against the Trial Chamber's Decision of 2 August 2004 Refusing Leave to File an Interlocutory Appeal, SCSL-04-14-T, 19-01-2005.

The Prosecutor v. Moinina Fofana and Allieu Kondewa, Judgment Partially Dissenting Opinion of Judge Renate Winter, SCSL-04-14-A, 28-05-2008.

The Prosecutor v. Moinina Fofana and Allieu Kondewa Appeal Judgment, SCSL-04-14-A, 28-05-2008.

The Prosecutor v. Issa Hassan Sesay, Morris Kallon and Augustine Gbao Decision on Prosecution Application for Leave to file an interlocutory appeal against Decision on Motion for Concurrent Hearing of Evidence Common to Cases, SCSL-04-15-PT-150 and and SCSL-2004-16-PT, SCSL-04-15-PT-150, 01-06-2004.

The Prosecutor v. Issa Hassan Sesay, Morris Kallon and Augustine Gbao Judgment Summary, SCSL-04-15-T, 25-02-2009.

Case Law—International Criminal Tribunal for the Former Yugoslavia

The Prosecutor v. Tadic Dusko and Goran Borovnica Amended Indictment, IT-94-1-I, 14-12-1995.

The Prosecutor v. Dragoljub Kunarac, Radomir Kovac, Zoran Vukovic Judgment, IT-96-23-T & IT-96-23-T & IT-96-23/1-T, 22-02-2001.

The Prosecutor v. Dragoljub Kunarac, Radomir Kovac, Zoran Vukovic Appeals Chamber Judgment, IT-96-23-A & IT-96-23/1-A, 12-06-2002.

The Prosecutor v. Zejko Mejakic, Momcilo Gruban, Dusko Knezevic Amended Indictment, IT- 95-4-I, 18-07-2001.

The Prosecutor v. Zdravko Mucić, Zejnil Delalic, Hazim Delic and Esad Landzo Judgment, IT- 96-21, 16-11-1998.

Other Sources of International Law Cited

African Charter on Human and Peoples' Rights, adopted 27 June 1981, OAU Doc. CAB/ LEG/67/3 rev. 5, 21 I.L.M. 58 (1982), entered into force 21 October 1986.

Protocol to the African Charter on Human and People's Rights on the Rights of Women in Africa (Maputo Protocol), OAU Doc. OAU/LEG/MIN/AFCHPR/ PROT.1 rev.2 (1997), entered into force 25 January 2004.

African Charter on the Rights and Welfare of the Child, adopted in July 1990, OAU Doc. CAB/LEG/24.9/49 (1990), entered into force 29 November 1999.

Beijing Declaration and Platform for Action, A/CONF.177/20 (1995) and A/ CONF.177/20/Add.1 (1995), adopted by the Fourth World Conference on Women: Action for Equality, Development and Peace, on15 September 1995.

Charter of the International Military Tribunal, annex to the Agreement for the Prosecution and Punishment of the Major War Criminals of the European Axis, 8 August 1945, 59 Stat. 1544, 82 UNTS 279.

Charter of the International Military Tribunal for the Far East, 19 January 1946, amended 26 Apr. 1946, T.I.A.S. No. 1589.

Charter of the United Nations and Statute of the International Court of Justice, signed on 26 June 1945, in San Francisco, entered into force on 24 October 1945.

Convention on the Elimination of All Forms of Discrimination Against Women, General Assembly resolution 34/180 (XXII) of 18 December 1979, entry into force 3 September 1981.

General Recommendation 12 *violence against women*, Committee on the Elimination of Discrimination against Women, (1989), established under article 21 of the Convention on the Elimination of All Forms of Discrimination against Women.

General Recommendation 19 *violence against women*, Committee on the Elimination of Discrimination against Women (1992), Discrimination against Women (1989), established under article 21 of the Convention on the Elimination of All Forms of Discrimination against Women.

Convention on the Prevention and Punishment of the Crime of Genocide, General Assembly Resolution 260 A (III) of 9 December 1948, entry into force 12 January 1951.

Convention on the Rights of the Child, General Assembly Resolution 44/25 of 20 November 1989, entry into force 2 September 1990.

General Act of the Brussels Conference for the Suppression of the Slave Trade held at Brussels, 18 November to 2 July 1890, adopted 2 July 1890.

UN General Assembly Resolution A/Res/59/137 Assistance to survivors of the 1994 genocide in Rwanda, particularly orphans, widows and victims of sexual violence, adopted 10 December 2004.

UN General Assembly Resolution A/Res/64/226 Assistance to survivors of the 1994 genocide in Rwanda, particularly orphans, widows and victims of sexual violence, adopted 22 December 2009.

Geneva Convention (I) for the Amelioration of the Condition of the Wounded and Sick in Armed Forces in the Field, adopted by the Diplomatic Conference of Geneva on 12 August 1949, entry into force 21 October 1950.

Geneva Convention (II) for the Amelioration of the Condition of Wounded, Sick and Shipwrecked Members of Armed Forces at Sea, adopted by the Diplomatic Conference of Geneva on 12 August 1949, entry into force 29 October 1950.

Geneva Convention (III) relative to the Treatment of Prisoners of War, adopted by the Geneva Diplomatic Conference for the Establishment of International Conventions for the Protection of Victims of War on 12 August 1949, entry into force 21 October 1959.

Geneva Convention (IV) Relative to the Protection of Civilian Persons in Time of War, adopted by the Geneva Diplomatic Conference for the Establishment of International Conventions for the Protection of Victims of War on 12 August 1949, entry into force 21 October 1959.

Protocol Additional to the Geneva Conventions of 12 August 1949, and Relating to the Protection of Victims of Non-International Armed Conflicts (Protocol II), adopted by the Diplomatic Conference on the Reaffirmation and Development of International Humanitarian Law applicable in Armed Conflicts on 8 June 1977, entry into force 7 December 1978.

Protocol Additional to the Geneva Conventions of 12 August 1949, and relating to the Protection of Victims of International Armed Conflicts (Protocol I), adopted by the Diplomatic Conference on the Reaffirmation and Development of International Humanitarian Law applicable in Armed Conflicts on 8 June 1977, entry into force 7 December 1978.

Hague Convention (II) with Respect to the Laws and Customs of War on Land and its annex: Regulations concerning the Laws and Customs of War on Land. Adopted at the First Peace Conference of The Hague, 29 July 1899, entry into force 4 September 1900.

Hague Convention (IV) Respecting the Laws and Customs of War on Land and its annex: Regulations Concerning the Laws and Customs of War on Land, adopted at the International Peace Conference on 18 October 1907, entry into force 26 January 1910.

High Court of Australia, The Queen and Wei Tang (2008) HCA 39 28, M5/2008, August 2008.

International Covenant on Civil and Political Rights, General Assembly Resolution 2200A (XXI) of 16 December 1966, entry into force 23 March 1969.

General Comment 16 Article 17 *right to privacy*, Human Rights Committee (1989), established under article 28 of the International Covenant on Civil and Political Rights.

General Comment 18 *non-discrimination*, Human Rights Committee (1989), established under article 28 of the International Covenant on Civil and Political Rights

General Comment 28 *the equality of rights between men and women*, Human Rights

Committee (2000), established under article 28 of the International Covenant on Civil and Political Rights.

International Covenant on Economic, Social, and Cultural Rights, General Assembly Resolution 2200A (XXI) of 16 December 1966, entry into force 3 January 1976.

International Convention on the Elimination of All Forms of Racial Discrimination, General Assembly Resolution 2106 (XX) of 21 December 1965, entry into force 4 January 1969.

General Comment 25 *gender-related dimensions of racial discrimination*, Committee on the Elimination of Racial Discrimination (2000), established under article 8 of the International Convention on the Elimination of All Forms of Racial Discrimination.

General Comment 27 *discrimination against Roma*, Committee on the Elimination of Racial Discrimination (2000), established under article 8 of the International Convention on the Elimination of All Forms of Racial Discrimination.

General Comment 29 Article 1 (i) *regarding descent,* Committee on the Elimination of Racial Discrimination (2002), established under article 8 of the International Convention on the Elimination of All Forms of Racial Discrimination.

General Comment 31 XXXI *on the prevention of racial discrimination in the administration and functioning of the criminal justice system* (2005), Committee on the Elimination of Racial Discrimination (2002), established under article 8 of the International Convention on the Elimination of All Forms of Racial Discrimination.

Lomé Peace Agreement between the Government of Sierra Leone and the Revolutionary United Front of Sierra Leone, 18 May 1999.

Report of the Preparatory Commission for the International Criminal Court, Finalized Draft Text of the Elements of Crimes (2000), UN Doc. PCNICC/2000/1/Add.2. 2 November 2000.

Rome Statute of the International Criminal Court, adopted by the United Nations Diplomatic Conference of Plenipotentiaries on the Establishment of an International Criminal Court on 17 July 1998, entry into force 1 July 2002.

Security Council Resolution 872, S/RES/872 Adopted by the Security Council at its 3296th meeting, on 21 October 1993.

Security Council Resolution 935, S/RES/935 Adopted by the Security Council at its 3400th meeting on 1 July 1994.

Security Council Resolution 955, S/RES/955 Adopted by the Security Council at its 3453rd meeting on 8 November 1994.

Security Council Resolution 1306, S/RES/1306 Adopted by the Security Council at its 4168th meeting, on 5 July 2000.

Security Council Resolution 1315, S/RES/1315, Adopted by the Security Council at its 4186th meeting, on 14 August 2000.

Security Council Resolution 1325, S/RES/1325, Adopted by the Security Council at its 4213th meeting, on 31 October 2000.

Security Council Resolution 1820, S/RES/1820, Adopted by the Security Council at its 5916th meeting, on 19 June 2008.

Security Council Resolution 1888, S/RES/1888, Adopted by the Security Council at its 6195th meeting, on 30 September 2009.

Security Council Resolution 1889, S/RES/1889, Adopted by the Security Council at its 6196th meeting, on 5 October 2009.

Slavery Convention signed on 26 September 1926, entry into force 9 March 1927 (amended by the Protocol done at the Headquarters of the United Nations, New York, on 7 December 1953, the amended Convention entered into force on 7 July 1955).

Statute of the International Court of Justice, annex to the Charter of the United Nations signed at San Francisco on 26 June 1945.

Statute of the International Criminal Tribunal for the Prosecution of Persons Responsible for Genocide and Other Serious Violations of International Humanitarian Law Committed in the Territory of Rwanda and Rwandan Citizens Responsible for Genocide and Other Such Violations Committed in the Territory of Neighboring States, between 1 January 1994 and 31 December 1994, adopted by Security Council Resolution 955 (1994) of 8 November 1994, amended by Security Council Resolutions 1165 (1998) of 30 April 1998, 1329 (2000) of 30 November 2000, 1411 (2002) of 17 May 2002 and 1431 (2002) of 14 August 2002.

Statute of the International Tribunal for the Prosecution of Persons Responsible for Serious Violations of International Humanitarian Law Committed in the Territory of the Former Yugoslavia since 1991, adopted by Security Council Resolution 827 (1993) of 25 May 1993, amended by Security Council Resolutions 1166 (1998) of 13 May 1998, 1329 (2000) of 30 November 2000, 1411 (2002) of 17 May 2002 and 1431 (2002) of 14 August 2002.

Statute of the Sierra Leone Special Court (2000), established by an Agreement between the United Nations and the Government of Sierra Leone pursuant to Security Council Resolution 1315 (2000) of 14 August 2000.

Truth and Reconciliation Commission. *Witness to Truth: Report of the Sierra Leone Truth and Reconciliation Commission.* Accra: Graphic Packaging Limited, 4 October 2004.

Truth and Reconciliation Commission Act. Supplement to the *Sierra Leone Gazette,* vol. 131, no. 9, 10 February 2000.

United Nations Declaration on the Elimination of Violence Against Women, General Assembly Resolution 48/104 of 20 December 1993.

Universal Declaration of Human Rights, General Assembly Resolution 217 A (III) of 10 December 1948.

Vienna Declaration and Program of Action, adopted by the Conference on Human Rights in Vienna, A/CONF.157/23, on 25 June 1993.

Women's Caucus for Gender Justice in the International Criminal Court, 1997/44. Recommendations and Commentary for August 1997 Preparatory Committee on the establishment of an International Criminal Court. 4-15 August 1997.

The Women's International War Crimes Tribunal for the Trial of Japanese Military Sexual Slavery in the matter of the Prosecutor and the Peoples of the Asia Pacific Region v. Emperor Hirohito et al. and the Government of Japan, summary of findings, 12 December 2000.

Index

Women (*cont'd*)
45, 44, 48, 107; indigenous, 35; Jewish,
26, 45, 172n20; Korean, 26, 32, 45, 48,
151, 161; migrant, 32; Muslim, 45, 48,
76, 149; pregnant felons, 27; Roma, 36;
and rural, 30, 32, 51, 101; sex
workers, 27, 32, 92, 136; small status,
18, 76, 78, 82, 84, 184n1; white middle-
class, 8, 33

World conferences: End of Decade
Conference (Nairobi, 1985), 50; Second
World Conference on Human Rights
(Vienna, 1993), 50, 51; Fourth World
Conference on Women (Beijing,
1995), 52

Zur, Judith, 163, 168n22
Zwingel, Susanne, 48

Acknowledgments

I wrote this book over many years. It was inspired by many places and events, but for the purposes of this space reserved for the expression of my gratitude and debt, let me say that my maturity as a researcher began in the small European city of Utrecht. As a researcher with Utrecht University's School of Law, I worked closely with some of Europe's leading human rights scholars, most notably Bas de Gaay Fortman, Cees Flinterman, and André Klip. Cees and André supervised my research projects in Europe and Africa, and they became familiar with my biblical mantra of "Who of you by worrying can add a single hour to his life?" But still, between them, they did worry about my research, my immigration status, my writing, my emotional state, my family in Zambia, and my missed deadlines. I thank them for the responsibility they took on when they first recruited me as a junior researcher in 2001. I also thank early role models from the University of Zambia. Carlson Anyangwe urged me to "research Africa. It's all happening here!" And Alfred Chanda (1959–2007) and Elizabeth Mumba (1949–2005) both encouraged me to pursue a research career in the field of international human rights law.

I must also express my gratitude to the young doctors Maria Nybondas, Irene Hadiprayitno, Mitja Kovač, Eline Hofman, Giuseppe Dari Mattiacci, Tendai Mugwagwa, Anne-Marie de Brouwer, and Paulien Muller. We began our academic pursuits at the same time, and they all published their books a year or even years ahead of me. But they never tired of urging on their slower sister until she too finished the race: thank you for sharing your families, fine cooking, and homes with me—you are my "Dutch family" and a great source of strength.

I gratefully acknowledge the sponsors that supported this work. A generous Mozaiek grant from the Netherlands Organization for Scientific Research made possible my residence over a five-year period with the School of Human Rights Research, a part of Utrecht University's School of Law. The Mozaiek supported my field visit to Sierra Leone and the G. J. Wiarda Institute for Legal Research supported my field visit to Rwanda. The editorial staff at Wiarda did a superb job preparing the first presentable draft manuscript of this book in March 2010.

The EU COST Action allowed me to develop an important institutional relationship that came with my three-month position as a visiting fellow with the Africa Center for Peace and Conflict Studies (now the John and Elnora Ferguson Center for African Studies) within the University of Bradford's Department of Peacekeeping in the United Kingdom. In particular, I thank Connie Scanlon, David Francis, and Kenneth Omeje for hosting me and fostering my maturity into an interdisciplinary researcher.

I thank Tom Zwart, who as Dean of Graduate Studies and Director of the School of Human Rights Research at Utrecht, provided moral and financial support for my sabbatical year in Washington, D.C. This crucial period of writing up the book was conducted at American University (AU) (2008–2009). Early manuscripts were reviewed and roundly critiqued by AU faculty at the Washington College of Law as well as at the AU School of International Service and AU's International Training and Education Program. I made a number of presentations based on my draft chapters throughout my stay in the United States, including at Cornell University's Institute for African Development, Georgetown Law, State University of New York (SUNY) Potsdam, SUNY Cortland, Emory University's Institute for Developing Nations, and the International Center for Research on Women. The dialogue these meetings engendered was invaluable in the final stages of writing as I worked to unite and finalize my arguments. I must thank Professors Muna Ndulo (Cornell), Susanne Zwingel (SUNY Potsdam), Abdullahi An-Na'im (Emory), and Pamela Scully (Emory) for their extraordinary hospitality and mentorship during this time.

The Pence Law Library could not be a more inviting refuge for a scholar, and I thank Adeen Postar and her colleagues at the AU Pence Law Library and the Bender Library for their support of my research efforts. I am indebted to Brenda V. Smith (AU Washington College of Law), Susan Shepler (AU), Teresa Godwin Phelps (AU Washington College of Law), Valerie Oosterveld (Western Ontario), and my academic sponsor, Diego Rodriguez-Pinzón (AU Washington College of Law) for their mentorship, friendship, and inspiration throughout my residence at AU. I also thank Meetali Jain (AU Washington College of Law), Wenjing Liu (visiting scholar), Jan Kratochvil (visiting scholar), and Noya Rimalt (visiting professor), whose friendship inside and outside of the library made the research task seem that much lighter.

In fall 2010, I was surprised to find myself in the Bronx as an assistant professor teaching human rights and international law in the department of political science at Lehman College, a senior college of the City University of New York (CUNY). I received a timely and generous PSC-CUNY grant, which has funded the crucial final stages of editing this manuscript under the careful guidance of University of Pennsylvania Press. I could not have asked for a more amicable and supportive editor than Peter Agree: may all authors enjoy such an affirming and respectful relationship. I am grateful to Peter for referring me to Mary Murrell, my development editor, and Noreen O'Connor-Abel, my project editor, both of whom have guided the last phase of the editing process with sure and steady directions.

My parents taught me to listen to stories and to tell stories. They are responsible for my eternal passion for voices hidden in the pages of books, and my eternal curiosity about gender and power and gender as power. I thank my parents, Joyce Ruby and Benjamin Ndabila, and my siblings, Chisala, Mwenzi, Chimango, Mayase, and Bweupe, for supporting what I was doing so long as it made me really happy. Sampa, Mwaba, Nkundwe, Chisala (small), Ndabila, Lucy, William, Mubanga and Tukupasha—you are my sunshine.

And, finally, let me acknowledge the generosity I encountered in the field. In Rwanda, I was hosted by the Rwanda Tribunal's sexual violence unit in Kigali and the Center for Conflict Management, a part of the National University of Rwanda in Butare. I cannot begin to express my gratitude to the police, psychologists, social workers, gynecologists, survivor groups, survivors, and prosecutors I met and spoke with in Butare and Kigali. Similarly, in Sierra Leone, I enjoyed a warm reception and cooperation from the police, military, survivors of civil war, and civil society organizations. The narratives gathered from these interactions underlie this work. I have returned to Sierra Leone and Rwanda since the completion of this manuscript and can confirm that my partners there continue to enlighten and enliven my approach to teaching and researching on the subject of narratives of gender and violence in human rights law and processes of justice.